the new polish cuisine

The New Polish Cuisine

Chef Michael J. Baruch

photography by **Gregory Bertolini**

lb cm

Jacket: Wild Mushroom, Barley, and Dill Soup

Text © Michael Baruch 2002
Photography © Gregory Bertolini 2002
Design and layout © La Baruch Cuisine Moderne 2002

First published 2002 by La Baruch Cuisine Moderne

LBCM Publishing, Inc.
P.O. Box 55
Del Mar, CA 92014-0055
www.TheNewPolishCuisine.com

Library of Congress Cataloging-in-Publication Data is on file with the publisher.
ISBN: 0-9715313-0-7

First U.S. edition, 2002
Manufactured in China

1 2 3 4 5 6 7 8 9 10

dedication

I'd like to dedicate this book to everyone who enjoys a really good bowl of hot soup
and a great piece of rye bread. Smacznego!

Also, a heartfelt special dedication for a true Polish American hero, World War II
ace pilot Francis S. Gabreski. May God bless you and I hope you are
having fun flying on the wings of angels.

—Chef Mike Baruch, 2002

*ac*knowledgements

I would like to express my gratitude to the following for their contributions of taste, creativity, and style. Without their tenacious pursuit of excellence, this yearlong project would have never come to fruition.

Panache of La Jolla For their generous contribution of exquisite china and tableware, and especially to Jerad Hollandsworth, my Russian friend, for his shared vision of Eastern European culture and elegance.

Greg Bertolini For my photographer Greg, with his gentle spirit, only your modesty surpasses your talent. Without his vision, the soul and beauty of our cuisine would have never been captured on film.

David Clarke Bringing this book to life turned out to be a much bigger task than I had originally planned, so I enlisted the much-needed help of David, my art director and friend that I have the greatest admiration for. His artistic brilliance speaks for itself in the book's layout and design.

Last but not least, I would like to thank all of my friends and family in Chicago that I have known through the years for embracing and teaching me all that is good about Polish culture and heritage.

table of contents

welcome

about the chef

Over the last 20 plus years, I've been blessed with the strength, talent, and luck to have worked for some of the best chefs in the world. Jovan's, Le Francais, Le Perroquet, Café Provencal, Aux armes de Brusselles, and Le Crocodile to name a few. Anyone in the culinary field knows their reputation not only for 4-star dining, but also for their work ethic, pursuit of excellence, and inner fortitude to strive to be the best and push the envelope just a little bit further. I like that philosophy because it kind of sums up my life.

Clients of mine are always amazed that I didn't graduate from some big chef school, (hell, I barely made it through high school, the teachers thought I asked too many questions), and they are dumfounded as to how I got all those great jobs. That's easy; get a haircut, put on a clean shirt, and knock on the back door. I'm proud of the fact that I made my bones the hard way on the back streets of the city of Chicago, a true workingman's town.

I've never considered myself to be a tyrannical chef of mammoth proportions who commands respect from his underlings, or a chef philosopher who bores his patrons with lectures on the virtues of the lonely artichoke. Chefs that I have worked for have christened me with the title "king of the braise," the master of one-pot cooking, and as of late considered me to have reincarnated as a firmly rooted Polish peasant with aristocratic tastes. I've never felt comfortable wearing a tall, white chef's hat but it's my experience in my profession that has propelled me to chef status without losing sight of my humble beginnings. I'm a cook. I put all of my awards and accolades in a box on the shelf, because the best compliment for me is to see a customer's face light up when they taste one of my creations, or to have a fellow chef reminisce in the late hours of the evening about a dish his mother used to make after he's had one of mine that's similar.

Early in my career, I worked at a few restaurants both here and abroad that specialized in Eastern European country cuisine. Most of these institutions were housed in old 3-story brown stones, and garnered their reputations as being family run, and food, service, and ambience oriented. The concepts worked and most are still around today. I liked the style, the comfort of the family, and the unpretentiousness of the service. The food was always great and chefs would always reiterate that customers come and go, but the food and service carries on for generations.

It took me a long time to grasp and incorporate that philosophy into my cooking style because most restaurant owners I've dealt with are number counters, not hospitable hosts reared on the old Eastern European tradition of style and service. I don't blame them; escalating rents, insurance, and employee problems plague the industry, and it's easy to lose sight of all those little niceties that make a restaurant shine.

Life is funny. I've strived to stay on the cutting edge of culinary expertise, but it's the lessons of my northwest side roots that have always kept my business busy and afloat. For the last 10 years, I've been working bi-coastally, helping failing or new concept restaurants find their niche in the market place. It's an arduous process. When people hire me, they are well-informed that I work off of 4 basic premises: 1. Use traditional culinary techniques. 2. Get back to your roots. 3. Get rid of any excess baggage. 4. My way or the highway! They are simple concepts that stand the test of time in the culinary world.

Through my work, I've met a lot of great chefs, cooked many a late night dinner party, put on a few extra pounds, but I've always been perplexed by these recurring questions, "What's a Polish kid doing in a French kitchen, how come there's no good Polish cookbooks, and do you have any good Polish recipes because I'm having a party? I've heard it from Wolfgang, Emeril, Julia, family Moet, and the list goes on. I've always shrugged it off as small talk because what would a highly successful chef want with such peasant style fare. As my business has grown, more chefs have asked those same haunting questions causing me to lose sleep, and inspiring me to write a great Polish cookbook. Easier said than done!

research and history

I'm a sixth generation Pole from the northwest side of Chicago. My family was middle class, my dad was an advocate for Polish and Hispanic immigrants rights, and my mom's side of the family was from Wausau, Wisconsin, the home of the dairy farmer. Norwood Park, my home, was a stones throw away from Milwaukee Avenue, a gateway to cultural and ethnic diversity in the city of Chicago. My neighborhood is known for its religious traditions and fervent devotion to ethnic heritage. I hung out with Irish, Italians, Poles, Germans, Greeks, cops, and firemen, people who had large families and well-rooted ties to the community. It wasn't uncommon to hang with guys whose parents owned small "mom and pop" grocery stores, taverns, sausage, or bakery shops. Most of these small stores were handed down from their grandparents who usually lived upstairs in comfortable but cramped quarters. That closeness seemed to really bring those families together, and there was a lot of hard work, love and joy that went into keeping those businesses alive and thriving over the years. Unfortunately, parents pass on and the children either sink or swim in taking over the business. Modern technology, pre-mixed dough, and prepared foodstuffs have replaced a lot of laborious tasks in kitchens these days, and though it might on the outset seem to make financial sense, that old world feel and generational recipe is lost. The very foundation of what made that family and that business successful is gone and the passing on of our culinary heritage is lost forever. A good example is to try a grocery store bought piece of rye bread and compare it to a corner bakery "made fresh daily" loaf. You know what I mean.

Polish cuisine up to this time has been very elusive, not because there aren't any great Polish restaurants around, but do to the fact that no one of any culinary authority has ever attempted to step up to the plate and lay it out in a clear, definitive manner. Don't get me wrong, there are a handful of Polish cookbooks that I own that are fair but are so outdated and incomplete that they in no way, shape, or form represent the goodness of Polish cooking. Great cookbooks are always judged on complete and workable recipes, not on half-truths and generalities. Let me put it to you another way. When you build a house, you always begin with a workable blue-print that starts from the foundation and works its way up. This is to insure that the structure is solidly built and will stand the test of time. On the other hand, if you don't follow the blueprint, your structure will inevitably weaken and fall. The same goes for cooking. Start out with a bad recipe and you will end up with a dish that failed. However, if you start out with a complete and precise recipe, you will most likely end up with a successful and delicious dish every time.

In researching this project, I was appalled by some of the culinary advice that the so-called Polish cooking experts were driveling to their readers. One writer, who lives in Warsaw, recommends that people save their pickle juice for a refreshing morning mouthwash. What planet are you from? And I was also amazed to find out that a Frenchman is at the helm of one of Poland's greatest hotel kitchens that serves nouvelle Polish cuisine. There are some 40 million Poles in Poland. So where are the great chefs at? I'm proud to be a Polish American and, call me crazy, but I take a lot of offense to anyone who inadvertently makes a mockery of Poles in general. No other country in world history has endured the hardships that Poland has, but there is one thing that is constant, the Poles have always persevered with their dignity and pride in tact. Traits that exemplify the true meaning of being a Pole. I would like to take on the culinary challenge of writing a great Polish cookbook to set the record straight for generations to come.

If you study food history all, and I mean all, Eastern European countries up until the 14th century ate the same monotonous medieval foods. Crude cuts of meat and birds went to the kings and queens, whereas the peasants were left with root vegetables and grains. Most people are surprised to learn that Poles were mostly vegetarian, which was due to the fact that they had so many religious holidays, and there was a lot of fasting going on. Any culinary history before the 14th century is sketchy, but it was at about this time that two great women significantly impacted and changed the Polish culinary world forever. Jadwiga of Anjou, a daughter of a Hungarian king of French ancestry was married off to a Lithuanian prince in the year 1386. History books note that the marriage was no more than one of convenience as she was a political pawn. However, she made the best of a bad situation by enjoying the luxuries of the queen's court and by spreading her wealth and vast knowledge of food to the peasants in the countryside. It was during her reign that refinement, style, and an assortment of dry spices were introduced to Polish cuisine. And it is also noteworthy, that although the Anjou's were considered French, they were in reality a type of Mediterranean Creole since they owned kingdoms in Cyprus, Syria, and Armenia. In 1518 the Poles got a blessing by the name of Princess Bona Sforza who married King Sigismund I. This Italian princess from Milan brought to the Poles a variety of Mediterranean vegetable staples such as celery, leeks, artichokes, asparagus, assorted tomatoes, and soup herbs. History also notes that the Byzantines were trading heavily in Milano at this time so she also is responsible for the infusion of olive oil, lemons, figs, oranges, chestnuts, and oregano to the Polish culinary landscape.

The Italian influence cannot be ignored because of Poland's special relationship to the papal see. Poland, due to its geographical location, has always had abundant streams, rich farmland and has been a haven for wild game and birds. Root vegetables grew along with assorted wild berries and endless fields of grain. For the next 200 plus years, Polish cuisine flourished and evolved. Kings and queens enjoyed the fruits of the peasant's labors, whereas the peasantry gained knowledge by glimpsing the way the aristocrats dined. It wasn't uncommon for the peasantry to be spectators at the lavish banquets held by the royalty. Throughout these years, food pilgrimages were made to Poland by neighboring countries with no real historical culinary impact. In 1682, Stanislaw Czerniecki, a nobleman and secretary to King Jan III Sobieski, wrote the first original Polish cook-book. It is also worthy to note that the first roadside Polish restaurant, called a Karczma, had its beginnings at that time.

There is a lot more history I would like to relate, but it isn't pretty. In 1772, Russia, Germany, and Austria, under self serving treaty agreements, erased Poland from the map, and Poland's political entity evaporated into thin air. That's some heavy stuff!

It's at this point that I began my Polish culinary journey. I've been cooking this food for years, never giving it any low marks as a viable and interesting cuisine. Heck, I've even cooked it for mayors, judges, governors, and CEO's with rave reviews. Over the last 20 some years, I've cooked, studied, and mastered most aspects of French and Italian cooking, and can clearly see their evolution. The question remained though, what can I bring to my fellow Poles that will put their treasured cuisine on the culinary map for the entire world to see? Should I reinvent all of the classics, or abandon them completely and start anew? I took my cause to the streets, but had a lot of doors shut in my face. In the last year, my dining room table has become my workspace and directly across from where I sit is a beautiful framed image of My Lady of Czestochowa with Child. Slipped into the frame is an old black and white photo of my great aunt, Sister Norbert, a Franciscan nun. Sometimes late at night when the kids are asleep, I'll be working at the table, and for some strange reason I subconsciously talk to the pictures for strength and guidance. If I get up and look into the picture, the only reflection I can see in the glass is myself. I guess they are saying to me just be yourself and look into your own heart.

the new Polish cuisine

A truly great inspirational chef and mentor from across the pond who I've admired throughout my career paraphrased peasant country cooking most beautifully and eloquently as "A cuisine that is founded on sympathy. It is only done well with deep instinctive feelings, and is done best if you have been familiar with it all your life." Very well put!

My cooking style has always had a rustic character, because it is based on the peasant country dishes that I've enjoyed through the years whether it be Polish, French, Greek, or Italian. I'm fortunate that I have tasted and savored all the warmth and joy of everyday Polish cooking firsthand. From my Aunt Minnie's chicken in the pot when I was 5 years old, to watching my grandmother make her famous pierogi, the aromas, tastes, and emotions associated with these memories are still etched in my mind. I've seen many hardened businessmen get teary eyed when they reminisce about their busia's cooking, and if they only had a written recipe that would duplicate that dish. It's unfortunate that the recipe was never written or handed down.

Polish cuisine, like many other cuisines, is based on maybe a dozen or so great local dishes that would simmer away for hours in iron pots on old stoves. The amount of meat in the pot might have been scarce, but the rest of the ingredients were the freshest available, usually locally grown, and full of flavor. Cooking was usually done by busia or matka, who devoted a great deal of their time in the kitchen to prepare meals for the family they loved. Polish history books show that cooking and entertaining were integral parts of the social life in villages and small towns. Polish crystal, hand-laced linen, and glistening silverware always adorned a host's table if visitors would come around. I like to think of Polish cooking and entertaining style as peasant hospitality serving gourmet fare.

The question still remained, how could I combine my classically trained culinary skills together with the peasant nature of Polish cooking, without losing the integrity of the original food? I would like the two to enhance each other but not go over the culinary edge. Professional kitchens usually have a good dozen trained cooks who prepare all sorts of food items such as stocks, sauces, or desserts, whereas the home cook is usually on their own. So this is what I've done in my first volume on Polish cooking:

I've reworked the most loved and recognizable Polish dishes by reducing the fat and sour content so they are healthier and have a broader appeal without losing the true integrity and flavor of the dish.

I've given the home cook for the first time an accurate and precise recipe that truly represents the taste and flavor of modern Polish American cooking.

The recipes utilize readily available ingredients and spices that are staples in most homes. Also, the recipes have been scaled down to a manageable size for a family, but can be easily doubled or tripled if desired.

I've also included other dishes that compliment the style of Polish cooking for those of you who are on the more adventurous side.

With that said, I give you *The New Polish Cuisine*. In this first volume, it was my intention to give the home cook a solid base and book of accurate recipes that represent the art of Polish cooking at its best. The dishes that are in this volume are those most familiar to me growing up on the northwest side of Chicago. If your favorite recipe does not appear in the book, don't be disappointed, I promise that it will show up in a subsequent volume in the near future. I hope that the beautiful pictures will inspire you to get into the kitchen and cook for yourself and your family.

—*Chef Mike Baruch, 2002*

*p*reparation

a well-tooled kitchen

Let Mikey give all of you "masters of the flame" a good piece of advice. If you're going to cook, do it right! Abandon all your old aluminum pots and pans, and get into the habit of using quality cookware. Not only will it make your life easier, but it will also make your food taste better. Professional chefs always bellow the phrase, "use the right tool for the right job." Trust me, it makes a difference. Over the past 20 some odd years, I think I've accumulated more useless cooking tools than any chef I know. Call it an obsession or just plain fascination; a well-tooled kitchen can be your best friend or worst enemy. "Let me digress."

Every year, some 1,000 or so new fangled cooking gadgets flood the market and are hocked by celebrity chefs on local cable channels as the utensil you can't live without. Some are good, but the majority because of cheap production costs could actually burn your house down. I dig cooking with real pots and pans that are slightly heavy –duty, non-stick, and available at a reasonable price. Now there are those purists that only cook with glistening copper (pretty to look at, but a pain in the neck to maintain), or those who swear by calphalon (handles break off and food sticks), or those who hit the restaurant stores and buy the standard aluminum based pans (stands the test of time, but are clunky, unattractive, and absorb odors from the food). Who am I to judge, I currently use a set of pans I like that are analon coated that I get in a set every couple of years for Christmas.

Years back, I was approached by a major upscale retail store to help young couples compile their wish list for cooking utensils in their bridal registry. The job paid very well, but I was abruptly dismissed, because I wasn't pushing the big-ticket items. Call me crazy, but do newly weds really need that 5-quart fish poacher, or that 8-burner fuel injected range from hell! That extra $2,500.00 would make a nice deposit toward a small condo. (I hope you appreciate my point.)

To research this preface, all I had to do was go through my entire kitchen, and to my amazement, I realized that I own the same knives that I started out with some 25 years ago. I also have a few really soft cotton chef shirts and aprons that are slightly tattered, been washed a million times, but have worn the test of time. When I think back of when I first purchased them, they were high quality products that weren't inexpensive, but I'm lucky I had good sales people helping me at quality stores. If you live in the Chicago land area and are somewhat confused about what and where to buy, I can recommend 4 great stores that I purchased my goods at. They are Marshall Fields, Crate and Barrel, Williams Sonoma, and Chef's Catalog. (Note: I am not sponsored by any of these stores, but they have great culinary departments and my all out favorite: a no hassle return policy. I recommend bringing in my kitchen list and let them help you out.) Please keep in mind that the following pages are just a guideline to a well-stocked kitchen. If you are on a budget, a good set of assorted pots and pans and assorted knives will hold you over for many years.

knives

The chef's best friend. When shopping for a knife, pick it up and see how it feels in your hand. Some knives will be well- balanced, while others will be blade or handle heavy. Try to find the happy medium knife with a thin, sharp blade. I advise you to invest in high-quality, high carbon, stainless steel knives. Be sure to keep your knives sharpened, cleaned, and stored properly.

2 paring knives, 3$^1\!/_2$ inches long

boning knife, 5$^1\!/_2$ inches long

chef's knife, 8 to 10 inches long

thin pointed carving knife, 10 inches long

serrated bread knife, 8 inches long

sharpening steel, 12 inches long

roasting fork, 7 inches long

1 set kitchen shears

cleaver, 7 inches long

1 large pizza cutter wheel

pots and pans

The second most important tool to a chef is a good quality set of pots and pans. As I've stated earlier there are endless varieties and types of pots on the market, so the choice is up to you. My advice to you is to go to a store and pick up a pan, feel its weight, see if the handles give under pressure, and so on. If you are a petite person you don't want a heavy set, but if you are cooking on a professional home range, you better pick something with good weight and durability.

2 non-stick medium-weight frying pans (skillets), 8 or 10 inches in diameter

3 qt. non-stick sauté pan, straight sided with a tight fitting lid

10 or 14-inch old-fashioned cast iron skillet

10-inch stovetop grill

12-inch non-stick wok

5 saucepans with lids: 2 cup, 1$^1\!/_2$ qt., 2 qt., 3 qt., and 4$^1\!/_2$ qt. capacity

5 qt. Dutch oven with tight fitting lid

8 qt. stockpot with tight-fitting lid

small shallow roasting pan

large high-sided roasting pan with rack

an assortment of colorful Le Creuset oven cookware, including roasting pans

collapsible vegetable steamer insert

utensils

Kitchen utensils are all of those little tchotchke things that seem to overflow everyone's kitchen drawers, but are indispensable. If you are an avid cook, let me give you a tip. Keep all of the spoons and ladles in decorative Polish crocks on your counter-tops for ease of use, and buy drawer organizers to separate all of the smaller stuff you rarely use. This little bit of organization could greatly help you out if your hands are full of cake batter, and you need something quick!

<table>
<tr><td>2 sets stainless steel measuring spoons</td><td>citrus zester</td></tr>
<tr><td>2 sets stainless steel measuring cups</td><td>apple corer</td></tr>
<tr><td>Pyrex glass-measuring cup – 1 cup</td><td>potato peeler</td></tr>
<tr><td>Pyrex glass-measuring cup – 4 cups</td><td>bottle opener</td></tr>
<tr><td>1 set assorted plastic funnels</td><td>corkscrew</td></tr>
<tr><td>assorted plastic spatulas</td><td>heavy-duty can opener</td></tr>
<tr><td>assorted long handled wooden spoons</td><td>bulb baster</td></tr>
<tr><td>long-handled stainless steel spoon</td><td>ice cream scoop</td></tr>
<tr><td>long-handled stainless steel slotted spoon</td><td>nutmeg grater</td></tr>
<tr><td>long-handled Chinese skimmer</td><td>egg slicer</td></tr>
<tr><td>2 stainless steel soup ladles, large and small</td><td>stainless steel whisk</td></tr>
<tr><td>large stainless steel grill spatula</td><td>meat mallet</td></tr>
<tr><td>assorted kitchen tongs</td><td>lemon juicer</td></tr>
<tr><td>8 non-stick grilling skewers, 12-inch</td><td>box grater</td></tr>
<tr><td>6 thin metal skewers, 6 to 8-inch</td><td>potato ricer</td></tr>
<tr><td>1 pack wood skewers, 6 to 8-inch</td><td>mortar and pestle</td></tr>
<tr><td>small wire mesh hand strainer</td><td>peppercorn mill</td></tr>
<tr><td>medium wire mesh hand strainer</td><td>salad spinner</td></tr>
<tr><td>small plastic colander with legs</td><td>instant-read meat thermometer</td></tr>
<tr><td>large plastic colander with legs</td><td>mercury oven thermometer</td></tr>
<tr><td>fine mesh chinois</td><td>candy thermometer</td></tr>
<tr><td>nut cracker</td><td>kitchen timer</td></tr>
</table>

baking equipment

Last but not least. Baking equipment over the past 10 years has really gone through an overhaul due to technological advances in plastics, and the general renewed interest in the art of baking. Depending on which style of pastry making you are in to, there are literally hundreds of gadgets you can acquire, but be forewarned they can get quite pricey. We are fortunate in Chicago to have some of the best baking utensil manufacturers around, so I think you can find what you are looking for.

1 set heavy-duty oven mitts

1 heavy-duty stand mixer, 5 to 6 qt. capacity

food processor, 6 to 7 cup capacity

marble pastry slab

wood pastry slab

dough scraper

1 thin and 1 heavy rolling pin

assorted clear plastic buckets for flour
and sugar

small digital pastry scale in ounces

large table scale, 2$^1/_2$ pound capacity in ounces

quality set stainless steel mixing bowls

quality set Pyrex glass bowls

2 double thick aluminum half sheet pans
with silpat

2 double thick aluminum quarter sheet pans
with silpat

2 10 x 18-inch stainless cooling racks

2 8$^1/_2$ x 4$^1/_2$-inch non-stick loaf pans

4 mini loaf pans

16 x 4-inch Italian bread pan

2 round non-stick 9-inch cake pans

9-inch spring form pan

rectangular 13 x 9-inch baking pan
with plastic lid

heavy jelly roll pan, 10 x 15-inch

2 regular pie tins

2 non-stick muffin tins, $^1/_2$-cup capacity
for 12 muffins

2 fluted tart pans, 8 or 10-inch

1 set cookie cutters

1 set circle cutter

1 boxed set pastry bag and tips

2 small and 2 large boar bristle pastry brushes

1 set heat resistant spatulas

thin metal icing knife

powdered sugar shaker

1 dozen 10-inch cardboard cake circles

water spray bottle

fresh breads

milwaukee avenue caraway rye bread

archer avenue light rye

pulaski sandwich rye with caraway and dill

pumpernickel bread

rustic country loaf

butter crunch top

farm house daily white

poppy seed twist

Let's face it, Poles love breads, the staff of life. And I'm not talking about store bought, I'm talking about Ma and Pa corner bakery made fresh daily. These people take their bread so seriously, that in Medieval times history books show that there have been bread wars, revolts, taxes on quality grain, church crusades, and hell, even a couple of famines to boot, all in the name of bread.

Up until the 18th century, light rye as we know it today was unavailable to the lower class peasants of Poland, and most of Eastern Europeans due to the fact that there were so many religious holidays, all of the best or light grain was given to the Church or the King as an offering. So the working class was left with a darker unrefined grain, which in some cases led to huge mortality rates due to molds and the unsanitary conditions in which the grains were stored. Man, what a way to go.

People in Chicago love all types of light rye. I'm talking about a tight crumb; slightly sour tasting, slightly chewy-crusted loaf with a hint of caraway. Oh, they love other breads too, but light rye is the workingman's daily choice. The lightness of the loaf lifts the workingman to aristocratic ranks whereas; the sourness of the bread keeps him well rooted in the peasant tradition. Chicago bakeries have a special lingo that one must know to order breads. Firstly, the shape and size, meaning does one want it long or short, bucket rolled or braided? Light or dark, meaning light rye or dark rye or pumpernickel. Next is seeded or unseeded, meaning with or without caraway seeds, poppy seeds, or sesame seeds. Finally, should it be sliced or whole. My advice to you is to get to the bakery early, grab a number, and pay close attention to the action, because by mid-morning all the good stuff is gone.

With that said, let's get to the heart of Polish cuisine. I've included in this book 8 breads that have been very loyal to me over the last 25 years. I wanted to give you a wide spectrum of lightness, tastes, flavors, and textures, and if you look very closely at the ingredients, you will see that they are all very similar in nature, but when baked are oh so different. Bread baking is a very easy, but sometimes very frustrating science. I've seen many a great chef break down and cry with frustration over the fact that their bread didn't turn out like the corner bakery. This is without question the most difficult chapter in the book, but these recipes (unrevealed until now) have been my most requested. There are six steps in making a good loaf of bread:

1. Mixing the flour, salt, yeast, and water to make a mass of dough.
2. Kneading the dough to form gluten that will give the dough its strength.
3. Resting the dough so that the yeast can activate with the gluten and rise.
4. Punching back the dough to release yeast bubbles and recharge the microorganisms in the dough.
5. Shaping the dough and letting it rise until it doubles in shape.
6. Baking and cooling.

Bread dough has a mind of its own. If it's too cold when mixed, it gets lethargic and moves really slowly. If it gets too hot, it just gets plain out ornery by rising too fast and taking on a yeasty taste. However, if you pay close attention to my directions, you will reach a happy medium and have dough that does exactly what you want it to do. I have one last piece of advice on bread making. Don't get frustrated if your loaves don't turn out like the ones at your local bakery. Commercial bakeries have all kinds of specialized equipment and ingredients that make their bread look perfect. Be more concerned with the taste than the appearance.

Mike, the apprentice Polish baker

I've got to be honest; I have a love-hate relationship with bread and pastry. I think it all stems from my earlier days as an apprentice cook working at a local bakery on the Northwest side of Chicago. When I was hired for the job over the phone, I was told by the owner in his broken English, "Yeah! You'll be working in the back with the bakers, so be here tomorrow at 6:00 a.m. sharp. And wear comfortable shoes." So with that said and a promise to make minimum wage, I went to bed early that night, so that I could be awake by 5:00 a.m. As I trudged 2 miles through the early morning snow, my thoughts of sweet anticipation could barely hold back my enthusiasm. Swirling hot Babkas, Almond Coffee Cakes, Rye Breads, and Tortes whipped through my head, and maybe a cup of hot cinnamon Krupnik to welcome the new kid on the job. As I turned up the alley, I could see the back of the bakery, and low and behold there were 4 bakers, 2 Poles and 2 Germans to be exact, sitting on old dairy crates waiting for me.

As I approached them, I was greeted with an enthusiastic "Hello," and at the same time I thought it was strange that they were all red-cheeked sitting there in 5 below weather, wearing nothing but white short sleeved T-shirts, stained aprons, and those crazy Chicago Tribune formed baker hats. One baker by the name of Stanley said, "Hey, you're early so have a cup of coffee," and then he offered me an unfiltered cigarette that he pulled from behind his ear. I declined the smoke but accepted the coffee that was in a mug, which resembled my grandfather's old shaving cup, and the coffee didn't taste much better. For an uneasy 5 minutes of small talk, all I could do was stare at their thick necks, and massive arms, which obviously were built by years of mixing dough, and hoisting pans into the hot ovens. Alas, one of the bakers let me into paradise. I could still remember it today; it was like walking into heaven, the warmth of the kitchen, and the sweet smell of fresh baked pastries and breads. As my eyes gleamed at the massive sized bakery, a long building with a center aisle of wood worktables down the middle, and baking equipment on each side, I was in awe. And while my coat and scarf was lifted off of me, I was donned with one of the bakers used aprons, and another's sweat filled hat was placed on top of my head. I was ready to bake! I asked with anticipation, "Wear do I start?" And now my new friend, Stanley put his arm around me and said, "You're going to work with the sugar."

"Oh," I said, "I always wanted to work with sugar." With that said, he handed me 2 wood-handled metal pastry scrapers, and said, "Now get on your hands and knees, and start scraping the trampled sugar off the oak floors, all the way up and all the way down." No joke! Two bowling alley sized lanes were laid out before me. As Stanley walked out the back door, he reminded me that the shop opened in 1 hour. So on my hands and knees, I began my apprenticeship. Every foot of the way was an adventure, huge tables to the left of me, huge containers full of sugar and flour to the right, and let's not forget, gargantuan baker's ovens, bowl, mixers, and a million stack trays. As I eagerly scraped, I noticed that I was eerily the only one in the dimly lit bakery, except for the voices speaking in Polish behind the red velvet curtain at the front of the store. "Scrape, scrape, scrape, crawl, crawl, crawl," Hey, I said to myself, this must be some kind of Polish joke, right. Maybe if I get up to the curtain, I'll be saved." Dare I not get up, but to stretch my aching back and swollen hands? So alas, in pain, I popped up and to my amazement, I saw that on the wood work tables were hundreds of fresh baked breads of all shapes and sizes, beautiful pastries, tortes, coffee cakes, chocolate pachki, cookies galore, and because it was around Christmas, Chrusticki and almond crescents gloriously coated with powdered sugar. My stomach reeled in pain from the cheap coffee, so I grabbed the closest item off the table to ease the pain, and now while I'm scraping again and choking on the powdered sugar crescents, I hear the distinct sound of Christmas bells emulating from the front of the shop. The store is open. I quietly crawl up to the velvet curtain, and peak my head through to see a beautiful wood paneled European storefront, with glass lined shelves adorned with dainty Polish lace, and two bread cutting machines running full tilt at 7:00 a.m. The steady clientele of Busias, dressed in car coats, scarves, and galoshes, were streaming through the front door fighting over the number machine. As I sat there in amazement watching this fevered excitement, my eyes were affixed to one of the countertops which had a spool of kitchen twine that was rapidly being wound around every box and package that left the store. At the same time, the velvet curtain was drawn, and I was knocked on my butt by one of the Polish girls hurriedly racing to get more rye breads and Babkas. Not a word was said, or an apology given, so dejectedly I went back to my scraping and table foraging, and just about the time I got down to where I had begun, I was tapped on the shoulder by one of the shop girls named Sophie. A big girl with a huge chest and a lot of makeup, and a hairnet to boot, she said in her sweet Polish accent, "Welcome to the bakery, and here's a cup of coffee and a chocolate pachki for you." She also added two other phrases that I will always remember;

"All employees get 50% off on all unsold bakery, and when you're done with the floor,
don't forget to clean the baking pans."

Bread Baker's Work Bench

There is nothing more satisfying in life than the smell of freshly baked bread coming from your kitchen, and with a little trial and error, anyone can knock out a beautiful loaf. Before you begin, please follow my guidelines and read about the ingredients that I use at home.

proper measuring

Every recipe in this book, whether it is bread or pastry, uses the spoon and sweep method. That is pouring a bag of flour into a plastic container, then using a large kitchen spoon, spoon the flour directly into a metal measuring cup, then using a flat icing spatula, remove any excess flour by running the flat edge across the top of the cup. (Do not dip your measuring cup into a bag of flour because it compacts the flour too much and the recipes won't work.)

proper mixing

Breads in this book are better kneaded in a heavy-duty tabletop mixer to build gluten. All of the breads can be mixed in a large capacity food processor but I prefer the other. One good word of advice is to never walk away from the machine while it is on because certain dough will torque the machine and may cause it to hop around the counter and land on the floor.

oven temperature

Always make sure that your oven is cleaned and properly calibrated. A few degrees off here and there can ruin your precious dough. It is wise to invest in a good oven thermometer.

ingredients

Never short yourself by buying inferior products. Good ingredients make all the difference in baking.

Active Dry Yeast—I only use Red Star (granular) in the jar, stored in the freezer to keep fresh. Rapid rise is a no-no, and fresh yeast is too hard to work with. Old recipes call for too much yeast, so please follow my guidelines for measuring yeast. Use ½ teaspoon yeast per cup for regular flour dough, and use 3/4 teaspoon yeast per cup for heavy and sweet dough.

Butter—I like good old Land O' Lakes Unsalted Butter for its never-ending consistency and exceptional taste.

Shortening—Crisco all vegetable shortening in the blue can is my favorite for its frying and baking consistency.

Vegetable Oil—Wesson Canola Oil is great because of its pure clean taste and versatility.

Eggs—Grade A large eggs are perfect for all of my recipes.

Milk—I only use Grade A pasteurized whole milk.

Powdered Milk—Powdered milk is sometimes used instead of whole milk to keep a bread or dough light and fluffy without adding extra fat or weight.

Sea Salt—I only use sea salt in all of my cooking for its clean and pure taste. Regular iodized table salt will give your food an unpleasant after taste.

Malt Syrup—A honey like syrup made of roasted grains that has a more concentrated taste than regular sugar. Dark honey can also be substituted if needed.

Molasses—Brer Rabbit green label molasses is excellent for providing flavor, color, and moisture to baked products.

Chef's Tip about flour: While the home cook depends almost exclusively on a product called all-purpose flour, the professional baker has available a wide variety of flours with different qualities and characteristics. It is vitally important that you seek out the best flour you can get your hands on to replicate the quality of bakery shop results.

Powdered Sour—An integral ingredient that gives rye bread its distinctive mellow, tangy, sour flavor. Powdered sour is available at any quality baking supply house or through mail order.

Vital Wheat Gluten—Not all flours are created equal so a tablespoon or 2 added to any bread dough will give your loaves more strength and boost while lightening the texture and promoting a good rise. I recommend using 1 teaspoon per cup of regular flour, and $1\frac{1}{2}$ teaspoon per cup of whole grain or rye flours.

All-Purpose Flour—Store bought flours are adequate. However, I like to search out and find quality flour milled from hard red winter wheat that has a significant amount of gluten producing protein in it. Most whole food markets carry a variety of great brands, but read the label for brands that carry a minimum of 11.7% protein.

Bread Flour—I prefer to use bread flour that is unbleached, unbromated, and that is made from hard red spring wheat. Bread flours naturally have higher protein content than other flours and this will give your loaves more structure. Try to find a brand that contains at least a 12.7% to 14.2% protein content.

Rye Flour—Rye flours come in so many different varieties that it is often difficult to know what to buy. I prefer using light rye flour, but sometimes I combine it with darker rye flours or whole rye meal (pumpernickel flour) to give my breads a richer taste or texture. Rye flours are naturally low in protein so most bakers use a rye bread improver or high protein wheat flour that gives the bread its chewy texture. My recipes use a combination of high protein bread flour and vital wheat gluten to give the loaves that extra lift.

Rye Blend—Whole food markets sometimes sell this mixture which is a combination of light rye and a strong wheat flour that is an excellent mix for the beginning rye bread maker. Feel free to substitute this blend for all the flour in any rye bread recipe.

Milwaukee Avenue Caraway Rye Bread

Ingredients

Sponge

1 cup warm water (about 110 degrees)
1½ teaspoons active dry yeast
1¾ cups rye flour
Pinch of sugar

Dough

1½ teaspoons active dry yeast
3½ cups bread flour
7½ teaspoons vital wheat gluten
1½ teaspoons powdered sour
2 tablespoons shortening, softened
2½ teaspoons sea salt
1 tablespoon caraway seeds
½ cup warm water (about 120–130 degrees)

Starch wash

¼ cup water
½ teaspoon cornstarch

One heavy sheet pan lined with parchment
   and dusted with cornmeal

About 25 years ago, I worked at a bakery on the Northwest side of Chicago around Milwaukee and Devon called Forest View. On my last day, my friend Stashu, the head baker, took me aside and said, "Mihawik, every young baker needs at least one good rye bread recipe." With that said, he handed me a recipe scribbled in Polish on a used flour sack. Needless to say, I was deeply touched, but also confused because I don't read Polish and the recipe was for 250 loaves. It wasn't until years later that I had the faded recipe interpreted and finally broken down to a manageable size. I consider this to be the best rye bread made in the city of Chicago. The recipe produces a smaller sized loaf, tight grained with slightly sour and caraway undertones, complimented by a shiny, chewy crust. This bread is just a tad darker than other ryes in the book, but that is just a play on the flour ratios. I recommend eating it with smoked Polish sausage, kraut and pork, bigos, or kiszka and eggs.

Chef's Tip!

Don't be tempted to add more flour to the semi sticky dough, that's the way it's supposed to be. For first time bakers, bake the bread in long tube pans.

Preparation

1. To make the sponge, place the water in a mixing bowl and whisk in the yeast. Stir in the flour and sugar until smooth, then cover with plastic wrap and let the sponge rise until doubled in volume, about 1 hour.

2. To mix the dough in a heavy-duty mixer, place the sponge and all the other ingredients, except the water in the mixing bowl, attach the paddle and mix on low speed for 1 minute to blend the ingredients. While the machine is still running on low speed, slowly add the warm water to the flour until the dough forms a mass around the paddle. Now turn the machine off, remove the paddle and replace with the dough hook. Knead the dough on medium low speed for about 5 minutes, or until the dough is smooth and elastic. If the dough is excessively soft and sticky, add 1 to 2 tablespoons more flour, one at a time, and knead a little longer.

3. Place the dough in a large oiled bowl and turn to coat all sides. Cover the bowl tightly with plastic wrap, and allow the dough to rise in a warm place until doubled in bulk, about 1 hour.

4. Turn the risen dough out onto a clean work surface, and divide the dough into two equal pieces. To form a loaf, use your hands to punch the dough back and flatten it out. Fold the piece of dough over onto itself away from you. Square the edges and push them an inch or so near the middle. Then roll the loaf up into a tight log, sealing the dough at each turn with the tips of your fingers. Pinch each end to seal. Now form the other loaf. Carefully lift up and place onto the prepared pan, seam side down, and equally spaced apart. Cover the loaves with oiled plastic wrap, and allow to rise in a warm place until ¾ risen.

5. While the loaves are rising, preheat the oven to 450°F.

6. When the loaves are ready, slash them 6 or 7 times with a razor blade across the top of the loaf, starting from about halfway up one side and ending halfway up the other side. Spray the oven a few times, using a spray bottle filled with water, and then bake the loaves for 30 minutes until the tops are golden brown.

7. While the loaves are baking, combine the water and cornstarch in a small pot and bring to a quick boil, then remove from the heat. Whisk with a spoon until smooth.

8. When the loaves are golden brown, remove from the oven and place on a cooling rack. While the loaves are still hot, using a pastry brush, lightly paint them with the starch wash.

Makes 2 loaves

Archer Avenue Light Rye

Archer Ave., with its bustling Polish community, is quickly becoming the new Warsaw in Chicago. Restaurants, sausage shops, bakeries, and even Polish soup kitchens are sprouting up everywhere. This rye is typical of what you will find in that area. The loaves are light in color and plump, tightly grained with a hint of sweetness. This rye is the perfect compliment for soups and sandwiches.

Chef's Tip!

When you form the loaves, it's important to roll them into a tight sausage shape, then tuck the ends underneath so that the dough has a nice tight rye bread appearance.

Ingredients

Sponge

1/2 cup warm water (about 110 degrees)
2 teaspoons active dry yeast
1/2 cup light rye flour
1 tablespoon caraway seeds

Dough

2 teaspoons active dry yeast
5 1/2 cups bread flour
1/2 cup light rye flour
6 teaspoons vital wheat gluten
1 teaspoon powdered sour
2 tablespoons shortening, softened
2 teaspoons sea salt
2 teaspoons malt syrup or honey
1 3/4 cup warm water (about 120–130 degrees)

Starch wash

1/4 cup water
1/2 teaspoon cornstarch

One heavy sheet pan lined with parchment
and dusted with cornmeal

Preparation

1. **To make the sponge,** place the water in a mixing bowl and whisk in the yeast. Stir in the flour until smooth, then cover with plastic wrap and let the sponge rise until doubled in volume, about 1 hour.

2. **To mix the dough** in a heavy-duty mixer, place the sponge and all the other ingredients, except the water in the mixing bowl, attach the paddle and mix on low speed for 1 minute to blend the ingredients. While the machine is still running on low speed, slowly add the warm water to the flour until the dough forms a mass around the paddle. Now turn the machine off, remove the paddle and replace with the dough hook. Knead the dough on medium low speed for about 5 minutes, or until the dough is smooth and elastic. If the dough is excessively soft and sticky, add 1 to 2 tablespoons more flour, one at a time, and knead a little longer.

3. **Place the dough** in a large oiled bowl and turn to coat all sides. Cover the bowl tightly with plastic wrap, and allow the dough to rise in a warm place until doubled in bulk, about 1 hour.

4. **Turn the risen dough** out onto a clean work surface, and divide the dough into two equal pieces. To form a loaf, use your hands to punch the dough back and flatten it out. Fold the piece of dough over onto itself away from you. Square the edges and push them an inch or so near the middle. Then roll the loaf up into a tight log, sealing the dough at each turn with the tips of your fingers. Pinch each end to seal. Now form the other loaf. Carefully lift up and place onto the prepared pan, seam side down, and equally spaced apart. Cover the loaves with oiled plastic wrap, and allow to rise in a warm place until 3/4 risen.

5. **While the loaves are rising,** preheat the oven to 450°F.

6. **When the loaves** are ready, slash them 6 or 7 times with a razor blade across the top of the loaf, starting from about halfway up one side and ending halfway up the other side. Spray the oven a few times, using a spray bottle filled with water, and then bake the loaves for 30 minutes until the tops are golden brown.

7. **While the loaves are baking,** combine the water and cornstarch in a small pot and bring to a quick boil, then remove from the heat. Whisk with a spoon until smooth.

8. **When the loaves are golden brown,** remove from the oven and place on a cooling rack. While the loaves are still hot, using a pastry brush, lightly paint them with the starch wash.

Makes 2 loaves

Pulaski Sandwich Rye with Caraway and Dill

Ingredients

1¾ cups rye flour
5 cups bread flour
7 teaspoons vital wheat gluten
4 teaspoons active dry yeast
1 teaspoon powdered sour
2 teaspoons caraway seeds
2 teaspoons dill seeds
2 tablespoons shortening, softened
2¼ cups warm water (about 120–130 degrees)
1 tablespoon sea salt
1 tablespoon malt syrup or honey

Two 8½ x 4½ x 2¾ inch loaf pans, oiled

I developed this recipe for those of you who just can't abandon every day white bread, but still enjoy the subtle taste of caraway rye. This is what I consider to be typical deli bread found at your local supermarket, without the preservatives. It is a plump pan loaf of medium grain, light in color with a slight caraway seasoning, and the slice-ability of sandwich bread. This is a great loaf for the lighter cuts of deli fare such as ham, smoked turkey, roast beef, egg salad, and even tuna. Load it up with tomato, lettuce, cheese, and mustard.

Chef's Tip!

Before you begin this recipe, I advise you to measure your loaf pans. If they're not the size I've indicated, your bread will be flat, but still good. Size does matter!

Preparation

1. **To mix the dough** in a heavy-duty mixer, place the flours, wheat gluten, yeast, sour, caraway and dill seeds, and shortening in the mixer bowl, attach the paddle and mix on low speed for 1 minute to blend the ingredients. Dissolve the salt and malt syrup into the warm water, and while the machine is still running on low speed, slowly add the warm liquid to the flour until the dough forms a mass around the paddle. Now turn the machine off, remove the paddle and replace with the dough hook. Knead the dough on medium low speed for about 5 minutes, or until the dough is smooth and elastic. If the dough is excessively soft and sticky, add 1 to 2 tablespoons more flour, one at a time, and knead a little longer.

2. **Place the dough** in a large oiled bowl and turn to coat all sides. Cover the bowl tightly with plastic wrap, and allow the dough to rise in a warm place until doubled in bulk, about 1 hour.

3. **Turn the risen dough** out on to a clean work surface, and divide it into two equal pieces.

4. **To form a loaf,** using your hands, stretch the dough into a rough rectangle. Fold in the short ends of the dough until it is approximately the length of the pan, and then fold the far long edge over to the middle. Fold over the other long side and compress to form a tight loaf. Place the loaf in the oiled pan, seam side down. Cover the

pan with plastic wrap. Repeat with the second piece of dough. Allow to rise in a warm place until almost ¾ risen.

5. **While the loaves are rising,** preheat the oven to 400°F.

6. **When the loaves are ready,** place in the oven and bake for about 30 minutes until they are golden brown and firm. Unmold the loaves to a rack to cool.

Makes 2 loaves

Pumpernickel Bread

Let's face it; pumpernickel breads can be plain out heavy, dry, and overly sweet. One day, I couldn't find any pumpernickel flour so I substituted rye flour instead, and "Holy Kiszka", one beautiful, light, airy, and heavenly sweet loaf was born. The bread has all of the taste characteristics of pumpernickel, medium crumbed and lusciously sweet from the molasses. The recipe yields 2 huge round loaves, and I recommend serving this bread with any smoked fish, pickled herring, or creamy cheese.

Chef's Tip!

To give these plump round loaves a rustic appearance, lightly dust the tops with some rye flour before placing them into the hot oven.

Ingredients

Sponge

½ cup warm water (about 110 degrees)
1 teaspoon active dry yeast
⅔ cup bread flour

Dough

5¼ cups bread flour
1¾ cups pumpernickel or rye flour
2¼ teaspoons active dry yeast
2 tablespoons unsalted butter, softened
1 tablespoon plus ¼ teaspoon sea salt
1¾ cups warm water (about 120–130 degrees)
¼ cup dark molasses
1½ teaspoons caramel (optional)

One heavy sheet pan lined with parchment
   and dusted with cornmeal

Preparation

1. **To make the sponge,** place the water in a mixing bowl and whisk in the yeast. Stir in the flour until smooth, then cover with plastic wrap and let the sponge rise until doubled in volume, about 1 hour.

2. **To mix the dough** in a heavy-duty mixer, place the sponge and all the other ingredients, except the water, dark molasses, and caramel in the mixing bowl, attach the paddle and mix on low speed for 1 minute to blend the ingredients. While the machine is still running on low speed, slowly add the warm water, dark molasses, and caramel to the flour until the dough forms a mass around the paddle. Now turn the machine off, remove the paddle and replace with the dough hook. Knead the dough on medium low speed for about 5 minutes, or until the dough is smooth and elastic. If the dough is excessively soft and sticky, add 1 to 2 tablespoons more flour, one at a time, and knead a little longer.

3. **Place the dough** in a large oiled bowl and turn to coat all sides. Cover the bowl tightly with plastic wrap, and allow the dough to rise in a warm place until doubled in bulk, about 1½ hours.

4. **Turn the risen dough** out onto a lightly floured work surface. Deflate the dough and divide it into two equal pieces. Now invert the bowl and cover the two pieces, and let them rest for exactly 10 minutes.

5. **To form a loaf,** remove any excess flour from the work surface. Using your hands, grasp the dough and form it into a rough shaped ball. Now gently using both hands, fold the dough underneath itself to create a tight ball. Repeat with the remaining dough, then place them onto a parchment lined sheet pan. Cover the loaves with oiled plastic wrap, and allow to rise in a warm place until doubled.

6. **When the loaves are almost doubled,** set a rack at the middle level of the oven and preheat to 475°F.

7. **When the loaves are ready,** place the pan into the hot oven. Spray the oven a few times, using a spray bottle filled with water, then bake the loaves for 10 minutes. Now reduce the temperature to 450°F., and bake for another 20 minutes until the crust is hard and well browned. Now turn the oven off and let the bread sit in the hot oven for 5 to 10 more minutes, until it appears that it can't go another minute without burning, then remove from the oven and cool for 45 minutes before slicing.

Makes 2 loaves

Rustic Country Loaf

Ingredients

3 cups bread flour
1 cup whole wheat flour
2½ teaspoons active dry yeast
1¼ teaspoon sea salt
Pinch of sugar
1⅓ cups warm water (about 120–130 degrees)

One heavy sheet pan lined with parchment
   and dusted with cornmeal

I t is well known that Poles have an affinity for all kinds of bread. Rye breads are well suited to most of the recipes in this book. However, there are also dozens of other breads that are eaten throughout Poland and many are wheat flour based. This firm, crusty loaf is the easiest of all breads to make, and when it is baking, it fills the kitchen with an enticing aroma. I usually advise people to make their dough in a heavy-duty mixer, but this is one of those dough's that is best made by hand to give it that rustic feel.

Chef's Tip!

This is a very versatile loaf. You can use all bread flour or substitute half of the bread flour with whole-wheat flour. All-purpose flour works well, too.

Preparation

1. **Put the flours,** yeast, salt, and sugar into a large mixing bowl. Stir with a wooden spoon to combine, and then make a well in the center. Now slowly add the warm water and using a heavy wooden spoon, stir the mixture until it forms a shaggy mass around the spoon.

2. **Using floured hands,** remove all of the shaggy mass from the spoon and place it onto a lightly floured work surface. Now using both hands, gently start to knead the dough until it becomes slightly smooth (if the dough seems sticky, sprinkle on a little more flour and work it into the dough). Form the dough into a tight ball, place it back into the bowl, cover the bowl with a kitchen towel, and let it rise in a warm place for about 1 hour or until it doubles.

3. **When the dough** has doubled in bulk, punch it down, and return it back to the bowl for another half hour to rise.

4. **After a half an hour,** remove the dough from the bowl, punch it down again, and gently knead it slightly, then form it back into a tight ball being careful to tuck the ends underneath. Place the ball onto the parchment lined sheet pan, cover again with a kitchen towel, and let it rise for another 30 to 40 minutes until almost doubled.

5. **While the dough** is rising, preheat the oven to 425°.

6. **When the dough** is risen, lightly dust it with some flour, and place it into the hot oven to bake on the middle rack for 25 to 30 minutes until it is a deep golden brown. Remove the loaf to a rack to cool.

Makes 1 plump loaf

Butter Crunch Top

You will find this Easter-time loaf in everyone's decorative basket, along with fresh Polish sausage, horseradish, hard-boiled eggs, and assorted goodies waiting to be blessed on Easter Sunday. This is a tight-grained loaf, slightly eggy and sweet, with the added bonus of an extra buttery crunch crust topping. It is the perfect "thin slicing loaf" for an Easter buffet. Excellent with smoked ham, horseradish, and Kosciusko mustard.

Chef's Tip!

Don't let the crunch topping throw you off, just lather it on as best as you can.

Ingredients

Dough

6 ¾ cups bread flour
5 teaspoons active dry yeast
3 tablespoons unsalted butter, softened
1 large whole egg and 1 yolk
1 tablespoon sea salt
1 ¾ cups warm water (about 120–130 degrees)
⅔ cup powdered milk
7 ½ tablespoons sugar

Crunch Topping

¼ cup warm water (about 110 degrees)
2 ½ teaspoons active dry yeast
⅓ cup bread flour
2 tablespoons unsalted butter, melted

Two 8 ½ x 4 ½ x 2 ¾ inch loaf pans, oiled

Preparation

1. **To mix the dough** in a heavy-duty mixer, place the flour, yeast, butter, eggs, and salt in the mixer bowl, attach the paddle and mix on low speed for 1 minute to blend the ingredients. Dissolve the milk powder and sugar into the warm water, and while the machine is still running on low speed, slowly add the warm liquid to the flour until the dough forms a mass around the paddle. Now turn the machine off, remove the paddle and replace with the dough hook. Knead the dough on medium low speed for about 5 minutes, or until the dough is smooth and elastic. If the dough is excessively soft and sticky, add 1 to 2 tablespoons more flour, one at a time, and knead a little longer.

2. **Place the dough** in a large oiled bowl and turn to coat all sides. Cover the bowl tightly with plastic wrap, and allow the dough to rise in a warm place until doubled in bulk, about 1 ½ hours.

3. **Turn the risen dough** out on to a lightly floured work surface. Deflate the dough and divide it into two equal pieces. Now invert the bowl and cover the 2 pieces, and let them rest for exactly 10 minutes.

4. **While the pieces are resting,** prepare the crunch topping. In a separate bowl, using a wooden spoon, combine the water, yeast, bread flour, and butter until they are the consistency of yogurt. Cover the bowl with plastic wrap and set aside for 15 minutes.

5. **To form a loaf,** remove any excess flour from the work surface, then using a rolling pin, stretch the dough into a rough rectangle.

Fold in the short ends of the dough until it is approximately the length of the pan, and then fold the far long edge over to the middle. Fold over the other long side and compress to form a tight loaf. Place the loaf in the oiled pan, seam side down. Cover the pan with plastic wrap. Repeat with the second piece of dough. Allow to rise in a warm place until doubled, about 1 hour.

6. **When the 15 minutes** has elapsed, it's time to apply the crunch topping to the loaves. Uncover the loaves, and very carefully using a soupspoon, equally spread the topping onto the rising dough. Recover again with plastic wrap.

7. **When the loaves** are almost doubled, set a rack at the middle level of the oven and preheat to 400°F.

8. **When the loaves are completely risen,** place in the oven and bake for about 25 to 30 minutes until they are golden brown and firm. Unmold the loaves to a rack to cool.

Makes 2 loaves

Farm House Daily White

Ingredients

6 cups bread flour
3 teaspoons active dry yeast
$^1/_4$ cup unsalted butter, softened
$2^1/_2$ teaspoons sea salt
2 cups warm water (about 120–130 degrees)
$^1/_3$ cup powdered milk
3 tablespoons sugar

Two $8^1/_2$ x $4^1/_2$ x $2^3/_4$ inch loaf pans, oiled

This is an excellent and easy bread to make if you are a beginner. I learned how to make this bread by hand from my Aunt Minnie, a dairy farmer up in Wausau, Wisconsin. This loaf was once the staple of every Midwestern table before the advent of store bought. You'll find the crumb light, airy, and slightly sweet while the crust has a nice, chewy crunch. Lather on the unsalted butter and homemade strawberry jam for a taste of the farm.

Chef's Tip!

Proper temperature, kneading, forming, and pan size are the key to making this easy bread. If it doesn't work out, I'll come to your house and teach you.

Preparation

1. **To mix the dough** in a heavy-duty mixer, place the flour, yeast, butter, and salt in the mixer bowl, attach the paddle and mix on low speed for 1 minute to blend the ingredients. Dissolve the milk powder and sugar into the warm water, and while the machine is still running on low speed, slowly add the warm liquid to the flour until the dough forms a mass around the paddle. Now turn the machine off, remove the paddle and replace with the dough hook. Knead the dough on medium low speed for about 5 minutes, or until the dough is smooth and elastic. If the dough is excessively soft and sticky, add 1 to 2 tablespoons more flour, one at a time, and knead a little longer.

2. **Place the dough** in a large oiled bowl and turn to coat all sides. Cover the bowl tightly with plastic wrap, and allow the dough to rise in a warm place until doubled in bulk, about 1½ hours.

3. **Turn the risen dough** out on to a lightly floured work surface. Deflate the dough and divide it into two equal pieces. Now invert the bowl and cover the 2 pieces, and let them rest for exactly 10 minutes.

4. **To form a loaf,** remove any excess flour from the work surface, then using a rolling pin, stretch the dough into a rough rectangle. Fold in the short ends of the dough until it is approximately the length of the pan, and then fold the far long edge over to the

middle. Fold over the other long side and compress to form a tight loaf. Place the loaf in the oiled pan, seam side down. Cover the pan with plastic wrap. Repeat with the second piece of dough. Allow to rise in a warm place until doubled, about 1 hour.

5. **When the loaves are almost doubled,** set a rack at the middle level of the oven and preheat to 400°F.

6. **When the loaves are completely risen,** place in the oven and bake for about 30 minutes until they are golden brown and firm. Unmold the loaves to a rack to cool.

Makes 2 loaves

Poppy Seed Twist

Ingredients

6½ cups bread flour
4 teaspoons active dry yeast
2 large whole eggs
2½ teaspoons sea salt
1½ cups warm water (about 120–130 degrees)
½ cup sugar
6 tablespoons canola oil

Egg wash

1 egg yolk well beaten with a little water
Poppy seeds or sesame seeds

One heavy sheet pan lined with parchment
    and dusted with cornmeal

My all time favorite, a.k.a. Egg twist or Challah. Who can resist a beautifully braided loaf, speckled with poppy seeds or white sesame seeds? I've reduced the traditional quantity of eggs in the recipe, and increased the sugar to produce a truly magnificent loaf. Medium grained, slightly sweet, and egg enriched, accentuates a soft but sliceable crust. Bakers in Poland sometimes add saffron water to the dough to give it a deeper color. Any leftovers make an excellent French toast.

Chef's Tip!

Care should be taken as to not let the braided dough re-rise more than three-fourths before baking, or the bread might lose its shape and volume when baked. Also, egg washing the braid twice gives it a deep, beautiful finish.

Preparation

1. **To mix the dough** in a heavy-duty mixer, place the flour, yeast, eggs, and salt in the mixer bowl, attach the paddle and mix on low speed for 1 minute to blend the ingredients. Dissolve the sugar into the warm water, and while the machine is still running on low speed, slowly add the warm liquid and oil to the flour until the dough forms a mass around the paddle. Now turn the machine off, remove the paddle and replace with the dough hook. Knead the dough on medium low speed for about 5 minutes, or until the dough is smooth and elastic. If the dough is excessively soft and sticky, add 1 to 2 tablespoons more flour, one at a time, and knead a little longer.

2. **Place the dough** in a large oiled bowl and turn to coat all sides. Cover the bowl tightly with plastic wrap, and allow the dough to rise in a warm place until doubled in bulk, about 1½ hours.

3. **Turn the risen dough** out on to a lightly floured work surface. Deflate the dough and divide it into four equal pieces. Now invert the bowl and cover the 4 pieces, and let them rest for exactly 10 minutes.

4. **To form a loaf,** remove any excess flour from the work surface, then using your hands roll each piece into a cylinder, 12 to 15 inches long. Arrange two strands side by side. Begin to braid in the

middle of the strands and braid to one end. Turn the dough around and braid from the middle to the other end.

5. **Now braid the other two strands.** Pinch each end to seal the strands together and turn the pinched parts under the loaves. Carefully lift up and place, onto the prepared pan, equally spaced apart. Cover the loaves with oiled plastic wrap and allow to rise in a warm place until doubled, about 1 hour.

6. **When the loaves are almost doubled,** set a rack at the middle level of the oven and preheat to 375°F.

7. **Brush the top and sides** of the risen loaves with the egg wash, and liberally sprinkle on the poppy seeds. Bake for 20 to 25 minutes, or until the tops are golden brown. Transfer to a rack to cool.

Makes 2 loaves

*b*uffets, kanapkis, and zakaski

*m*ike the chef on buffets

*m*ike the chef on kanapkis

*m*ike the chef on zakaski

*m*eat and pasztet arrangements

*f*ish platter arrangements

*c*lassic cheese combinations

*t*able compliments

*c*hef's kanapkis

*s*avory salads

*p*arty skewers

*w*hite wine pickled herring

*p*ickled herring in sour cream

*f*ancy smoked salmon roulade

"*p*arty" paszteciki

*e*asy chicken liver mousse

*d*uck liver pasztet polski

*c*ountryside paté

Mike the chef on buffets

Most people around the country usually identify me with a four star restaurant or such, but my real loyal fans know me from a small catering company I used to own way back when. I had a simple premise: allow me to use all of your precious china, silverware, linens and such, and I'll set you a Polish style buffet table that will blow your mind, "literally." The concept worked!

The ritual of buffet table dining has held its place in Polish history for centuries. Of any cultural group, the Poles have had more treaties, exiles, and religious holidays substantiated over a little food and Vodka. Although the circumstances were not cause for celebration at times, the Polish spirit of hospitality became legendary.

Entertaining and noshing go hand in hand in Polish culture. Poles have always had an affection for the past, and tradition and hospitality have always been a part of their heritage and daily lives. If you are fortunate to have read books about Polish customs, you are well aware of the fact that at least once or twice a month there is something to celebrate. The confusing fact is that most of the celebrations revolve around religious holidays or saint days that actually turn out to be major feasts, so where do you start, and what is the easiest and most economical way to keep these cherished Polish customs alive? You guessed it, have a buffet! I couldn't think of a better way to bring together close family, friends, and new acquaintances, and show them in our own special way the custom of Polish hospitality. Our holidays offer us an opportunity to create a very special social scene, to carry on old traditions, and also to pass them on to new generations with a minimum of effort. The concept is not new, but sometimes people make it too complicated with too much heavy food.

Think of a buffet as a dainty vignette, nice, plain, simple food that is accentuated by a beautifully dressed and adorned table. You're probably saying to yourself, "Oh, that's good for you, Mike the chef, but what about us peasant folks that don't cook?" Let me tell you my secret. When I'm in Chicago, I take a day and visit all of the nice little Polish sausage shops and bakeries that I like. I talk to the owner, tell him or her what I'm doing, and they set me up. I get cold cuts, sausages, smoked fish, kraut, cheese, bread (if I don't make my own), ham, some pastry, and liquor, and man, my car smells for a week. Then I go home, cook the ham, arrange my platters, set the table, have a beer, and I'm done. Don't get me wrong, I like to cook and I always make a couple of things on my own, but my local shops who have been around for generations specialize in Polish goods that I couldn't duplicate at home. It's not inexpensive, but if you hunt around and get creative, a little bit goes a long way and your guests will appreciate it. Cold hors d'oeuvres and appetizers can be found at most Polish affairs, whether it be the traditional Easter feast which contains hard boiled eggs, ham, sausage, fresh homemade bread, salads, and such to a more elaborate cocktail party which could contain such delicacies as caviar, kanapkis, patés, cold platters, and a hearty cocktail service. Poland's turbulent history and multiple occupations have undoubtedly contributed to its adoption of some of its Western European refinements. The Baltic Sea has blessed the Poles with an abundant supply of caviar and herring while the neighboring border countries have contributed unbelievable charcuterie that we now call our own.

The buffet table is a very easy and adaptable form of entertaining. The only limitations of course are the size of the party, occasion, and your depth of cooking skills to pull it off. I've always thought of a buffet table as a warm and inviting meeting place. My parents and their close friends threw great parties year round both inside and out, which when I look back were masterful and flawless events. Since my father was an attorney and extremely active in the Polish community, governors or heads of state were commonplace in our home. My mother was always cool-headed, took things in stride, and always served buffet style. She would always say, "Big deal, the big shots here! I'm serving what I like, and what I know how to do. I don't have to impress anybody, my Polish charm will do." As I've said, the parties were flawless and usually started in the early evening with quality cocktails followed by interesting hors d'oeuvres that were passed around, and then there was the beautifully decorated table that was adorned with artfully arranged cold platters, a substantial hot dish, and a finale that consisted of cheesecake, coffee, and cordials. Simple but elegant! The food was great, but it was the dynamic mix of the people that were there that made the party enjoyable and memorable.

Mike the chef on kanapkis

I guess you can tell by now, I take my entertaining very seriously. Nothing satisfies me more than seeing the glowing response on people's faces when they bite into one of my creations. I've always liked little bits and tastes when I eat. You know, you can have a little bit of smoked salmon on pumpernickel, then move to a skewered sausage and horseradish tidbit, converse, sip your drink, then go back for seconds. Easy, relaxed, not too filling, that's the way I like it!

Kanapkis are a great invention. Think of them as small 2-inch round open-faced sandwiches without the crust. Kanapkis and hors d'oeuvres fall into the same category on the food chain. They're both usually served before a main meal to fill you up slightly, but the difference between the two is in the mind of the creator. I prefer the kanapki type over the hors d'oeuvre because it lends itself to more creativity whereas the other can be plain out boring. I think of kanapkis as nice little jewels of delectable delicacies such as smoked oyster and red caviar kanapki, or **Spicy Shrimp with Mango and Capers** kanapki.

Throughout the book I have repeated the phrase, "use your imagination, but also use your common sense." Old Polish cookbooks describe kanapkis as being butter laden and aspic coated concoctions, a practice whose time has come and gone. I prefer to use seasoned cream cheese because it holds up better and people seem to enjoy the clean, neutral taste of it. My concepts are simple, I use good quality Polish foodstuffs that I can buy locally, and I arrange them artfully in a beautiful fashion. When I create, I like a variety of tastes but I also stay within a workable theme while trying to combine the old with the new. Kanapki making is very easy, just be sure to have all of your ingredients in front of you and ready to go. I've given you a general explanation of how to assemble the kanapkis (study the color photos), and you can find my recipes for the seasoned cheese bases in the Pantry section of the book.

Mike the chef on zakaski

When you entertain in the Polish buffet style, kanapkis play a big role but platters are the real mainstay of the buffet table. As I've mentioned earlier, Poles have a preference for cold appetizers whether it be a simple stuffed egg or a marinated mushroom salad. Just like their Russian neighbors where it's called Zakooskas hour, the Polish people enjoy Zakaski , a few hours of meet and greet as their favorite way of entertaining. The concept is simple because the hostess sets a beautifully adorned table with assorted food items and the guests usually congregate around the table helping themselves, exchanging remarks about delicacies, and then going back for another treat. The table can be set up anywhere in the house and usually contains small plates, forks, and napkins which are arranged in neat stacks and rows. I usually set up a bar area on another table and the pastry is always served out of the kitchen so as not to interfere with the mingling and jingling of the guests who contribute a big part to the festivities.

Artists create on a plain canvas, whereas chefs create beauty with foods. In my experience, a party with a guest list of 20 to 30 people comfortably calls for a buffet table decorated with 6 large platters. To make it easier on yourself, consider that one of the platters will contain a hot item (I remove the sixth platter and replace it with a large sterno heated chafing dish) that accommodates either sausage and kraut, bigos, stuffed cabbage, assorted pierogi and sausages, or chicken and potatoes just to name a few. These food items can easily be prepared up to 3 or 4 days in advance. I also consider the first platter an easy fix because it always contains assorted cheeses and fruits that come ready to go from the deli. So you are actually left with 4 platters to concentrate on because the pastry, and the bar set up are pretty much self-serve items.

Trying to pull together 4 paintings is difficult, but arranging 4 platters is fairly easy as long as the theme flows smoothly. Since this is a Polish cookbook, I always keep my themes along the lines of my heritage and foodstuffs because it all meshes together. If you're a little confused, let me give you an example of a classic Polish buffet.

Sample Classic Polish Buffet

Assorted passed kanapkis and finger sandwiches

Hot item to include smoked sausage and sauerkraut

Cold platters to include assorted pierogis with cheese, potato, cabbage, and fruits

Smoked salmon, sledge, and chubs with whipped horseradish cream

Polish cold cuts and baked ham with assorted mustards, pickles, and breads

3 assorted Polish cold salads

Cheese and fresh fruits

Dessert table

This is just an example of what your buffet can be. If you go through my book, there is an unlimited amount of interchanging that can be done with the hot and cold platters. You can plan your menu according to the seasons of the year, the amount of guests you're entertaining, and depending on what occasion you're celebrating. Use your common sense and creativity and you will have a successful event.

Popular meat and pasztet arrangements for platters:

Lightly smoked boneless ham, Canadian bacon Polish style, stuffed veal breast, Krakowska sausage, Zywiecka sausage, and Cyganska sausage.

Pepper loaf, Prasky caraway sausage, beer sausage, onion old-fashioned loaf, Vienna style loaf, minced ham sausage, and Polish style bologna.

White headcheese, country style head cheese, black headcheese, hot headcheese with paprika, and jellied tongue.

Smoked gypsy ham, Polish style spiced ham, home-style smoked country ham, and juniper smoked boneless ham.

Duck liver mousse with port, country paté with black pepper, and savory liver terrine with cognac.

My most popular fish platter arrangements:

Alderwood smoked salmon—Pacific Northwest alderwood smoked salmon is pre-sliced and artfully arranged on a beautiful oval platter that is adorned with half lemon slices, tiny capers, chopped boiled eggs, and accompanied by thin pumpernickel slices and fresh horseradish whipped cream.

Chubs and trout—Carefully picked over succulent smoked chub and trout meat is gracefully adorned onto bite-size blini or potato pancakes that are garnished with a small dollop of fresh chive whipped cream, imported caviar, and a dill sprig.

Herring and Salmon salad—Spicy seasoned and cured herring and salmon are presented in a high-sided etched Polish crystal bowls that are nestled in beautifully folded lace napkins. Both of the salads are then garnished with thin slices of red onion rings and sprinkling of fresh dill and herbs.

Caviar service—A regal bowl of pristine caviar is presented in a small block of garnished ice. An accompanying platter is classically garnished with finely chopped onion, chopped hard cooked egg whites and yolks, tiny lemon pieces, and homemade toast points or blini.

Chef's Classic Cheese Combinations:

American Classic—Vermont cheddar, Dry Jack, Maytag Blue, Classic blue goat.

Wisconsin Classic—Mild Colby, Baby Swiss, Jalapeño Jack, Mild Cheddar, Smoked Cheddar

Accented Wisconsin—Bacon, Salami, Smoked Swiss, Smoked Cheddar, Jalapeño Jack

Blue Cheese Veined—Maytag Blue, Stilton, Roquefort, Cambozola

Italian Classic—Parmigiano-Reggiano, Pecorino Toscana, Gorgonzola, Smoked Buffalo Mozzarella

English Style—Cheshire, Cheddar, Stilton

Table compliments that I recommend for a perfect party:

Baby dill pickles

Cornichons style pickles

Imported green olives

Imported black olives

Fresh white horseradish

Fresh red horseradish

Mild Polish mustard

Polish horseradish mustard

Kosciusko mustard

Chef's Kanapkis

Stuffed Baby Tomato with Horseradish

Preparation

Base (see page 252)
A round kanapki of bread is spread with a little herbed cheese base.

Ingredients
Small cherry tomatoes, cut in half, horseradish cheese base

Assembly
Using a pastry bag fitted with a small star tip, pipe the horseradish cheese base onto the center of the kanapki. Carefully place a tomato half onto the horseradish cheese base and pipe some more onto the cut tomato. Place the other half on top.

Savory Sardine and Radish

Preparation

Base (see page 252)
A round kanapki of bread is spread with a little seasoned cheese base.

Ingredients
Smoked salmon cheese base, 1 tin marinated sardines, small radishes, thinly sliced, hard boiled eggs, finely chopped

Assembly
Using a pastry bag fitted with a small star tip, pipe the smoked salmon cheese base onto the center of the kanapki. Garnish the kanapki with a piece of sardine, 3 slices of radish, and a sprinkling of chopped egg.

Herring a la "Russe"

Preparation

Base (see page 252)
A round kanapki of bread is spread with a little smoked salmon cheese base.

Ingredients
Herbed cheese base, pickled herring pieces, salmon caviar, dill sprigs

Assembly
Using a pastry bag fitted with a small star tip, pipe the herbed cheese base onto the center of the kanapki. Garnish the kanapki with a piece of pickled herring, salmon caviar, and a sprig of dill.

The Russian

Preparation

Base (see page 252)
A round kanapki of bread is spread with a little herbed cheese base.

Ingredients
Horseradish cheese base, hard boiled egg, finely diced, small lemon wedges, black caviar

Assembly
Using a pastry bag fitted with a small star tip, pipe the horseradish cheese base into a small circle on top of the kanapki. Spoon some of the caviar into the center, then garnish with the diced egg and lemon wedge.

Chef's Kanapkis

Spicy Shrimp with Mango and Capers

Preparation

Base (see page 252)
A round kanapki of bread is spread with a little herbed cheese base.

Ingredients
Herbed cheese base, baby shrimp marinated in salsa, 1 small mango, tiny capers

Assembly
Using a pastry bag fitted with a small star tip, pipe the herbed cheese base onto the center of the kanapki. Garnish the kanapki with 3 small shrimp, 3 tiny capers, and a piece of mango in the center.

The Debutante

Preparation

Base (see page 252)
A round kanapki of bread is spread with a little herbed cheese base.

Ingredients
Horseradish cheese base, 1 tin smoked oysters, salmon caviar, thinly sliced pearl onions, watercress leafs

Assembly
Using a pastry bag fitted with a small star tip, pipe the horseradish cheese base onto the center of the kanapki. Garnish the kanapki with a smoked oyster, salmon caviar, pearl onion rings, and a watercress leaf.

Smoked Salmon Kanapki

Preparation

Base (see page 252)
A round kanapki of bread is spread with a little herbed cheese base.

Ingredients
Thin slices of smoked salmon, herbed cheese base, small lemon wedges, watercress leafs

Assembly
Cut the salmon into circles that will fit on the top of the bread, place onto the bread, and using a pastry bag fitted with a small star tip, pipe the herbed cheese base onto the center of the salmon then garnish with a lemon wedge and a watercress leaf.

Crab with Avocado and Chives

Preparation

Base (see page 252)
A round kanapki of bread is spread with a little horseradish cheese base.

Ingredients
Fresh flaked or canned crabmeat, well drained of moisture, herbed cheese base, 1 small avocado, chives

Assembly
Using a pastry bag fitted with a small star tip, pipe the herbed cheese base onto the center of the kanapki to form a mound. Place the crabmeat into a small bowl, then carefully the kanapki into the crabmeat and garnish with a piece of avocado and chives.

Savory Salads

Horseradish Egg Salad Dip

Ingredients

8 hard-boiled eggs, chopped
½ cup mayonnaise, full fat
1 tablespoon white prepared horseradish
1½ teaspoons Dijon mustard
⅛ teaspoon sea salt
⅛ teaspoon freshly ground black pepper
Dash of lemon juice, Tabasco, Worcestershire sauce,
    and garlic powder
Chopped chives

Preparation

1. **Place the chopped eggs** into a small mixing bowl, and in another bowl thoroughly combine the remaining ingredients until smooth, then gently fold into the eggs, and serve in a cold decorative serving bowl.

Makes about 2 cups

Curried Crab Salad Dip

Ingredients

1½ pounds fresh lump crabmeat, cleaned
½ cup mayonnaise, full fat
2 teaspoons quality curry powder
2 teaspoons mango chutney
1 medium sized apple, finely diced
1 large celery rib, finely diced
1 green onion, minced
Dash of lemon juice, Tabasco, celery salt, pepper,
    garlic powder, and Worcestershire sauce

Preparation

1. **Place the cleaned crabmeat** into a small mixing bowl, and in another bowl, thoroughly combine the remaining ingredients until smooth, then gently fold into the crab, and serve in a cold decorative serving bowl.

Makes about 2 cups

Sweet Pickled
Garden Vegetables

Ingredients

2 pounds assorted fresh
    vegetables such as
    Kirby cucumbers,
    baby carrots, celery,
    cauliflower, red
    peppers, and pearl
    onions, cut into florets,
    washed and dried
2½ cups cooled water

¼ cup cider vinegar
¼ cup sugar
1½ teaspoons sea salt
1 teaspoon pickling spice
1 teaspoon whole black
    peppercorns
8 sprigs fresh dill

Preparation

1. **Combine the water,** vinegar, sugar, sea salt, pickling spice, and peppercorns in a glass bowl and stir until well mixed. Place the vegetables and dill into another glass bowl, then pour all of the brine over them. Cover with plastic wrap and refrigerate for 3 to 4 days before using.

Makes 1 quart

Marinated Mushroom
Salad

Ingredients

1½ pounds small mushrooms, cleaned
3 tablespoons olive oil
3 large garlic cloves, minced
1 small onion, diced
1 small red pepper, diced
Large pinch of fresh thyme, sugar, bay leaf, sea salt,
    and pepper
2 tablespoons lemon juice
¾ cup light olive oil
¼ cup red wine vinegar

Preparation

1. **Heat the 3 tablespoons** of olive oil in a large skillet, and sauté the garlic, onion, red pepper, and mushrooms for exactly 4 minutes, then add the rest of the ingredients, cook for exactly 2 minutes more, then remove from the fire, and pour into a glass serving bowl and chill.

Makes 1 quart

Party Skewers

Bacon, Shrimp, and Sage

Ingredients

20 thin slices bacon, halved
40 raw shrimp, peeled and de-veined
40 fresh sage leaves
40 small button mushrooms
40 small wood skewers

Preparation

1. **Preheat the oven** to 400°. Lay the bacon strips horizontally out on to a clean piece of parchment paper, and then place a fresh sage leaf and one shrimp on top of that then roll up tightly. Skewer the package, and then crown it with 1 button mushroom. Repeat with the remaining skewers, and then bake in the hot oven for 8 to 10 minutes.

Makes 40 pieces

Asparagus and Prosciutto

Ingredients

20 thin asparagus spears
10 thin slices of prosciutto ham
Freshly ground black pepper
20 small wood skewers

Preparation

1. **Preheat the oven** to 400°. Peel the ends of the asparagus spears, and then blanch in boiling salted water for 2 to 3 minutes. Drain and refresh in iced water. Carefully cut each asparagus spear into 4 short even lengths. Cut each slice of ham into 8 strips and wrap one around each asparagus tip. Thread 3 pieces on to each skewer, season with the pepper, and bake in the hot oven for 5 to 6 minutes.

Makes 80 pieces

Provolone, Olive, and Salami

Ingredients

1 pound chunk provolone cheese
20 pickled peppers, quartered
40 thin slices of salami, halved
40 small green olives with pimento
40 small black olives, pitted
40 wood skewers

Preparation

1. **Cut the provolone** cheese into 40 small cubes and wrap a thin piece of pepper around each cube. Fold each piece of salami over twice and thread 2 on to each skewer with one green and one black olive and 2 cubes of cheese.

Makes 40 pieces

Pastrami and Pickled Vegetables

Ingredients

12 ounces whole pastrami piece
1 large Kosher pickle
1 jar pickled baby corn, halved
40 pickled martini onions
40 wood skewers

Preparation

1. **Cut the pastrami** and Kosher pickle into 80 small bite size cubes. Thread 2 pieces of pastrami, a pickle slice, piece of baby corn, and martini onion onto each skewer and serve cold.

Makes 40 pieces

White Wine Pickled Herring

Ingredients

3 pounds salted herring
2 cups dry white wine
½ cup white vinegar
¼ cup water
1 small onion, chopped
2 large garlic cloves, chopped
1 tablespoon pickling spice
2 teaspoons sugar
1 large carrot
1 large celery stalk
5 thin lemon slices
2 small whole red chili peppers
3 small bay leaves
1 medium red onion, thinly sliced
1 tablespoon freshly grated horseradish root, optional

Preparation

1. **Soak the salt herring,** refrigerated in a large pot of water for 24 hours. Change the water twice.

2. **Make the pickling solution** by combining the white wine, vinegar, water, onion, garlic, pickling spice, and sugar. Place all of these ingredients into a pot that is non-reactive, and bring the solution to a quick boil over high heat, then lower the heat and simmer for exactly 10 minutes and remove from the fire. Pour the liquid into a clean glass bowl and when cool enough, place into the refrigerator to chill overnight.

3. **The next day** remove the herring from the water, and using a sharp chef's knife, fillet the herring and remove any small bones with a pair of pliers. Cut the fish into finger size pieces, and then place into a large glass mixing bowl or a wide mouth mason jar. Again using the sharp chef's knife, cut the celery and carrot on a diagonal into thin pieces, and then place them with the lemon slices into the bowl.

4. **Remove the brine** from the refrigerator, taste, and re-adjust with more seasoning if needed. Carefully pour the brine through a fine mesh strainer over the herring and vegetables, and gently mix until well combined. Sprinkle the remaining ingredients over the top of the herring, and again mix until well combined.

5. **Cover the bowl tightly** with plastic wrap, and refrigerate for at least 3 or 4 days to let the fish cure and the seasonings mellow before eating. (Each day I recommend giving the bowl a good swirl without uncovering to redistribute the brine.)

Makes about 1 quart

Pickled Herring and Sour Cream

Ingredients

3 pounds salted herring
1¼ cups water
1¼ cup white wine vinegar
2 teaspoons sugar
1 tablespoon pickling spice
1 large red onion, thinly sliced
2 large garlic cloves, chopped
2 cups sour cream, full fat
2 dashes Tabasco
Dash of cayenne
2 tablespoons fresh dill, chopped, optional
1 tablespoon freshly grated horseradish root, optional

Preparation

1. **Soak the salt herring,** refrigerated in a large pot of water for 24 hours. Change the water twice.

2. **Make the pickling solution** by combining the water, white wine vinegar, sugar, and pickling spice. Place all of these ingredients into a pot that is non-reactive, and bring the solution to a quick boil over high heat, then lower the heat and simmer for exactly 5 minutes and remove from the fire. Pour the liquid into a clean glass bowl and when cool enough, place into the refrigerator to chill overnight.

3. **The next day** remove the herring from the water, and using a sharp chef's knife, fillet the herring and remove any small bones with a pair of pliers. Cut the fish into finger size pieces, and then place into a large glass mixing bowl or a wide mouth mason jar. Sprinkle the onion slices and chopped garlic over the herring pieces, and gently mix to combine.

4. **Remove the brine** from the refrigerator, taste, and re-adjust with more seasoning if needed. Now whisk into the brine, the remaining ingredients until well blended, then pour the entire mixture over the fish. Using a wooden spoon, carefully combine all the ingredients in the bowl, cover the bowl tightly with plastic wrap, and refrigerate undisturbed for at least 4 to 6 days before using. (Each day I recommend giving the bowl a good swirl without uncovering to redistribute the brine.)

Makes about 1 quart

Fancy Smoked Salmon Roulade

Ingredients

1½ pounds smoked salmon, thinly sliced

Cream Cheese Base

8 ounces cream cheese, softened
2 tablespoons heavy cream
¼ teaspoon garlic powder
⅛ teaspoon onion powder
¼ teaspoon celery salt
⅛ teaspoon freshly ground white pepper
Dash of paprika
Dash of Tabasco

Preparation

1. **Place the cream cheese** and heavy cream into a medium sized mixing bowl, and using a heavy wooden spoon, blend until smooth and well combined. Now add the rest of the ingredients and stir vigorously until well incorporated.

2. **Carefully place** a 14-inch long piece of plastic wrap onto a clean work surface so that it is horizontally in front of you. Gently lay 2 pieces of smoked salmon onto the center of the plastic wrap horizontally so that they are overlapping just a bit. (You should now have a strip of smoked salmon that is 8-inches long by 2-inches wide.)

3. **Using a small** icing spatula, thinly spread some of the seasoned cheese base onto the smoked salmon being careful not to run over the edges.

4. **Repeat procedures** 2 and 3 until all of the salmon and cheese base is used. (The top layer should be salmon.)

5. **Now fold the** plastic wrap over the top of the roulade, and twist the ends of the plastic wrap in opposite directions until you form a tight sausage shape. Secure both ends with twisty ties to keep the roulade tight, and then refrigerate overnight.

6. **The next day,** using a sharp serrated knife, cut the roulade into 16 thin slices and arrange on a serving platter.

Yields 16 pieces

"Party" Paszteciki

Ingredients

1 pound puff pastry dough

3 large shallots, minced
2 tablespoons unsalted butter
¾ pound pork butt, finely ground
1 tablespoon cognac
1 tablespoon port
¼ teaspoon sea salt
¼ teaspoon freshly ground black pepper
1 large egg yolk
Pinch of paté spice, optional
1 heaping tablespoon fresh dill or marjoram, chopped

1 large whole egg

Preparation

1. **In a small skillet,** melt the butter and sauté the minced shallots for exactly 2 minutes, then set aside to cool.

2. **In a medium sized** mixing bowl, combine the port, cognac, port, salt, pepper, yolk, spice, and fresh dill, and then add the chilled shallots. Using a heavy wooden spoon, blend the ingredients until well combined. Cover the bowl with plastic wrap and refrigerate over night.

3. **The next day** lightly flour a work surface, and place the dough on top of it. Using a rolling pin, gently roll out the dough into a large square about ⅛-inch thick. Now using a 1½-inch round cutter, cut the dough into 32 to 40 round pieces.

4. **Using a small spoon,** equally divide among half of the pieces, the meat mixture on to the center of each round of dough. Moisten the edges of the filled dough with a little water, and then place the other rounds of pastry on top sealing the edges carefully. Beat the remaining egg with a little water, and brush the tops of the paszteciki with egg wash.

5. **Place the paszteciki** onto a parchment lined sheet pan and refrigerate 1 hour before baking. After 1 hour, preheat the oven to 400°, re-glaze the tops, and bake for 20 to 25 minutes until golden brown.

Yields 16 to 20 pieces

Easy Chicken Liver Mousse

Ingredients

¹⁄₂ pound plus 2 tablespoons unsalted butter, softened
2 large shallots, minced
1 pound chicken livers, cleaned
¹⁄₂ teaspoon sea salt
¹⁄₄ teaspoon freshly ground black pepper
¹⁄₂ teaspoon paté spice, optional
¹⁄₄ cup Madeira
1 tablespoon green peppercorns, optional
1 tablespoon finely chopped truffle pieces, optional

Preparation

1. **Heat 2 tablespoons** of the unsalted butter in a large non-stick skillet over medium high heat. Add the shallots, and quickly sauté until they have softened but not browned, about 2 minutes.

2. **Add the cleaned chicken** livers to the pan and cook for exactly 2 minutes more until they are slightly colored but not brown. (The livers should just take on a little bit of color, it is important not to over cook them.) Season the livers with the salt, pepper, and paté spice, then remove from the fire and place them into the work bowl of a food processor fitted with a metal blade.

3. **Return the skillet** to the fire, add the Madeira to the pan, and reduce by half, then remove from the fire to cool slightly.

4. **After the chicken** livers have cooled slightly, attach the cover to the food processor, and pulse the livers until they are smooth. Remove the cover, scrape down the sides with a small plastic spatula, and then add the remaining butter to the bowl. Now again replace the cover and pulse the mixture until it is well combined and completely smooth. Carefully using a spatula, gently fold in the optional ingredients if used, and then place the mousse into a decorative mold to chill at least 8 hours before serving.

Makes about 3 cups

Duck Liver Pasztet Polski

Ingredients

2 pounds fresh duck or chicken livers
1 cup whole milk
Pinch of sea salt
2 tablespoons unsalted butter, softened
8 tablespoons unsalted butter, melted
1 small onion, finely diced
1 large garlic clove, minced
¹⁄₂ cup dry white wine
1 teaspoon sea salt
1 teaspoon white pepper
3 tablespoons brandy or Madeira
¹⁄₂ cup heavy cream
2 whole large eggs
1¹⁄₂ tablespoons green peppercorns, optional
1¹⁄₂ tablespoons finely chopped truffle pieces, optional

Preparation

1. **Preheat the oven** to 325°.

2. **Place the cleaned** duck livers, milk, and salt into a glass mixing bowl to soak for 15 minutes to remove any impurities and excess blood.

3. **Using the 2 tablespoons** of softened butter, generously coat the inside of a 5 to 6 cup earthenware terrine mold (round or square), then place it into the refrigerator until needed.

4. **Heat 4 tablespoons** of the unsalted melted butter in a large non-stick skillet over medium high heat, add the onion and garlic, and stir cook for exactly 2 minutes, then add the white wine and let it reduce until it turns to a syrup-like consistency.

5. **Quickly drain the livers** (discarding the milk) into a small colander, then immediately pour them into the hot skillet, and stir cook again until the livers are just an off-pink color. Remove the pan from the fire to cool slightly. Do not overcook.

6. **Using a plastic spatula,** scrape the entire liver mixture into the work bowl of a food processor fitted with a metal blade. Now add the rest of the ingredients including the reserved amount of melted butter (not the optional ingredients), attach the lid, and pulse the mixture until it is well blended and the ingredients are incorporated.

7. **Strain the mixture** through a very fine strainer to eliminate any liver fibers or sinews. (Now that the liver mixture is strained, you may add one or the other of the optional ingredients to the paté. Using a plastic spatula, very carefully stir it into the mix until it is incorporated.) Gently ladle the paté mixture into the chilled mold, then place it into a *bain marie* filled with enough water that reaches to 1-inch from the top of the mold. Bake the pasztet for 45 to 65 minutes until the paté sets, and a skewer comes out clean when the mold is pierced.

8. **Allow the pasztet** to cool for 2 hours, then refrigerate covered overnight. The next day un-mold the paté onto a serving platter.

Yields one 5-cup terrine

Countryside Paté

Ingredients

Forcemeat

2½ pounds pork (pork butt or Boston butt),
  coarsely ground
½ pound veal shoulder, coarsely ground
3 large garlic cloves, minced
⅓ cup shallots, minced
⅓ cup pistachio nuts
¼ cup dry white wine
2 tablespoons cognac
1 tablespoon cornstarch
1 tablespoon sea salt
2 teaspoons paté spice
¼ teaspoon saltpeter, optional

Paté Garnish

½ pound veal shoulder, sliced ½-inch thick
8 chicken livers
¼ pound ham steak, sliced into long ½-inch
  thick strips
½ teaspoon freshly ground black pepper
2 tablespoons cognac

Terrine Liner

8 oz. piece of caulfat, thinly sliced
3 bay leaves
½ teaspoon thyme

Paté Spice

Ingredients

½ teaspoon powdered bay leaf
½ teaspoon thyme
½ teaspoon mace
¾ teaspoon cinnamon
1 teaspoon nutmeg
1 teaspoon cloves
½ teaspoon white pepper
½ teaspoon rosemary
½ teaspoon basil
Pinch of cayenne

Preparation

1. **Place all of the ingredients** into a small glass jar with a tight fitted lid, shake vigorously, and store in a cool place until needed.

Makes about ¼ cup

Preparation

1. **Place 2 medium-size** mixing bowls onto a clean counter, and add the ingredients for the forcemeat of the recipe in one, then place the garnish ingredients in the other. Carefully using your hands, thoroughly combine each of the ingredients in their separate bowls.

2. **Line a 6-cup terrine** mold with the caulfat.

3. **Gently press a third** of the forcemeat into the bottom of the mold to make an even layer about 1-inch thick. Now on top of the forcemeat, arrange about half of the veal strips end to end to form 2 even rows running the length of the paté mold. Cover the veal strips with about 1-inch more of the forcemeat, then arrange the chicken livers directly down the middle of the terrine from end to end. Place some of the ham strips on each side of the chicken livers running the length of the paté mold, and then repeat with any remaining forcemeat and garnish until it is all used up.

4. **Carefully turn** the overhanging edges of caulfat on top of the paté mixture to cover, then trim off any excess with kitchen shears. Place the 3 bay leaves and thyme on top of the caulfat, and tightly seal the assembled paté with plastic wrap, then refrigerate for 3 days to mellow.

5. **After 3 days,** preheat the oven to 325°, remove the plastic wrap and tightly cover the paté with 2 sheets of aluminum foil. Set the mold into a roasting pan filled with enough water to come half way up the sides of the mold, then bake in the hot oven for 1¾ hours until the internal temperature of the paté registers 155° on a meat thermometer. Remove the paté from the oven and let it cool on a baking rack for a few hours while still covered with the aluminum foil. Refrigerate for at least 2 days before unmolding and serving.

Yields one 6-cup terrine

simple salads
and great vegetables

summer lettuce salad

cucumber salad with dill

roma tomato, cabbage, and pickling cucumber salad

celery seed cabbage salad

beet, green bean, tomato, and red onion salad

backyard party summer potato salad

mustard celery root salad

debutante's ball fancy chopped salad

hail thaddeus caesarski salad

polish picnic potato salad

roasted carrots with dill

roasted brussels sprouts polonaise

smokey green beans

excellent stuffed artichokes and tomatoes

cauliflower gratinée

creamed spinach with mushrooms

split pea purée

sweet and sour red cabbage

There was a time in history that most Poles rejected fresh lettuces and baby vegetables as rabbit food, and would rather eat cold gruel as a healthy mainstay! I guess every ethnic group has their misgivings, but great salads and vegetables in today's society are always a welcome addition for anyone who is living a heart healthy lifestyle. Most European countries distinguish between two different types of salads, one of just plain greens, or the salad type served on buffet carts that contains an assortment of chopped vegetables or such. The first would usually be served as a small garnishment for a piece of paté or liver mousse. While the second is usually some bizarre mix of diced vegetables, fruit, nuts, smoked tongue, or salted herring that is combined with a thick mayonnaise base and is listed under the heading salad a la Russe. One of Poland's biggest exports is cold packed pickled salads that are usually produced during the summer season and sold around the world to be enjoyed during the winter. These includes such delicacies as cucumbers in brine, pickled mixed vegetable salads, sauerkraut with cumin seeds, and cabbage, mushrooms, carrots, and onion salads to name a few.

I love working with salads and vegetables. As a young chef, I was always fascinated with the different kinds and varieties of exotic goods we would get our hands on at different times of the year. Beautiful greens, exotic mushrooms, heirloom tomatoes, multi-colored asparagus and beets would be brought to the back door of the restaurant by small local farmers who would barter a dinner for payment of these little jewels. Each leaf and vegetable had their own personality and inventing light vinaigrettes and dressings to compliment them was always a welcome challenge.

I've always loved the simple style of Polish salads, because they are cool, crisp, and refreshing. All my aunties on the farm had ample stocked larders of homemade flavored vinegars, mustards, spices, and horse-radish, which they added to salads and vegetables to give them that certain pucker and distinctive Polish flavor. One of my most treasured cookbooks is a tattered volume of *Blue Ribbon Award Winners of Midwestern Fairs*, which gives actual recipes of pickled salads, vegetables, and assorted greens that cheerfully line farmer's root cellars. The recipes are clear and precise, and use no preservatives, just the best of the crop with a little seasoning, spice, and a lot of love. The French also have an admiration for salads and vegetables that are simply dressed, as do the Italians who set lavish tables based on the art of salad and vegetable cooking alone.

When I first started cooking, fanciful salads heavily laden with dressings were served before or after a meal, but this is not the case anymore. Chefs of the new guard have turned the average salad into the main event. The infusion of nouvelle cuisine has brought such beautiful concoctions as warm goat cheese salad, grilled duck breast, endives, and raspberry salad, and even a warm grilled Portobello steak on fancy greens salad. The beauty of this new preparation is that the natural cooking juices became the salad's dressing with a small splash of vinegar and quality olive oil to round out the dish. Chefs took it a step further by adding grilled baby vegetables and an occasional splattering of fresh fruit to brighten up the taste.

There are literally dozens of Polish salads and vegetables dishes that I could have included in this chapter. In my mind, the easier preparations always win over the complex because salads and vegetables should be a simple and light compliment to the main course. Most Poles that I know pride themselves on having summer gardens which include cucumbers, tomatoes, cabbages, green beans, fresh dill, and possibly some baby beets. These are also the vegetables that were most familiar to me growing up in a Polish household. Rather than masking the freshness of their taste, I have chosen to give them simple preparations because it seems to bring out the best of each one of these individual salads or vegetables on the whole.

Most of my salads and vegetables can be served in many ways. Sometimes I'll forgo a heavier meat entrée and just feature a **Cesarski Salad** as the main course and serve it with a side cup of split pea soup and a loaf of rye bread, or if the weather in July is exceedingly hot, a chilled bowl of beet borscht with mushroom uszka goes well with **Cucumber Salad and Dill**. I love to grill, so a fresh bratwurst topped with **Celery Seed Cabbage Salad** is very refreshing, but I've also been partial to a slightly chilled fresh **Beet, Green Bean, Tomato, and Red Onion Salad** that my wife sprinkles with feta cheese and Italian olives.

Summer Lettuce Salad

Ingredients

1 medium sized head lettuce
$\frac{1}{2}$ cup sour cream, full fat
2 teaspoons canola oil
1 teaspoon lemon juice
$\frac{1}{2}$ teaspoon sea salt
$\frac{1}{8}$ teaspoon freshly ground black pepper
$\frac{1}{2}$ teaspoon sugar
Dash of garlic powder

Preparation

1. **Remove any bad leaves** from the head of lettuce, then using a sharp kitchen knife, quarter the head then quarter it again. Chop the pieces into medium sized chunks, then set aside in a large mixing bowl.

2. **Combine the rest** of the ingredients in a small mixing bowl, cover with plastic wrap, and refrigerate for 1 hour.

3. **Re-stir the dressing,** pour over the chopped lettuce, then mix with your hands to combine.

Serves 4

Cucumber Salad with Dill

Ingredients

2 large seedless cucumbers
$1\frac{1}{2}$ teaspoons sea salt
1 cup sour cream, full fat
2 teaspoons lemon juice
$\frac{1}{4}$ teaspoon celery salt
$\frac{1}{4}$ teaspoon freshly ground white pepper
$1\frac{1}{2}$ teaspoons sugar
2 dashes Tabasco
2 dashes garlic powder
2 tablespoons dill, chopped

Preparation

1. **Cut the cucumbers** into $\frac{1}{8}$-inch pieces, and place into a large mixing bowl. Sprinkle on all of the sea salt, then using your hands, gently mix so all the salt is evenly distributed. Now pour the cucumbers into a colander set over a bowl to drain excess liquid, and cover the colander with plastic wrap then set aside for $\frac{1}{2}$ hour.

2. **Combine the rest** of the ingredients in a small mixing bowl, cover with plastic wrap, and refrigerate for $\frac{1}{2}$ hour.

3. **After $\frac{1}{2}$ hour,** gently squeeze out any excess water from the draining cucumbers, then place into a medium sized mixing bowl. Using a plastic spatula, fold in the dressing, cover with plastic wrap, and refrigerate for a few hours before serving.

Serves 4

Roma Tomato, Cabbage, and Pickling Cucumber Salad

Ingredients

6 plump Roma tomatoes
6 plump pickling cucumbers
1/4 small head red or green cabbage, shredded
1 small red onion, sliced
1/2 cup Greek feta cheese, crumbled
24 Kalamata olives
1/2 cup olive oil
1/4 cup red wine vinegar
1/4 teaspoon sea salt
1/8 teaspoon freshly ground black pepper
10 large basil leaves

Preparation

1. **Cut the tomatoes** into quarters, and slice the cucumbers into 1/4-inch pieces. Place into a large mixing bowl with the cabbage, onion, cheese, and olives, then set aside.

2. **In a medium-sized** mixing bowl, combine the olive oil, vinegar, salt, and pepper, and gently ladle over the tomato salad. Combine with your hands, re-season, cover with a piece of plastic wrap, and refrigerate for 1 hour. Just before serving, shred the basil leaves and combine with the salad

Serves 4

Celery Seed Cabbage Salad

Ingredients

2 pounds red or green cabbage, cored and shredded
1/2 cup canola oil
2 tablespoons sugar
3 tablespoons red wine vinegar
1 1/2 teaspoons stone ground mustard
1 1/2 teaspoons celery seeds
2 teaspoons prepared horseradish
1/2 teaspoon sea salt
1/8 teaspoon freshly ground white pepper
2 Red Delicious apples, cored and thinly sliced, optional
1 tablespoon lemon juice
1 medium red onion, thinly sliced

Preparation

1. **Place the shredded cabbage** into a large mixing bowl and set aside.

2. **In another small** mixing bowl, whisk together the oil, sugar, vinegar, mustard, celery seeds, horseradish, salt, and pepper with a whisk until thoroughly combined. Adjust the seasoning more or less to your taste.

3. **Combine about** 6 to 7 tablespoons of the dressing with the cabbage, and toss together using your hands. (This is the amount that I recommend for this amount of cabbage.)

4. **Cover the salad** bowl with a piece of plastic wrap and refrigerate for at least 1 hour.

5. **Just before serving** the salad, combine the apple slices, lemon juice, and onion, and gently mix into the salad.

Serves 4

Beet, Green Bean, Tomato, and Red Onion Salad

Ingredients

4 medium sized beets, unpeeled
$\frac{1}{2}$ pound green beans, trimmed
4 large Roma tomatoes
1 medium red onion, peeled
$\frac{1}{4}$ cup raspberry vinegar
$\frac{1}{4}$ cup light olive oil
Large pinch of sugar
$\frac{1}{4}$ teaspoon sea salt
$\frac{1}{8}$ teaspoon freshly ground black pepper

Ever since I was a kid, my family always had a small vegetable garden that seemed to blossom more tomatoes and beans than we could possibly eat. Chicago's summer heat always produced beautiful plump red Roma tomatoes, long pole green beans, and an assortment of baby beets that were sugary sweet. Raspberry vinaigrette is a mouth watering and refreshing compliment to the fresh vegetables, and really brings out the full taste of summer.

Chef's Tip!

This simple salad is really at its best when the vegetables are at their peak ripeness. Also try experimenting with different fruit flavored vinegars because they all go beautifully with the fresh vegetables.

Preparation

1. **In a small mixing bowl,** combine the vinegar, olive oil, sugar, salt, and pepper, and whisk until smooth.

2. **Place the beets** into a medium sized saucepot, cover by 2 inches with cold water, add $\frac{1}{4}$ teaspoon of salt, bring to a boil, and simmer for 20 to 30 minutes until a knife pierces the beets easily. When the beets are cooked, remove from the water, cool slightly, and gently rub off their skins with a paper towel, then set aside.

3. **Bring 1 quart** of lightly salted water to a boil, and cook the green beans until they are crisp to the taste. Immediately remove with a kitchen skimmer to a bowl containing ice cubes and water to stop the cooking process. When the green beans are cool, drain thoroughly in a strainer, then dry with a paper towel.

4. **Using a sharp** kitchen knife, slice the beets $\frac{1}{4}$-inch thick, then place into a large mixing bowl, and add the green beans. Now cut the red onions into $\frac{1}{4}$-inch slices, and quarter the tomatoes.

5. **Re-stir the dressing,** add about half to the green beans and beets, and very gently using your hands, toss to mix. Now add the onions and tomatoes to the bowl, and again gently toss to mix. Re-season if needed, cover the bowl with a piece of plastic wrap, and refrigerate for at least 1 hour.

Serves 4

Beet, Green Bean, Tomato, and Red Onion Salad

Backyard Party
Summer Potato Salad

Ingredients

6 medium red potatoes with skins
4 hard boiled eggs, chopped
½ medium red onion, sliced
½ cup olive oil
2 tablespoons red wine vinegar
1 tablespoon Dijon mustard
2 teaspoons garlic, minced
¼ teaspoon sea salt
⅛ teaspoon freshly ground black pepper
¼ cup parsley, chopped

Preparation

1. **Cut the potatoes** across the width into ¼-inch slices, then place in a colander and rinse under cold running water until the water runs clear.

2. **Bring a medium-sized** pot of salted water to a boil, add the potatoes, and cook until slices are barely fork tender, about 4 to 6 minutes. Drain and cool in a colander.

3. **Combine the remaining** ingredients in a medium sized bowl, add the potato slices and eggs, then toss to combine. Cover the bowl with plastic wrap and refrigerate for a couple of hours.

Serves 4

Mustard Celery
Root Salad

Ingredients

1½ pounds celery root, cleaned and cut julienne
3 tablespoons lemon juice
½ teaspoon sea salt
2 Granny Smith apples, cored and thinly sliced
¾ cup mayonnaise, full fat
1 tablespoon Dijon mustard
1 tablespoon Polish dill gherkins, finely minced
1 tablespoon capers, finely minced
1 tablespoon parsley, chopped
Pinch of freshly ground white pepper
Pinch of garlic powder
2 dashes of Tabasco

Preparation

1. **In a large mixing bowl,** combine the celery root, lemon juice, salt, and apple slices, and set aside for 5 minutes.

2. **In another medium-sized** mixing bowl, combine the remaining ingredients and gently fold together with a plastic spatula.

3. **Pour off any excess** liquid that has accumulated in the celery root bowl, then gently fold in the dressing. Cover the bowl with plastic wrap and refrigerate for 2 hours before serving.

Serves 4

Debutante's Ball
Fancy Chopped Salad

Ingredients

4 thick slices Polish bacon
1 small head iceberg lettuce; trimmed, washed, and dried
1 small head romaine; trimmed, washed, and dried
1 large California avocado; pitted, peeled, and diced
2 large plum tomatoes, diced
4 hard boiled eggs, chopped
1 medium red onion, chopped
1/4 pound Roquefort cheese, crumbled
1/4 cup grainy mustard
2 large garlic cloves, minced
2 tablespoons fresh lemon juice
2 tablespoons red wine vinegar
3 teaspoons honey
1/4 teaspoon sea salt
1/8 teaspoon freshly ground black pepper
1/2 cup light olive oil

Preparation

1. **In a small mixing bowl,** combine the mustard, garlic, lemon juice, vinegar, honey, salt, pepper, and olive oil, and whisk until well blended. Refrigerate for at least 2 hours before using.

2. **In a medium-sized** skillet over medium high heat, cook the bacon until it renders its fat and turns lightly brown and crisp. Remove the bacon from the pan and when cool enough to handle, roughly chop then set aside.

3. **Using a sharp** kitchen knife, finely chop the lettuces into small bite size pieces.

4. **Place all the ingredients** except the dressing into a large mixing bowl, cover with plastic wrap, and refrigerate for at least 1 hour.

5. **To prepare the salad,** gently using your hands, toss the ingredients until evenly mixed. Pour half of the dressing onto the salad, and gently mix. Taste and if needed, re-season with more dressing.

Serves 4

Hail Thaddeus Caesarski
Salad

Hey, give a Polish kid a break, the editor wanted more filler.

Ingredients

2 small heads Romaine lettuce, cleaned and chopped
3 thick slices rye bread, cubed
1/4 cup olive oil
2 garlic cloves, peeled and minced
1/2 pound smoked kielbasa sausage, sliced
1/2 cup freshly grated Parmigiano-Reggiano cheese

Caesarski Dressing

1 whole large egg
2 anchovy fillets
2 large garlic cloves, peeled
1 teaspoon whole black peppercorns
1/2 teaspoon celery salt
1/4 cup Parmigiano-Reggiano cheese
1 teaspoon Dijon mustard
2 tablespoons lemon juice
3 tablespoons red wine vinegar
2 dashes Tabasco
2 dashes Worcestershire sauce
1/2 cup olive oil or canola oil

Preparation

1. **To prepare the dressing,** place the anchovies, garlic, peppercorns, celery salt, Parmesan cheese, Dijon mustard, lemon juice, vinegar, Tabasco, and Worcestershire sauce into the bowl of a food blender. Now place the whole egg into a small saucepot filled with water, bring to the boil, and simmer for exactly 1 1/2 minutes. (This kills any bacteria in the egg.) Immediately remove the egg and crack it into the blender with the other ingredients. Cover and pulse the blender a few times, now remove the center cap from the cover, and with the machine running, slowly pour in the olive oil until well blended and the dressing is smooth. Refrigerate the dressing for at least 1 hour before using.

2. **While the dressing** is cooling, prepare the croutons. Heat the olive oil in a medium sized skillet over medium high heat until hot, then add the garlic and swirl the pan for 30 seconds. Now add the diced rye bread and cook for 3 to 5 minutes until the bread is lightly browned and crisp. Remove to a small bowl until needed.

3. **Return the skillet** to the fire, add the Polish sausage pieces, and sauté on both sides until brown and crisp.

4. **Place the cleaned** and chopped Romaine leaves into a large mixing bowl, then sprinkle on the croutons. Pour on some of the chilled dressing, and using a kitchen tong, gently toss the salad, and then divide evenly among 4 dinner plates.

5. **Carefully arrange** the browned kielbasa slices in a decorative fashion onto each salad, then sprinkle on the remaining Parmesan cheese and serve.

Serves 4

Polish Picnic Potato Salad

Ingredients

2 pounds small red new potatoes, cleaned
   and halved
1/3 cup olive oil
1/4 cup apple cider vinegar
3/4 teaspoon sea salt
1/2 teaspoon freshly ground black pepper
2 large garlic cloves, minced
2 medium stalks celery, finely chopped
4 green onions, white and some of the green part,
   finely chopped
8 radishes, sliced
1 large dill pickle, finely chopped
4 tablespoons fresh dill, chopped
2 tablespoons parsley, chopped
2 hard boiled eggs, coarsely chopped

Everyone enjoys a summer picnic, and potato salad has always been my favorite. Classic "mayo"-type salads don't hold up very well in the hot sun, but don't fret because I invented this salad just for you. Small red potatoes are combined with a Polish style garnish of pickles, dill, and egg, and are then dressed with a puckery apple cider dressing. I love this salad with grilled barbeque chicken or smoked Polish sausage.

Chef's Tip!

Keep your eye on the potatoes while they're steaming; overcooking them will produce a salad that is mushy and unappealing. Also, if you like, you can add a tablespoon or so of pickle juice to really perk it up a bit.

Preparation

1. **Steam the new potatoes** in a vegetable steamer placed over 1 inch of hot water for 12 to 15 minutes until tender. Remove to a large mixing bowl and cool slightly.

2. **While the potatoes** are steaming, combine the olive oil, cider vinegar, salt, pepper, and garlic cloves and mix well.

3. **In another large mixing bowl,** combine the remaining ingredients until well blended, then add the dressing and stir slightly with a wooded spoon until well mixed.

4. **Arrange the slightly cooled** potatoes in one layer, cut side up onto a serving platter, then gently spoon all the mixed dressing onto the potatoes. This dish is best served at room temperature.

Serves 4

Roasted Carrots with Dill

Ingredients

8 large carrots, peeled and cleaned
2 tablespoons olive oil
¾ teaspoon sea salt
¼ teaspoon freshly ground black pepper
Pinch of sugar
3 tablespoons dill, chopped

Preparation

1. **Preheat the oven** to 400°F.

2. **Place the carrots** onto a clean work surface and carefully, using a sharp kitchen knife, slice the carrots on a diagonal into 2-inch pieces.

3. **Place all the carrots** into a large mixing bowl and season with the olive oil, salt, pepper, and sugar, and using your hands, toss to coat.

4. **Pour the carrots** onto a heavy-duty nonstick sheet pan and arrange the carrots so that there is equal space between them. Place the pan in the oven and roast the carrots for 20 to 25 minutes until fork tender, not mushy.

5. **Remove the pan** from the oven and cool the carrots slightly, then place them into a serving dish and sprinkle on the dill.

Serves 4

Roasted Brussels Sprouts Polonaise

Ingredients

1½ pounds Brussels sprouts, cleaned
3 tablespoons olive oil
¼ teaspoon sea salt
⅛ teaspoon freshly ground black pepper

1 recipe Savory Polish Topping *(see page 252)*

Preparation

1. **Preheat the oven** to 400°F.

2. **Place the Brussels** sprouts into a large mixing bowl and season with the olive oil, salt, and pepper, and using your hands, toss to coat.

3. **Pour the Brussels** sprouts onto a heavy-duty nonstick sheet pan and arrange the sprouts so that there is equal space between them. Place the pan in the oven and roast for 30 to 40 minutes until fork tender, not mushy.

4. **Remove the pan** from the oven, and cool the sprouts slightly, then place them back into a mixing bowl. Sprinkle on the savory Polish topping and toss the bowl to coat, then pour it into a serving dish.

Serves 4

Smokey Green Beans

Ingredients

2 thick slices Polish bacon, minced
2 large garlic cloves, minced
1 medium sized red onion, diced
1½ pounds green beans
⅛ teaspoon sea salt
⅛ teaspoon freshly ground black pepper

Preparation

1. **Preheat the oven** to 425°F.

2. **In a medium-sized** nonstick skillet, lightly brown the minced bacon until it renders its fat, then add the garlic and onion and sauté for 2 minutes more. Remove the pan from the fire and pour off all but 1 tablespoon of bacon fat.

3. **Place the green beans** into a large mixing bowl, and pour on the bacon-onion mixture, then season with the salt and pepper. Toss gently with a kitchen tong, then pour the green beans onto a heavy-duty nonstick sheet pan, and roast for 30 minutes until the green beans are fork tender.

4. **When the green beans** are cooked, remove to a serving dish.

Serves 4

Excellent Stuffed Artichokes and Tomatoes

Ingredients

8 pre-cooked artichoke hearts
4 plum tomatoes, halved
¾ cup fresh breadcrumbs
6 tablespoons Parmigiano-Reggiano cheese
½ pound mozzarella cheese, shredded
4 garlic cloves, minced
¼ cup parsley, minced
1 heaping tablespoon Pesto *(see page 168)*
⅛ teaspoon sea salt
⅛ teaspoon freshly ground black pepper
6 tablespoons olive oil

Preparation

1. **Preheat the oven** to 375°. In a medium-sized mixing bowl, combine the breadcrumbs, Parmesan, mozzarella, garlic, parsley, pesto, salt, and pepper, and thoroughly mix until well blended.

2. **Pour 3 tablespoon**s of the olive oil onto the bottom of a medium sized oval earthenware casserole, then artfully arrange the artichoke hearts and tomatoes (cut-side up) on top of that. Now drizzle the remaining olive oil on top of the artichokes and tomatoes, then sprinkle on about half of the prepared cheese stuffing being sure that all of the vegetables are evenly covered. (Store the remaining cheese mixture in an airtight container and freeze for later use.)

3. **Place the pan** into the hot oven and bake for 20 to 25 minutes until the breadcrumbs and cheese are lightly browned.

Serves 4

Cauliflower Gratinée

Ingredients

2 pounds cauliflower florets, pre-cooked al dente
2 tablespoons unsalted butter, melted
2 tablespoons all-purpose flour
2 cups heavy cream
½ teaspoon sea salt
¼ teaspoon freshly ground black pepper
⅛ teaspoon nutmeg
⅛ teaspoon garlic powder
Dash of Tabasco
2 tablespoons unsalted butter, softened
2 tablespoons freshly grated Parmigiano-Reggiano cheese
    or
½ cup grated Colby, jack, or Swiss cheese

Preparation

1. **Preheat the oven** to 375°. In a small saucepan over medium heat, combine the melted butter and flour, and cook stir for exactly 2 minutes with a wooden spoon. Now add the heavy cream, salt, pepper, nutmeg, garlic powder, and Tabasco, and bring to a boil. Reduce the heat, and stir cook the sauce with a whisk for another 2 to 3 minutes then remove from the fire.

2. **With the remaining butter,** heavily coat the bottom of a medium sized earthenware oval casserole, and then place the cooked florets on top of it. Now spoon the warm sauce over the cauliflower pieces, sprinkle on the grated cheese, and bake in the oven for 20 to 30 minutes until bubbly and golden brown.

Serves 4

Creamed Spinach with Mushrooms

Ingredients

4 pounds fresh spinach leaves, cleaned and pre-blanched
4 tablespoons unsalted butter, melted
2 slices hickory smoked bacon, minced
1 pound domestic mushrooms, sliced
6 large garlic cloves, minced
2 cups heavy cream
½ scant teaspoon sea salt
¼ teaspoon freshly ground black pepper
⅛ teaspoon nutmeg
Large dash of Tabasco
Large dash of Maggi
2 tablespoons unsalted butter, chilled

Preparation

1. **Place the blanched** spinach leaves onto a clean kitchen towel, and fold the long ends over each other. Now grasping both ends of the towel, twist to squeeze the excess liquid out of the spinach. Coarsely chop the spinach using a sharp kitchen knife, and set aside in a bowl until needed.

2. **Place a medium-sized** nonstick skillet over medium high heat, and when the pan turns white-hot, add the butter, bacon, mushrooms, and garlic, and sauté quickly until the mushrooms start to release their liquid. When the liquid starts to dissipate, add the heavy cream, salt, pepper, nutmeg, Tabasco, Maggi, and chopped spinach, and bring to the boil. Now reduce the heat, and simmer slowly until the cream thickly coats the back of a wooden spoon about 8 to 10 minutes.

3. **Remove the skillet** from the fire, re-season the mixture, and stir in the butter.

Serves 4

Split Pea Purée

Ingredients

1 small piece smoked ham rind, pre-blanched
1 cup green split peas
2 tablespoons olive oil
4 large garlic cloves, minced
1 small onion, diced
1 small carrot, diced
1 small celery stalk, diced
1 bay leaf
½ teaspoon dried marjoram
½ teaspoon dried thyme
2½ cups chicken stock
¼ teaspoon sea salt
⅛ teaspoon freshly ground black pepper
2 large dashes Tabasco
2 large dashes Maggi
Dash of garlic powder

Preparation

1. **Heat the olive oil** in a small pot over medium heat; add the garlic, onion, carrots, and celery and cook, stirring, until slightly softened, about 3 minutes. Do not let the vegetables brown.

2. **Now add the bay leaf,** marjoram, and thyme and cook for exactly 1 minute to release their oils.

3. **Add the rest** of the ingredients to the pot, bring it to a boil, then reduce the heat and simmer slowly for about 1 hour.

4. **Using a heavy wooden spoon,** or better yet, an electric hand mixer, puree the peas and vegetables until smooth. (Don't be tempted to add more stock at this point, the puree will produce more liquid.)

5. **Let the puree cook** for another 5 to 10 minutes until thick. Re-season and serve.

Serves 4

Sweet and Sour Red Cabbage

Ingredients

2 pounds red cabbage, cored and shredded
2 tablespoon red wine vinegar
2 tablespoons sugar
2 tablespoons duck fat
1 small onion, diced
1 medium sized tart apple, peeled, cored, and diced
1 tablespoon honey
½ cup dry red wine
1 cup chicken stock
1 bay leaf
½ teaspoon sea salt
¼ teaspoon freshly ground black pepper
Pinch of cinnamon
Pinch of cloves
¾ teaspoon caraway seeds, optional

Preparation

1. **Place the shredded cabbage** into a medium sized mixing bowl, then pour on the red wine vinegar and sugar, and toss with your hands until evenly coated and the sugar has dissolved. Cover the bowl with plastic wrap and refrigerate for at least 8 hours.

2. **Heat the duck fat** in a medium pot over medium high heat, then add the onion and apples, and cook stirring until slightly softened, about 2 minutes. Add the honey and cook stir for another minute. Now add the red wine, and cook it until it has reduced by half. Add the rest of the ingredients, including the marinating cabbage and its liquid, stir with a wooden spoon, cover the pot, then reduce the heat and simmer slowly for about 1 hour. Be sure to stir the cabbage every 15 minutes.

Serves 4

*m*ushrooms

*h*unter's delight with pancetta and marjoram

*m*ushrooms escargots

*k*ing bolete with green peppercorns

*s*autéed wild mushrooms on "garlic croutes"

*b*usia's chicken livers with chanterelles

*c*ocktail party mushrooms

*s*icilian-style stuffed mushrooms

As I write, there are some thirty-eight thousand different varieties of wild mushrooms throughout the world. Some are edible but most are not. In Poland alone, the government has issued a culinary declaration that 31 wild varieties will be designated for sale, whereas 15 other varieties can be dried and sold around the rest of the world for a premium.

While most Americans might treasure the start of football season, most Eastern Europeans anticipate the mushroom harvest and the feast of the forest that they bring. I've personally witnessed this sometimes futile phenomenon and seen neighbor pitted against neighbor, busia against busia, all in a mad scurry into the damp autumn woods, hunting, scouring, and hiding behind trees to protect their secret places where maybe a few giant cepes or a scattering of golden chanterelles might be nesting.

As a kid, I remember driving along with my Grandpa John up around Devon and Peterson, and on one or two occasions, he would abruptly pull the car over to the side by the woods, hop out with the ignition still on, and disappear into the then densely tree lined woods. He would appear five minutes later with an arm full of mushrooms, dirt and all. He'd hop back in the car and say, "Hey boy, I could smell those things a mile away," and then I was given the riot act about keeping this spot a secret. Years would go by, and I would always see people park their cars, run into the woods quickly, and return with arms full of goodies. Courtesy of the Cook County Forest Preserves!

To begin with, unless you are a trained professional, or hang with a qualified mycologist (mushroom expert), I urge you not to go running into the woods to pick your own. It is an often confusing and extremely dangerous proposition if you don't know what you're doing. In this country, fresh mushrooms are available on a daily basis at any local market and there are endless varieties. The most popular are **chanterelle** – mild, apricot nutty taste; **cremini** – earthy flavor; **enoki** – very mild and fragile; **morel** – full, strong, heavy flavored; **oyster** – delicate, soft taste; **porcini** – rich and meaty, nutty; **Portobello** – meaty flavor and texture; **shitake** – meaty, earthy flavor; and **wood ear** – musty, mild flavored. Undoubtedly to the Poles, the finest tasting mushroom would be the **borowik** or **King Bolete**, which is similar to the French cepe or the Italian porcini. To avoid confusion, the name Bolete is used to describe a wide range of mushrooms with similar tastes and appearance, so it is best to concentrate on the American varieties.

Mushrooms have been a Polish mainstay for centuries, due to the climatic conditions of the region. It wasn't uncommon for a small family on a weekend to pick a year's worth, to later be dried, lightly smoked, canned, pickled, or even sold to purveyors for pennies of what they were worth on the market. Mushroom dishes are considered more as a main dish than as a garnishment to the Poles, but with the current cost of fresh at the local stores, I'd rather treat them as an appetizer or an accompaniment to a ragout or stew. I've never been partial to using dried mushrooms because of the cost, and I've noticed over the years that the taste varies dramatically depending on which purveyor you use. Mushroom powders are a better value because a little bit goes a long way to sup up a soup or stew.

It is said that "mushrooms know no national boundaries," so there are literally thousands of preparations known to man, but the simplest are the best. I've always enjoyed mushrooms simply sautéed in a hot skillet with a little butter, garlic, and fresh herbs. Italian chefs that I know are partial to marinating and grilling Portobello mushrooms, whereas French chefs that I know like the classic mushroom escargots with its extra sauce that can be sopped up with a piece of country bread. The Poles favor cold mushroom salads, but also have been known to treat these little gems majestically by adding chicken livers or other savory charcuterie. The dishes that I have listed have been my most requested throughout the years and actually can be cooked very quickly as long as you have all of the ingredients at hand.

As with all fresh mushrooms, there are some important guidelines to choosing and preparing them for the skillet. Always buy mushrooms that are whole without any blemishes, pit marks, or have an ammonia like smell to them. Wild mushrooms should never be washed because their open pores absorb water like a sponge. There might be an occasion where the dirt cannot be removed from the surface with a soft brush so a quick rinse and dry will have to suffice. Always store clean mushrooms in between layers of paper towels (not in plastic bags where they will mold) and use as quickly as possible.

Hunter's Delight
with Pancetta and Marjoram

Ingredients

2 tablespoons unsalted butter, melted
¼ cup Pancetta ham, sliced thin and diced
2 pounds assorted field mushrooms, quartered,
   such as cepes, shitakes, oyster, or cremini
¼ cup Madeira
½ cup chicken or veal stock
Pinch of sea salt
Pinch of freshly ground black pepper
Dash of Maggi
1 tablespoon fresh marjoram, chopped
1 tablespoon parsley, chopped
¼ cup heavy cream, optional

If your old man comes back from the big hunting trip up North with a bag full of assorted mushrooms, this is the recipe for you. When I teach young chefs about mushroom cooking, I always tell them that the secret is to cut the mushrooms into equal pieces and to use a skillet that is heated "white hot and smokin'." Pancetta, Madeira, stock, and marjoram are the perfect contrast to the muskiness of the mushrooms.

Chef's Tip!

If you are an adventurous cook, you can create an elegant dinner appetizer by pre-baking store bought puff pastry shells, and stuffing the cooked mushroom mixture into them. This fun appetizer comes together in a snap!

Preparation

1. **Place a medium-sized** nonstick skillet over medium high heat, and when the pan turns white-hot, add the butter and pancetta, and cook for 1 minute. Add the mushrooms, and sauté quickly until the mushrooms start to release their liquid. When the liquid starts to dissipate, and the mushrooms start to brown at the edges, remove the pan from the heat, and pour in the Madeira. Return the pan back to the fire and tilt it slightly towards the flame so the Madeira will ignite. Shake the pan until the flames die down, then lower the heat to medium low.

2. **Now add** the chicken stock and cook stir for 1 minute until slightly reduced, then add the rest of the ingredients, and cook for 3 to 5 minutes until the sauce lightly coats the back of a spoon.

Serves 4

Mushrooms Escargots

Ingredients

1 tin canned snails
½ cup dry white wine
½ cup chicken stock
1 bay leaf
2 sprigs fresh thyme
Dash of sea salt
Dash of freshly ground black pepper
2 tablespoons unsalted butter, melted
1½ pounds cepes or porcini mushrooms, quartered

Herbed Butter

½ small head garlic cloves, peeled
1 tablespoon dry white wine
1 teaspoon brandy
1 teaspoon lemon juice
1 teaspoon sea salt
⅛ teaspoon freshly ground white pepper
Pinch of nutmeg
Pinch of cayenne
Dash of Tabasco
½ cup parsley, chopped
1 pound unsalted butter, chilled

When I was a young cook, I worked my way through a couple of really great continental restaurants, and I served a big Texan 6 orders of this dish one late evening. I've always been amazed at how many people have asked me for this simple recipe over the years, so here it is!

Chef's Tip!

Although this is an easy dish to prepare, it is vitally important that you drain the cooked snails of all residual liquid before placing them into the oven with the butter on top. If the snails are wet when they heat up, they have a tendency to pop and will make a mess of your clean oven.

Preparation

1. **Drain the snails** in a small strainer, then rinse under cold running water for 1 minute. Place the snails into a small saucepan with the white wine, stock, bay leaf, thyme, salt, and pepper, and bring to a quick boil, then reduce to a slow simmer and cook for 5 minutes. Let the snails cool in the liquid, then cover with plastic wrap and refrigerate.

2. **Now prepare the herbed butter** by placing all of the ingredients into the work bowl of a food processor, attach the lid, then pulse 4 to 5 times. Remove the cover, scrape down the sides of the bowl with a plastic spatula, recover, and pulse again until the mixture is smooth. Remove the butter to a small bowl, cover with plastic wrap, and refrigerate.

3. **Preheat the oven** to 350°F.

4. **Drain the snails** of all liquid and set aside. Place a medium sized heavy-duty cast iron skillet over medium high heat, and when the pan turns white-hot, add the butter and mushrooms, and cook for 1 minute. Now add the snails, and cook stir with a wooden spoon for 1 minute more, then remove the pan from the fire.

5. **Remove the herbed butter** from the refrigerator, and using a tablespoon, scoop one-fourth of it out of the bowl and place directly on top of the mushroom-snail mixture. Place the pan into the hot oven, and cook for 10 minutes until the butter bubbles without burning.

Serves 4

King Bolete with Green Peppercorns

"Borowik or King Bolete" is undoubtedly the finest tasting mushroom known to man. Comparable to the French cepes and the Italian porcini, you'll find it's taste semi-nutty with mellow woodsy aftertones. Whenever you see imported dry mushrooms, Bolete is 99% of the time the culprit, but why use dried when you can obtain fresh in most markets? This regal specimen deserves special treatment, so I've combined it with Cognac, cream, and green peppercorns; a combination I'm sure you'll love.

Chef's Tip!

Although the recipe calls for cepes or porcinis, feel free to substitute any assortment of wild mushrooms that strike your fancy. I recommend using a hardier variety because they seem to stand up better to this regal sauce.

Ingredients

2 tablespoons unsalted butter, melted
1½ pounds cepes or porcini mushrooms, quartered and sliced
1 tablespoon Cognac
¼ cup heavy cream
½ cup veal stock
1 teaspoon whole green peppercorns
Pinch of sea salt
Pinch of freshly ground black pepper
Dash of Maggi

Preparation

1. **Place a medium-sized** nonstick skillet over medium high heat, and when the pan turns white-hot, add the butter and the mushrooms, and sauté quickly until the mushrooms start to release their liquid. When the liquid starts to dissipate, and the mushrooms start to brown at the edges, remove the pan from the heat, and pour in the Cognac. Return the pan back to the fire and tilt it slightly towards the flame so the Cognac will ignite. Shake the pan until the flames die down, then lower the heat to medium low.

2. **Now add** the heavy cream and cook stir for 1 minute until slightly reduced, then add the rest of the ingredients, and cook for 3 to 5 minutes until the sauce lightly coats the back of a spoon.

Serves 4

Sautéed Wild Mushrooms
on "Garlic Croutes"

Ingredients

12 thin slices Rustic Country Loaf (*see page 22*)
⅓ cup olive oil
2 large garlic cloves, minced
½ cup freshly grated Parmigiano-Reggiano cheese
2 tablespoons unsalted butter, melted
2 large garlic cloves, minced
1 small onion, finely diced
¼ cup pancetta ham, sliced thin and diced
1½ pounds assorted field mushroom, quartered
1 tablespoon parsley, chopped
1 tablespoon fresh rosemary or sage, chopped
Dash of sea salt
Dash of freshly ground black pepper

Sometimes in life it is best to leave things well enough alone. Freshly picked wild mushrooms are at their peak taste for only a few hours, and the best way to enjoy their natural taste is to give them a quick sauté in some really good butter, a few seasonings, and that's it.

Chef's Tip!

This quick and easy mushroom sauté can also compliment a small grilled butt steak or can even be a filling for a savory cheese omelet. Remember to always a use a skillet that is heated "white hot" before sautéing.

Preparation

1. **Preheat the oven** to 400°, and place the sliced bread onto a baking pan. Using a pastry brush, lather on the olive oil, sprinkle on the minced garlic and grated cheese, then bake in the hot oven for 15 minutes until slightly golden brown. Set aside until needed.

2. **Place a medium-sized** nonstick skillet over medium high heat, and when the pan turns white-hot, add the butter, garlic, onion, and pancetta, and cook for 1 minute. Add the mushrooms, and sauté quickly until the mushrooms start to release their liquid. When the liquid starts to dissipate, and the mushrooms start to brown at the edges, season with the fresh herbs and a dash of salt and pepper, then remove from the fire.

3. **Place the crisped croutes** onto a serving platter, then carefully spoon the mushroom mixture on top and serve immediately.

Serves 4

Busia's Chicken Livers with Chanterelles

I know of a little Polish restaurant on Devon Ave. that serves fresh chicken livers with tiny golden chanterelle mushrooms, and rumor has it that the mushrooms are picked from the local woods and cemeteries that surround the area. Unless you're an avid and experienced mushroom picker, I wouldn't recommend this practice but hey, for "$1.95" a plate, I'm there!

Chef's Tip!

Personally, I am not partial to chicken livers, and if you feel the same, you can easily substitute 4 small pieces of fresh calves liver in this recipe.

Ingredients

3 tablespoons unsalted butter, melted
1 pound fresh chicken livers
1 teaspoon Polish spice #1 *(see page 251)*
¼ cup all-purpose flour
½ small onion, finely diced
1 pound baby golden chanterelles
2 tablespoons dry sherry
½ cup heavy cream
½ cup chicken stock
Dash of sea salt
Dash of freshly ground black pepper
Dash of nutmeg
Dash of Maggi

Preparation

1. **Place the chicken livers** onto a plate lined with a paper towel, and pat the livers with another paper towel to remove all excess moisture. Discard the towels and season the livers with the Polish spice.

2. **Over medium high heat,** heat a medium sized nonstick skillet until white-hot, add the butter, then quickly dredge the chicken livers into the flour. Sauté the livers on both sides until golden brown, about 1 to 2 minutes on each side, then remove to a clean plate.

3. **Using the same skillet,** add the diced onion and cook stir for 1 minute, then add the mushrooms and cook until they start to release their liquid. When the liquid starts to dissipate, remove the pan from the heat, and pour in the sherry. Return the pan back to the fire and tilt it slightly towards the flame so the sherry will ignite. Shake the pan until the flames die down, then lower the heat to medium low.

4. **Now add the heavy cream** and cook stir for 1 minute until slightly reduced, then add the rest of the ingredients, including the livers, and cook for 3 to 5 minutes until the sauce lightly coats the back of a spoon.

Serves 4

Cocktail Party Mushrooms

Ingredients

2 pounds assorted mushrooms, such as field
    mushrooms, cepes, or cremini
1/2 cup all-purpose flour
3 whole large eggs
2 cups fresh breadcrumbs
2 teaspoons Polish spice #3 *(see page 251)*
2 cups Canola oil or vegetable shortening for frying

Dipping Sauce

1 cup mayonnaise, full-fat
1 1/2 to 2 tablespoons beet horseradish
2 teaspoons Dijon mustard
1/8 teaspoon celery salt
1/4 teaspoon garlic powder
1/8 teaspoon freshly ground black pepper
Large dash of Worcestershire sauce
Large dash of Tabasco

If you're having a small party and really want to impress your friends, this is a great recipe!

Chef's Tip!

You can really impress your vegetarian guests by also gently frying some thin zucchini slices, baby eggplants, sweet potato slices, and onion rings. Just follow the basic recipe, but double the proportions so you will have enough.

Preparation

1. **Combine all** the dipping sauce ingredients in a small bowl and refrigerate until needed.

2. Place all the **mushrooms** onto a clean work surface, and using a sharp kitchen knife, cut the mushrooms and stems into equal bite sized pieces.

3. **Place the whole eggs** into a large mixing bowl and whisk until well blended.

4. **In another large mixing bowl,** combine the breadcrumbs with the Polish spice.

5. **Combine the mushrooms** and the flour until the mushrooms are well coated, then pour into a large strainer and shake off all the excess flour. Now carefully, one by one, dip the floured mushrooms into the eggs, then roll in the breadcrumbs until well coated, then place onto a parchment lined sheet pan. Repeat until all the mushrooms are coated, then place the pan directly into the freezer to rest for 10 minutes.

6. **Heat the oil** in a deep fat fryer or a medium sized heavy-duty soup pot until the temperature reaches 375°F. (I highly recommend using a frying thermometer to gauge the temperature. It is imperative that the temperature remains in the 375°F range for proper cooking.)

7. **When the oil is hot** enough, deep fry the mushrooms in batches for 2 to 3 minutes until crispy and golden brown, then remove to a napkin lined serving basket. Serve with the dipping sauce.

Serves 4

Sicilian-style Stuffed Mushrooms

As you have read in an earlier chapter, Poles are great noshers, and this recipe could easily be classified as a meal in itself. When you have a cocktail party, always use foodstuffs that are fairly economical and easy to prepare ahead of time. I've spruced up a basic mushroom filling recipe, and I think you and your guests will enjoy it!

Chef's Tip!

If you're stressed for time and do not want to make your own sausage filling, just skip step #1 and substitute 1 pound of prepared Italian sausage of your choice.

Ingredients

¾ pound pork butt, ground for sausage
¼ teaspoon sea salt
¼ heaping teaspoon freshly ground black pepper
¼ heaping teaspoon fennel seeds
Pinch of red pepper flakes
2 tablespoons Parmigiano-Reggiano cheese, grated
2 tablespoons breadcrumbs
1 tablespoon parsley, chopped
32 medium-sized white domestic mushrooms with stems
3 tablespoons olive oil
2 large garlic cloves, minced
½ small onion, diced
½ medium sized red pepper, diced
¼ cup black Italian olives, pitted and diced
Grated Parmigiano-Reggiano cheese for sprinkling
Olive oil for sprinkling

Preparation

1. **In a medium-sized** mixing bowl, using a heavy-duty wooden spoon, combine the pork, salt, pepper, fennel seeds, red pepper flakes, cheese, breadcrumbs, and parsley until well blended. Cover the bowl with plastic wrap and place into the refrigerator until needed.

2. **Carefully remove** the stems from the mushrooms, and using a sharp kitchen knife, finely chop the stems.

3. **Heat the olive oil** in a medium sized nonstick skillet over medium high heat, then add the garlic, onion, and red pepper, and sauté for 2 minutes. Now add the diced mushroom stems and sauté for another 2 to 4 minutes until the mushrooms release their liquid. When the liquid evaporates, remove the skillet from the fire, and stir in the black olives.

4. **When the mushroom-onion** mixture has cooled, gently fold it into the fresh sausage and set aside until needed.

5. **Preheat the oven** to 450°F.

6. **Working quickly,** using a small soupspoon, scoop about 1 tablespoon of the savory stuffing into the caps of the mushrooms. (It is important to press the stuffing completely into the mushroom cap.) Repeat with the remaining mushrooms and stuffing, and place onto a large nonstick sheet pan.

7. **When all** the stuffed mushrooms are on the pan, liberally sprinkle on olive oil and grated cheese, then place the pan into the hot oven and cook for about 15 minutes until bubbling and well browned. Let the mushrooms cool for 5 minutes before serving.

Serves 4

*p*ierogi, dumplings,
noodles, and potatoes

old potato pierogi dough

new sour cream pierogi dough

church festival flour pierogi dough

fresh cabbage filling

sauerkraut and mushroom filling

potato and cheese filling

bacon, cheddar cheese,
and potato filling

fresh blueberry filling

fresh golden or red cherry filling

fresh plum filling

fresh prune and golden raisin filling

"greek style" with spinach and feta

spicy "sicilian style"

meat-filled "kolduny litewsky" filling

vegetable-filled "kolduny litewsky"
filling

lazy man's cheese and potato
pierogi/dumplings

kopytka

tavern pan sinkers

parsley dumplings

drop noodle dumplings

peasant noodles with cottage cheese
and ham

busia's buttered noodles with eggs

kapusta with egg noodles

quick vegetarian noodles

egg noodles with wild mushrooms
and rosemary

mushroom uszka with brown butter
and sage

parsley potato pancakes

latkes with chives and parsley

red pepper, zucchini, and potato cake

caramelized onion and ham
potato cakes

savory stuffed twice baked potatoes

cheesy potato gratinée

Old Polish saying: Swiety jacek z pierogami! Meaning: St.Hyacinth and his pierogi!

Lately I keep having this reoccurring dream that Ray Kroc visits me in my sleep and wants to replace the French fries on his menu and put pierogis in its place! Could you imagine how many billions he would have sold? All kidding aside, the Pole's beloved pierogi has finally found its place onto the American table as a truly wonderful dish. Some call it a stuffed dumpling and others call it a variation on the ravioli, but the Polish people have always known it as a pierogi!

Now I'm not going to get into some long-winded sermon about the history of pierogi, because we all know what it is. And I don't want to get any e-mails from busias around the country that say that I stole their recipe because there are hundreds of recipes for pierogi dough and hundreds of fillings for this delectable little treat. Also, depending upon where you live, humidity and elevation can play havoc on your dough, so it really becomes a little bit of this and a little bit of that kind of pierogi making process. The easiest way to start a Polish revolution is to proclaim who has the best peirogi, but in essence they're all good.

I've always considered Polish cuisine to be a well-rounded cultural experience, but it seems that peirogi has found its way onto other ethnic tables as well. Different cultures have adapted such fillings as goat cheese and mango, or even pineapple, ham, and cheese, but I'm a traditionalist when it comes to pierogi. Busias that I've known have always favored dough that was made out of old potatoes, because it reminds them of what their mothers used to make in Poland. When I give cooking lessons on the road, younger Poles that I meet reminisce about busia's pierogi and the time it took to make them properly. Chefs around the country have created more fashionable, thinner pierogi dough that's more pasta like and easier to roll out, but the process is still time consuming. I've tried to include in this chapter a wide range of doughs and popular fillings that have never been put in print and that should satisfy any discerning pierogi connoisseur.

Along with the hundreds of recipes for pierogi come the words dziatki, galeczki, galuszki, haluski, kluski, knedle, kolduny, kopytka, przasniki, sliziki, and zacierki, which all in some form or another translate to dumplings and noodles or anything farinaceous. History books show that a lot of potato and noodle dishes were brought to Poland from other countries so these words can be found in Hungarian, Ukrainian, and Slavic cookbooks as well. The Poles also have a preference for dumplings and most people are surprised at how light they can be. **Lazyman's Cheese and Potato Dumpling** along with the more traditional **Kopytka** are less time consuming than pierogi making because they don't contain any filling, but are just as tasty and are usually topped with savory breadcrumbs or served along with any roasted meat dishes as a great accompaniment. I invented **Tavern Pan Sinkers** for those of you who need a quick dumpling fix with a minimum of time and effort expended. If you have a family of growing boys, trust me, pan sinkers are the way to go to fill them up!

Noodle and potato dishes have always been a Polish favorite, and again the varieties are endless. In researching this chapter, I've found that most noodle dishes had a tendency to be overly sweet and baked which clearly shows their roots to a more Ukrainian and Jewish influenced culinary tradition. My earlier memories involving noodles were based more on the Kluski type that you would find in soup, although my mother also used to make a dish of **Kapusta with Egg Noodles** or the simple **Buttered Noodles with Eggs and Cheese** on a Friday meatless dinner night. Polish style noodles are softer in texture compared to what most people would be familiar with as a spaghetti type noodle so I've included a few recipes to compliment this type.

Last but not least is my favorite, the potato. Over the last ten years, the potato has been kicked around the block as not being good for you, too many carbs, too much sugar, and so on and so forth. I don't necessarily agree with that philosophy. I've always loved potato dishes whether they are my mom's **Garlic Whipped** with her famous pork loin and gravy, or my mother-in-law's **Red Pepper, Zucchini, and Potato Cake** that she serves cold as a light lunch. The preparation is usually what makes a potato dish fattening such as, French fries or others that are loaded with butter, but I don't know anyone that can resist a platter full of freshly made **Parsley Potato Pancakes** or **Latkes with Chives.** The recipes in this book are a small collection of my favorites and I hope that you will give them a try and enjoy them as much as I do.

Old Potato Pierogi Dough

Ingredients

2 cups dry mashed potatoes, chilled
3 cups all-purpose flour
3 whole large eggs
2 teaspoons sea salt
$1/2$ cup to $3/4$ cup cool water

This is an old fashioned Pierog dough that I learned from Busia. Back in the days when potatoes and flour were plentiful, and when worked with old frail hands, the end product was pure poetry. This dough produces a firm, slightly heavy, chewy dough, depending on how thin you roll it out.

Chef's Tip!

When mashing the potatoes for pierogi dough, don't be tempted to add any liquid, such as milk or chicken stock, as this will throw the whole recipe off. All you want is cooked mashed potatoes.

Preparation

1. **Place the mashed potatoes** into a large mixing bowl, then sprinkle on the salt. Beat the eggs in another bowl until frothy, then add to the potatoes. Using a heavy wooden spoon, thoroughly combine the egg and potato mix until very smooth.

2. **Now add to the potato mixture** a quarter cup of water, and stir with the spoon to combine.

3. **Place a medium-sized** fine mesh strainer over the potato bowl, and working with a 1 cup measuring scoop, add exactly 1 cup of flour to the strainer, and then sift onto the potatoes. Again using the heavy spoon, thoroughly incorporate the flour into the potatoes until smooth.

4. **Repeat again** with another quarter cup of water, then another cup of sifted flour until smooth.

5. **(At this point,** be careful as to how much water the potatoes will take.) Now sift the remaining flour onto the potatoes, and combine until you form a smooth dough. If more water is needed, add it tablespoon by tablespoon.

6. **Pour the dough** out onto a lightly floured work surface, and knead until smooth and elastic, not sticky. Refrigerate the dough for at least 2 to 3 hours before using.

Makes about 40 pieces

New Sour Cream Pierogi Dough

Ingredients

5 cups all-purpose flour
One 16 ounce container sour cream, full fat
2 tablespoons olive oil
3 whole large eggs
2 teaspoons sea salt

The "nouvelle" pieorgi dough. A basic but excellent dough that is lightened by the use of sour cream. Most chef's that I've made this for agree that it's their choice among the three, but only if it is made correctly. The dough produces a beautifully soft well-textured pierog, with just the right amount of bite.

Chef's Tip!

When you mix the dough, make sure that all the ingredients are chilled, as this will help the dough blend together more easily. Also, don't run the food processor too long or this will warm your dough.

Preparation

1. **To mix the dough** in a food processor, place the eggs, salt, and oil in the work bowl fitted with a metal blade. Run the machine continuously for 1 minute. Remove the cover, and add the sour cream and exactly 4½ cups flour. Recover and run the machine until a soft but sticky ball forms inside the bowl.

2. **Using the extra flour,** pour exactly 1 tablespoon of flour onto a work surface. Carefully using a plastic spatula, remove all of the dough from the bowl and place it on top of the floured surface. Now place on top of the dough 1 more tablespoon of the reserved flour, and gently knead it into the dough until it is all absorbed.

3. **Repeat the process** again using 2 more tablespoons of the reserved flour. The dough should be soft and pliable—if not, work in 1 more tablespoon of flour.

4. **Divide the dough** into 2 equal portions, and very gently, using your knuckles, push the dough into 2 six by six squares. Now flip each square over, and using a soft pastry brush, remove any excess flour from the dough. Now place each square into it's own Ziploc bag, put on a small sheet pan, and refrigerate overnight.

5. **Reserve the excess flour** for rolling out the dough.

Makes about 40 pieces

Church Festival Flour Pierogi Dough

I f you've got to make a ton of Pierogi, and you have a few dozen ladies, try this recipe. This dough, which is close to a pasta dough, is very basic, but also very forgiving. It mixes well, freezes well, and best of all can be rolled out through a pasta machine if necessary. The dough produces a semi-soft, but slightly firm Pierogi. I highly recommend it for first time Pierogi makers.

Ingredients

1 large whole egg
3 tablespoons sour cream, full fat
1 cup whole milk
1 cup water
1½ teaspoons sea salt
5 to 5⅓ cups all-purpose flour

Chef's Tip!

If you roll the dough through a pasta machine, make sure that the setting isn't too thin or your fillings will poke through the dough when you form the pierogi.

Preparation

1. **To mix the dough** in a food processor, place the egg, sour cream, milk, water, and salt in the work bowl fitted with a metal blade. Run the machine continuously for 1 minute. Remove the cover, and add exactly 5 cups flour. Recover and run the machine until a soft but sticky ball forms inside the bowl.

2. **Using the extra flour,** pour exactly 1 tablespoon of flour onto a work surface. Carefully using a plastic spatula, remove all of the dough from the bowl and place it on top of the floured surface. Now place on top of the dough 1 more tablespoon of the reserved flour, and gently knead it into the dough until it is all absorbed.

3. **Repeat the process** again using 2 more tablespoons of the reserved flour. The dough should be soft and pliable, if not, work in 1 more tablespoon of flour.

4. **Divide the dough** into 2 equal portions, and very gently, using your knuckles, push the dough into 2 six by six squares. Now flip each square over, and using a soft pastry brush, remove any excess flour from the dough. Now place each square into it's own Ziploc bag, put on a small sheet pan, and refrigerate overnight.

5. **Reserve the excess flour** for rolling out the dough.

Makes about 40 pieces

Pierogi Fillings

Fresh Cabbage

Ingredients

1 slice hickory smoked bacon, diced
2 tablespoons olive oil
2 teaspoons garlic puree
1 small onion, finely diced
1 medium head green cabbage, decored and diced
½ teaspoon sea salt
¼ teaspoon freshly ground black pepper
2 tablespoons chicken stock
2 dashes of Tabasco

Preparation

1. **In a large pot** over medium high heat, cook the bacon until it renders its fat and turns lightly brown, not crisp. Pour the bacon into a small strainer set over a bowl to collect the excess fat.

2. **Return the pot** to the fire, then add the olive oil. When hot add the garlic and onion, and cook stir for about 1 minute. Now add the cabbage and cook stir for about 3 to 4 minutes until the cabbage starts to wilt.

3. **Reduce the heat** to low, add the rest of the seasonings and the bacon, and cook slowly, covered, for about 20 minutes.

Makes about 2 cups

Sauerkraut and Mushroom

Ingredients

1 slice hickory smoked bacon, diced
2 teaspoons garlic puree
½ small onion, finely diced
¼ pound green cabbage, shredded
½ pound sauerkraut, drained and rinsed, twice
½ pound domestic mushrooms, sliced
1 tablespoon all-purpose flour
1 bay leaf
1 teaspoon Polish spice #2 *(see page 251)*
1 tablespoon tomato paste
1 cup chicken stock

Preparation

1. **In a medium pot** over medium high heat, cook the bacon until it renders its fat and turns lightly brown, not crisp. Carefully, using a slotted kitchen spoon, remove the bacon into a small bowl, and discard all but 2 tablespoons of the bacon fat.

2. **Return the pot to the fire,** add the garlic and onions, and cook for 1 minute. Now add the green cabbage, sauerkraut, and mushrooms and cook stir for 3 to 4 minutes until the vegetables are slightly softened. Stir in the flour, then add the rest of the ingredients including the bacon and bring to the boil.

3. **Reduce the heat to low,** cover tightly, and cook for about 45 minutes to 1 hour.

Makes about 2 cups

Pierogi Fillings

Potato and Cheese

Ingredients

1 cup farmer's or ricotta cheese
1 cup dry mashed potatoes, chilled
¾ teaspoon sea salt
¼ teaspoon freshly ground white pepper
¼ teaspoon garlic powder
¼ teaspoon onion powder
⅛ teaspoon freshly ground nutmeg
1 large egg yolk

Preparation

1. **Place all the ingredients,** except the farmer's cheese into a large mixing bowl, and using a heavy wooden spoon thoroughly combine the egg and seasoning with the potatoes until very smooth.

2. **Now using a plastic spatula,** gently fold the farmer's cheese into the potato mixture until fully and evenly incorporated.

Makes about 2 cups

Bacon, Cheddar Cheese, and Potato

Ingredients

2 pieces bacon, minced
1 cup cheddar cheese, finely grated
1 cup dry mashed potatoes, chilled
¼ teaspoon sea salt
¼ teaspoon freshly ground white pepper
¼ teaspoon garlic powder
¼ teaspoon onion powder
⅛ teaspoon freshly ground nutmeg
1 large egg yolk

Preparation

1. **Heat a small skillet** over medium heat and add the minced bacon. Cook stir with a wooden spoon until the bacon renders it's fat and turns lightly brown and crisp. Pour the bacon into a small strainer set over a bowl to collect the excess fat. Cool the bacon and set aside.

2. **Now place all the ingredients,** except the cheddar cheese into a large mixing bowl, and using a heavy wooden spoon thoroughly combine the egg, bacon, and seasoning with the potatoes until very smooth.

3. **Using a plastic spatula,** gently fold the cheddar cheese into the potato mixture until fully and evenly incorporated.

Makes about 2 cups

Pierogi Fillings

Fresh Blueberry

Ingredients

2 pints fresh blueberries, stemmed and cleaned
1 teaspoon Vanilla Sugar *(see page 258)*
Dash of lemon juice

Preparation

1. **Place the blueberries** into a medium sized mixing bowl, then sprinkle on the vanilla sugar and lemon juice. Grasp the bowl by the sides and gently toss the berries and sugar together until well combined. Let the mixture rest for 5 minutes, pour onto a nonstick sheet pan, and distribute the berries so that each one is sitting directly on the sheet pan. Place the pan in the freezer for 10 to 15 minutes until the berries are slightly frozen and firm. (Proceed to roll out your pierogi dough, and only remove as many berries as you need to fill the circles in front of you. This method will help to prevent the juices from discoloring your pierogi dough.)

Makes about 2 cups

Fresh Golden or Red Cherry

Ingredients

1 pound fresh ripe cherries, pitted and quartered
1 teaspoon Vanilla Sugar *(see page 258)*
Dash of lemon juice
Large dash of cinnamon

Preparation

1. **Place the quartered cherries** into a medium sized mixing bowl, then sprinkle on the vanilla sugar, lemon juice, and cinnamon, and using your hands, gently toss so the cherries are well coated. Let the mixture rest for 5 minutes before using.

Makes about 2 cups

Fresh Plum

Ingredients

12 fresh ripe Italian plums, pitted and quartered
1 to 2 teaspoons Vanilla Sugar *(see page 258)*
Dash of lemon juice
Large dash of cinnamon

Preparation

1. **Place the quartered plums** into a medium sized mixing bowl, then sprinkle on the vanilla sugar, lemon juice, and cinnamon, and using your hands, gently toss so the plums are well coated. Let the mixture rest for 5 minutes before using.

Makes about 2 cups

Fresh Prune and Golden Raisin

Ingredients

1½ cups pitted prunes
½ cup golden raisins
2 teaspoons Vanilla Sugar *(see page 258)*
1 teaspoon lemon juice
½ cup water

Preparation

1. **Place all of the ingredients** into a medium sized nonstick saucepot, and stew over medium low heat for 20 to 25 minutes until the prunes are tender. Cool for at least 3 hours before using.

Makes about 2 cups

Pierogi Fillings

"Greek Style" with Spinach and Feta

Ingredients

1 recipe New Sour Cream Pierogi Dough (*see page 84*)

Filling

1 large bunch fresh spinach, cleaned and dried
2 tablespoons unsalted butter, melted
1 large garlic clove, minced
1 small green onion, chopped
$1/2$ pound feta cheese
$1/2$ pound small curd cottage cheese
1 tablespoon Parmigiano-Reggiano cheese
2 tablespoons fresh dill, chopped
1 large egg yolk
$1/4$ teaspoon sea salt
$1/8$ teaspoon freshly ground black pepper
Dash of nutmeg

Topping

6 tablespoons unsalted butter
$1/4$ cup parsley, chopped
Coarsely ground black pepper

Preparation

1. **To prepare the filling,** remove the stems from the fresh spinach, and coarsely chop the leaves. In a medium sized skillet over medium high heat, melt the butter, then add the garlic and green onion, and stir cook for exactly one minute. Add the spinach, and stir cook again until the leaves start to wilt and release their liquid. Place the cooked spinach into a small colander set over a mixing bowl and let the mixture cool for 10 minutes.

2. **While the spinach is cooling,** place the remaining ingredients for the filling in a large mixing bowl, and using a heavy wooden spoon, combine until well mixed and slightly smooth. Now add the cooled spinach mixture, and again combine until smooth.

3. **Roll out the dough** on a lightly floured work surface as thinly as possible and stuff with the spinach-cheese mixture as you would for making pierogi.

4. **When all of your pierogi** are made, cook in lightly salted boiling water for 3 to 4 minutes. When they float to the top, remove to a colander and drain thoroughly.

5. **In a large non-stick** skillet over medium high heat, heat the butter until melted then add your pierogi, give the skillet a few quick flips so that they are covered in butter, and then sprinkle on the chopped parsley and coarsely ground black pepper. Give the pan a few more flips, then serve immediately.

Serves 4

Spicy "Sicilian Style"

Ingredients

1 recipe Church Festival Pierogi Dough (*see page 85*)

Filling

$1^1/2$ pounds ricotta cheese, drained overnight
$1/3$ cup Parmigiano-Reggiano cheese
1 large egg yolk
$1/4$ cup parsley, chopped
$1/4$ teaspoon sea salt
$1/8$ teaspoon freshly ground black pepper
Dash of garlic powder

Spicy Tomato Sauce

2 tablespoons olive oil
1 large garlic clove, minced
Pinch of red pepper flakes
One 28 oz. can plum tomatoes, crushed
Dash of sea salt
$1/4$ teaspoon freshly ground black pepper
$1/2$ teaspoon dried oregano

3 to 4 cups canola oil for frying

Preparation

1. **To prepare the filling,** place all of the ingredients into a medium sized mixing bowl, and using a heavy wooden spoon, combine the mixture until well-blended then set aside.

2. **To prepare the spicy sauce,** heat the olive oil in a medium sized saucepot over medium heat, then add the garlic and red pepper flakes, and stir cook for exactly 1 minute. Add the rest of the ingredients, bring the sauce to a boil, and then reduce the heat and simmer slowly for 20 minutes.

3. **Roll out the dough** on a lightly floured work surface as thinly as possible and stuff with the cheese mixture as you would for making pierogi.

4. **When all your pierogi** are made, heat the oil in a deep fat fryer or a medium sized heavy-duty soup pot until the temperature reaches 375°. Carefully place about 6 to 7 pierogi in the hot oil and cook until crisp and lightly brown.

5. **When the peirogi** are cooked, carefully remove with a skimmer to a paper-lined basket, and serve with the spicy tomato sauce. Repeat with the remaining pierogi.

Serves 4

Pierogi Fillings

Meat-filled "Kolduny Litewskie"

Ingredients

1 recipe Church Festival Pierogi dough *(see page 85)*

Filling

1 pound cooked beef from Braised Beef Short Rib recipe, chilled *(see page 152)*
½ cup sauce from Braised Beef Short Rib recipe
1 large whole egg
⅓ cup Parmigiano-Reggiano cheese
Dash of sea salt
Dash of freshly ground black pepper

Topping

6 tablespoons unsalted butter
¼ cup parsley, chopped
2 tablespoons Parmigiano-Reggiano cheese

Preparation

1. **To prepare the filling,** cut the beef into small pieces, then put it into a food processor and pulse the machine on and off until it is coarsely chopped. Add the sauce, egg, and cheese, and season with the salt and pepper. Pulse the machine on and off again to blend the mixture. (Do not over process the meat, it should retain a bit of its coarse consistency.) Remove the meat mixture to a bowl and set aside.

2. **Roll out the dough** on a lightly floured work surface as thinly as possible and stuff with the meat mixture as you would for making pierogi.

3. **When all your kolduny** are made, cook in lightly salted boiling water for 3 to 4 minutes. When they float to the top, remove to a colander and drain thoroughly.

4. **In a large nonstick skillet** over medium high heat, heat the butter until melted then add your kolduny, give the skillet a few quick flips so that they are covered in butter, and then sprinkle on the chopped parsley and cheese. Give the pan a few more flips then serve immediately.

Serves 4

Vegetable-filled "Kolduny Litewskie"

Ingredients

1 recipe Church Festival Pierogi dough *(see page 85)*

Filling

1 pound cooked vegetables from Braised Beef Short Rib recipe, chilled (including onions, carrots, celery, mushrooms, and potatoes) *(see page 152)*
1 large whole egg, beaten
⅓ cup Parmigiano-Reggiano cheese
Dash of sea salt
Dash of freshly ground black pepper

Topping

6 tablespoons unsalted butter
¼ cup parsley, chopped
2 tablespoons Parmigiano-Reggiano cheese

Preparation

1. **To prepare the filling,** cut all of the vegetables into bite size pieces, and then place into a medium sized mixing bowl. Add the egg, cheese, salt, and pepper, and mix gently just to combine.

2. **Roll out the dough** on a lightly floured work surface as thinly as possible and stuff with the vegetable mixture as you would for making pierogi.

3. **When all your kolduny** are made, cook in lightly salted boiling water for 3 to 4 minutes. When they float to the top, remove to a colander and drain thoroughly.

4. **In a large nonstick skillet** over medium high heat, heat the butter until melted then add your kolduny, give the skillet a few quick flips so that they are covered in butter, and then sprinkle on the chopped parsley and cheese. Give the pan a few more flips then serve immediately.

Serves 4

Lazy Man's Cheese and Potato Pierogi/Dumplings

If you have limited time or you just can't stand working Pierogi dough, this is the recipe for you. Cheese, potatoes, and savory seasonings are combined to produce an easy but tasty alternative to the more labor intensive Pierog. Serve it with a side of Kapusta and sausage for a heavenly treat.

Chef's Tip!

It is important that your farmer's or ricotta cheese is thoroughly drained of any excess moisture.

Ingredients

1 cup farmer's, cottage, or ricotta cheese
1 cup dry mashed potatoes, chilled
¾ teaspoon sea salt
¼ teaspoon freshly ground white pepper
¼ teaspoon garlic powder
¼ teaspoon onion powder
⅛ teaspoon nutmeg
¾ to 1 cup all-purpose flour
¼ cup unsalted butter, melted

Two quarts lightly salted water plus
    1 tablespoon olive oil

Preparation

1. **The night before** making the pierogi, place the cheese of your choice into a medium sized fine mesh strainer set over an empty bowl. Cover with plastic wrap and store in the refrigerator overnight to drain excess liquid.

2. **The next day** put the mashed potatoes into a large mixing bowl, and using a heavy wooden spoon, thoroughly incorporate all of the seasoning except the flour and butter until the mixture is smooth.

3. **Now add** the drained cheese to the bowl and thoroughly combine until well mixed.

4. **Place a medium** sized fine mesh strainer over the potato bowl and working with a quarter cup measuring scoop, add exactly ¾ cup flour to the strainer, and then sift on to the cheese potato dough. Now using the heavy spoon, thoroughly incorporate the flour into the mixture until smooth. At this point, the dough should be smooth and soft. If it still feels sticky, add 1 to 2 more tablespoons of flour into the dough. Remove the dough from the bowl and place onto a lightly floured work surface.

5. **Heat 2 quarts** of lightly salted water to boiling, and add the olive oil, then reduce to a slow simmer.

6. **Now using your hands,** lightly flatten the dough to a 6 by 6-inch square. Using a sharp chef's knife, make 5 vertical cuts through the dough equally spaced. Then repeat the process and make 5 horizontal cuts through the dough equally spaced. You should have 36 one-inch squares.

7. **Using lightly floured** hands, pick up a piece of cut dough and very carefully with your thumb and forefinger indent the center of the dough on both sides. Working in batches of six, place directly into the salted simmering water. Let the dumplings cook just until they float to the surface, then remove with a slotted kitchen spoon to a platter. Repeat with the remaining dough.

8. **Heat the melted butter** in a large nonstick skillet over medium heat, and add the pierogi one by one shaking the skillet often. Sauté for about 2 minutes on one side until lightly browned, then using a kitchen tong, flip the pierogi over and brown on the other side for another 2 minutes until lightly browned. Place a cover over the skillet for exactly one minute then remove and season the tops with freshly ground black pepper and serve.

Makes about 36 pieces

Kopytka

Ingredients

1¼ pound baking potatoes
1 large whole egg
2 tablespoons unsalted butter, melted
1 teaspoon sea salt
¼ teaspoon freshly ground white pepper
⅛ teaspoon freshly ground nutmeg
¾ to 1 cup all-purpose flour

5 tablespoons unsalted butter, melted
1 recipe Savory Polish Topping *(see page 252)*

2 quarts lightly salted water
1 tablespoon olive oil

The Polish equivalent of the Italian gnocchi, but better. Light and puffy pillows of seasoned potato are rolled into finger shapes, lightly poached and sautéed in butter, then adorned with a savory Polish topping. Be fore-warned, Kopytka are highly addictive, but require a lot of patience to master.

Chef's Tip!

Variations in potato moisture and flour can throw this recipe way off, so follow this general chef's rule if making a large quantity. To every 3 pounds of boiled potatoes, add exactly 2 cups of all-purpose flour, 1 extra large egg, and 1 teaspoon of sea salt.

Preparation

1. **Peel the potatoes,** rinse under cold water, and cut into large equal cubes. Put the potatoes into a medium saucepan, cover with cold water and bring to a boil. Cook until tender about 10 to 12 minutes. Drain thoroughly in a colander.

2. **Transfer the warm potatoes** to a large mixing bowl, and using a heavy wooden spoon, completely mash until very smooth, then cool slightly.

3. **In another small bowl,** whisk together for 1 minute the egg yolk, butter, salt, pepper, and nutmeg.

4. **Now using a heavy** wooden spoon, thoroughly combine the egg seasoning mix with the potatoes until very smooth.

5. **Place a medium-sized** fine mesh strainer over the potato bowl, and working with a quarter cup measuring scoop, add exactly ¼ cup flour to the strainer, and then sift on to the potatoes. Now using the heavy spoon, thoroughly incorporate the flour into the potatoes until smooth.

6. **Repeat again** with another quarter cup of sifted flour until smooth.

7. **Then repeat again** with another quarter cup of sifted flour until smooth.

8. **At this point,** the dough should be smooth and soft. If it still feels sticky, add 1 to 2 more tablespoons of flour into the dough. Remove the dough from the bowl and cut into 4 equal pieces with a sharp chef's knife and set aside.

9. **Heat 2 quarts** of lightly salted water to boiling, and add the olive oil, then reduce to a slow simmer.

10. **On a lightly floured** surface, using your hands, roll out one piece of the dough into a ½-inch thick by 14-inch long cylinder. Again using a sharp chef's knife cut the dough into 2-inch long pieces. Now with lightly floured hands, pick up a piece of cut dough and very gently rub between your hands to elongate the shape, and place directly into the salted simmering water. Let the dumplings cook just until they float to the surface, then remove with a slotted kitchen spoon to a platter. Repeat with the remaining dough.

11. **In a large nonstick** skillet, heat the butter, then add the dumplings, and cook over medium low heat for 2 to 3 minutes on each side until golden brown. When the dumplings are browned, sprinkle on the savory Polish topping, and serve immediately.

Makes about 30 pieces

Tavern Pan Sinkers

I love Mom and Pop taverns, you know, the ones that are full of tchotchkes, and that serve (help-yourself) lunch at the end of the bar. Years back, I helped a few ailing local joints boost their lunch sales by creating Tavern Sinkers, a great alternative to the laborious Kopytka. Potatoes, bread, and seasoning are combined, quickly poached, then sautéed in melted butter and covered with savory topping to produce a real working man's gut sinker. Trust me, cops and yuppies love them!

Chef's Tip!

I cannot stress to you enough the importance of using sea salt in the poaching liquid. Using regular table salt will make your sinkers take on an unpleasant aftertaste.

Savory Polish Topping

Ingredients

4 tablespoons unsalted butter, melted
1 slice hickory smoked bacon, minced
2 large garlic cloves, minced
1 small onion, finely diced
1 cup fresh breadcrumbs
2 hardboiled eggs, diced
2 tablespoons parsley, minced
¼ cup dill, minced
Dash of sea salt
Dash of freshly ground black pepper

Preparation

1. **In a large nonstick skillet** over medium high heat, heat the butter, add the bacon, and cook for exactly 1 minute.

2. **Now add the garlic** and onion, and cook for another minute until the onion is slightly soft.

3. **Add the breadcrumbs** and eggs, and gently toss the skillet until the mixture is well blended. Turn the heat off, and stir in the rest of the ingredients until well seasoned.

Makes about 1 cup

Ingredients

1 cup dry mashed potatoes, chilled
½ cup all-purpose flour
1 thick slice homemade white bread, crumbled
1 large whole egg
2 tablespoons unsalted butter, melted
Large dash of Tabasco
1 teaspoon Polish spice #1 *(see page 251)*
    or
½ teaspoon sea salt
¼ teaspoon freshly ground black pepper
Large dash of nutmeg
Large dash of garlic powder
Large dash of onion powder

4 tablespoons unsalted butter, melted
1 recipe Savory Polish Topping

2 quarts lightly salted water
1 tablespoon olive oil

Preparation

1. **Heat 2 quarts** of lightly salted water to boiling, and add the olive oil, then reduce to a slow simmer.

2. **In a large mixing bowl,** combine the potatoes, flour, bread, egg, butter, Tabasco, and desired seasoning, and using your hands, mix the dough until well blended.

3. **Turn the mixture out** onto a lightly floured work surface, and knead the dough until it becomes semi-stiff to the touch. (It's okay to add a little more flour to the dough, but not too much. The mixture will always feel pasty.)

4. **Using floured hands,** pinch off about a walnut size piece, and roll it into a ball. Now place the ball onto a clean work surface, and roll until it forms a 2½-inch long finger. Repeat with the rest of the dough, then cook in the salted, simmering water until they float to the surface, then cook for 2 minutes more. Remove the dumplings with a slotted kitchen spoon to a platter.

5. **In a large nonstick skillet,** heat the butter, then add the dumplings, and cook over medium low heat for 2 to 3 minutes on each side until golden brown. When the dumplings are browned, sprinkle on the savory Polish topping, and serve immediately.

Makes 20 to 24 pieces

Parsley Dumplings

Ingredients

2 cups all-purpose flour
3 teaspoons baking powder
1 teaspoon sea salt
1/4 teaspoon freshly ground white pepper
1/4 cup parsley, minced
3 tablespoons unsalted butter, softened
3/4 cup whole milk

Preparation

1. **In a large mixing bowl,** stir together the flour, baking powder, salt, pepper, and parsley.

2. **Working quickly,** cut the butter into the flour mixture with a pastry blender, until the mixture is evenly distributed.

3. **Now add the milk** and stir with a wooden spoon until the dry ingredients are just moistened, and the dough holds its shape.

4. **Turn out the dough** onto a lightly floured surface, and carefully with floured hands pat out the dough into a 6 inch by 6 inch square, about 1/2-inch thick. Now using a sharp chef's knife cut the dough into 1-inch squares.

5. **Using your hands,** lightly roll the squares into little round pieces and very gently place the parsley dumplings one by one into the simmering stew, making sure to leave a little space between each dumpling.

6. **Cover the pot** with a tight fitting lid and cook very slowly for 25 minutes. Do not lift the lid until 25 minutes has passed.

Makes about 30 pieces

Drop Noodle Dumplings

Ingredients

2 large whole eggs
1/2 scant teaspoon sea salt
1/4 teaspoon freshly ground white pepper
1/8 teaspoon freshly ground nutmeg
1 tablespoon olive oil
2 tablespoons water
1 3/4 cups all-purpose flour, sifted

2 quarts lightly salted water plus 1 tablespoon olive oil

Preparation

1. **In a mixing bowl,** whisk together the eggs, salt, pepper, nutmeg, olive oil, and water for exactly one minute. Now with a heavy flat wooden spoon vigorously stir in the sifted flour until you have a smooth, thick batter, and let the mixture rest for 15 minutes.

2. **Bring a large pot** of salted water to a boil over high heat, then reduce to a bubbling simmer. Add the olive oil.

3. **Now place over** the simmering water, a colander with large holes, then put the paste into the colander and using a plastic spatula, press down on the paste to force it through the holes into the simmering water. Cook for about 2 to 4 minutes until the noodles rise to the surface.

4. **Remove the cooked noodles** with a slotted spoon to a bowl full of ice water to stop the cooking. Drain from the ice water until thoroughly dry and then set aside.

Serves 4

Peasant Noodles with Cottage Cheese and Ham

Ingredients

1 pound wide Kluski noodle ribbons
4 tablespoons unsalted butter, melted
½ cup fresh baked ham, diced
1 cup small curd sweet cottage cheese or ricotta
Dash of sea salt
Dash of freshly ground black pepper

Preparation

1. **Bring a large pot** of lightly salted water to a boil and cook the kluski ribbons for 4 to 6 minutes until al dente or firm to the bite.

2. **While the noodles** are cooking, heat the butter in a small nonstick skillet over medium high heat and sauté the ham for 2 to 3 minutes until it turns lightly brown.

3. **Place the cottage cheese,** salt, pepper, and the cooked ham into a tabletop serving bowl, and gently mix until combined. When the noodles are cooked, thoroughly drain into a colander to remove any excess water, then mix into the ham and cheese mixture until well combined. Serve immediately.

Serves 4

Busia's Buttered Noodles with Eggs

Ingredients

1 pound thin Kluski noodle ribbons
4 large whole eggs
⅓ cup freshly grated Parmigiano-Reggiano cheese
2 tablespoons parsley, chopped
Dash of sea salt
¼ teaspoon freshly ground black pepper
4 tablespoons unsalted butter

Preparation

1. **Bring a large pot** of lightly salted water to a boil and cook the kluski ribbons for 4 to 6 minutes until al dente or firm to the bite.

2. **While the pasta** is cooking, place the eggs, grated cheese, parsley, salt, and pepper into a medium-sized mixing bowl, and beat with a whisk until well combined.

3. **When the noodles** are almost cooked, melt the butter in a large nonstick skillet over medium heat. Quickly drain the pasta in a colander, add it to the skillet, and toss briefly to coat it with the butter.

4. **Now add the egg** mixture to the skillet and using a flat wooden spoon, mix quickly together for less than a minute until the eggs and noodles become creamy and thick. (Do not cook the eggs too long or they will scramble and ruin the dish.) Serve immediately.

Serves 4

Kapusta with Egg Noodles

Ingredients

1 pound extra wide egg noodles
1 slice hickory smoked bacon, diced
2 tablespoons olive oil
2 teaspoons garlic puree
1 small onion, finely diced
1 medium head green cabbage, cored and diced
½ teaspoon sea salt
¼ teaspoon freshly ground black pepper
2 tablespoons chicken stock
2 dashes of Tabasco
Freshly ground black pepper
Freshly grated Parmigiano-Reggiano cheese,
  optional

Polish comfort food at its best! Slow braised cabbage, bacon, onion, and garlic are lightly seasoned, then combined with fresh Kluski noodles. Throughout my career, I have made this dish at midnight for many a weary traveling executive when nothing else was to be had in the larder.

Chef's Tip!

The secret to this dish is to prepare everything at the last minute. Also, I highly recommend that you thoroughly clean out any pots or pans that you use to prepare this dish because the noodles pick up subtleties of different flavors left lingering on the skillet.

Preparation

1. **In a large pot** over medium high heat, cook the bacon until it renders its fat and turns lightly brown, not crisp. Pour the bacon into a small strainer set over a bowl to collect the excess fat.

2. **Return the pot** to the fire, then add the olive oil. When hot add the garlic and onion, and cook stir for about 1 minute. Now add the cabbage and cook stir for about 3 to 4 minutes until the cabbage starts to wilt.

3. **Reduce the heat** to low, add the rest of the seasonings and the bacon, and cook slowly, covered, for about 20 minutes.

4. **While the cabbage** is cooking, bring 2 quarts of lightly salted water to a boil, then add the noodles, and cook until firm to the bite. Drain in a colander, then add to the cabbage. Gently, using a heavy wooden spoon, stir the noodles into the cabbage mixture to combine.

5. **Using a kitchen tong,** divide the kapusta among 4 dinner plates, and sprinkle on freshly grated ground black pepper, and Parmesan cheese.

Serves 4

Quick Vegetarian Noodles

Ingredients

1 pound wide Kluski noodle ribbons
1 pound cauliflower florets, pre-cooked al dente
1 pound broccoli florets, pre-cooked al dente
¼ cup olive oil
2 large garlic cloves, finely chopped
Pinch of dried red pepper flakes
1 medium sized red pepper, diced
½ pound assorted wild mushrooms, thinly sliced
Dash of sea salt
Dash of freshly ground black pepper

Preparation

1. **Bring a large pot** of lightly salted water to a boil and cook the kluski ribbons for 4 to 6 minutes until al dente or firm to the bite.

2. **While the noodles** are cooking, heat the olive oil in a large nonstick skillet over medium high heat. Add the garlic, red pepper flakes, red pepper, and mushrooms, and quickly sauté until the mushrooms release their liquid and start to turn golden brown. Now add the cauliflower and broccoli florets, toss to coat, then add the drained noodles to the skillet along with a little bit of the pasta water. Toss together for 1 minute over the heat, then serve immediately.

Serves 4

Egg Noodles with Wild Mushrooms and Rosemary

Ingredients

1 pound flat egg noodles, pre-cooked al dente
2 tablespoons unsalted butter
1 large garlic clove, minced
2 large shallots, minced
½ pound assorted wild mushrooms, thinly sliced
2 tablespoons parsley, finely chopped
1 tablespoon rosemary, finely chopped
½ cup dry white wine
½ cup chicken stock
½ cup heavy cream
Dash of sea salt
Dash of freshly ground black pepper
Dash of Tabasco
¼ cup Parmigiano-Reggiano cheese, optional

Preparation

1. **Heat the butter** in a large nonstick skillet over medium high heat, and add the garlic and shallots, and stir cook for exactly 1 minute. Now add the wild mushrooms and stir cook again for 3 to 4 minutes, then add the parsley and rosemary.

2. **Add the dry white wine** to the skillet, and let it reduce until the liquid evaporates. Add the chicken stock, heavy cream, salt, pepper, and Tabasco to the pan, and let it cook until it lightly coats the back of a wooden spoon.

3. **Now add the pre-cooked noodles** and stir with a wooden spoon until they are thoroughly coated with the sauce. Divide the noodles and mushrooms into 4 serving bowls, sprinkle on the cheese and serve immediately.

Serves 4

Mushroom Uszka with Brown Butter and Sage

"Who's got the uszka, I've got the uszka!" Right here, my friends and it's a great recipe. Mushroom uszka are better known as a soup garnishment for the classical beet borscht, but I've also served them as a pasta appetizer that people really seem to enjoy. A filling of pancetta, mushrooms, and fresh herbs are stuffed into homemade noodle dough, then cooked and adorned with brown butter, lemon, and sage to create a simply delicious Polish treat.

Chef's Tip!

If you're short on time, you can always purchase a frozen package of won ton skins that are available at any Asian market. The dough is already rolled and pre-cut so the dish comes together in a snap.

Ingredients

1 recipe Kluski noodle dough
2 tablespoons unsalted butter, melted
2 large garlic cloves, minced
1 small onion, finely diced
¼ cup pancetta ham, sliced thin and diced
2 pounds assorted field mushroom, finely diced
1 tablespoon parsley, chopped
1 tablespoon fresh marjoram, chopped
Dash of sea salt
Dash of freshly ground black pepper

4 tablespoons unsalted butter
8 fresh sage leaves
Juice of ½ lemon
¼ cup Parmigiano-Reggiano cheese

Preparation

1. **Place a medium-sized** nonstick skillet over medium high heat, and when the pan turns white-hot, add the butter, garlic, onion, and pancetta, and cook for 1 minute. Add the mushrooms, and sauté quickly until the mushrooms start to release their liquid. When the liquid starts to dissipate, and the mushrooms start to brown, season with the fresh herbs and a dash of salt and pepper, then remove from the fire.

2. **On a lightly floured** work surface, carefully roll out the pasta dough as thinly a possible (about ⅛-inch thick). Using a sharp knife, cut the dough into 1½-inch squares. Place a little of the cooled filling onto a square slightly off center, then fold in half to form a triangle, and pinch the edges together. Gently pull the 2 bottom corners together and join by pinching. Cook the uszka in lightly salted water for 2 to 4 minutes or until they float to the top.

3. **When the uszka** are almost cooked, melt the butter in a medium sized nonstick sauté pan over medium high heat, and cook until a golden brown color appears. Add the sage leaves and remove from the heat, then stir in the lemon juice. Drain the uszka in a colander, gently pour them into the sauté pan, and return to the heat. Add the cheese, toss to coat, and serve immediately.

Serves 4

Kluski Noodles

Ingredients

4 large whole eggs
1 scant teaspoon sea salt
1 tablespoon olive oil
2 cups bread flour

Preparation

1. **To make the dough** in a food processor, place the eggs, salt, and oil in the work bowl fitted with a metal blade. Pulse several times to mix. Now add the flour to the bowl and pulse the 8 to 10 times until the dough forms a ball. If the dough is excessively soft and sticky, add 1 to 2 tablespoons more flour, one at a time, and pulse, until the dough forms a coherent ball. Remove the dough to a lightly floured work surface and gently knead until it is completely smooth. Place into a Ziploc bag and refrigerate for at least 2 hours.

Makes about 1 pound

Parsley Potato Pancakes

Ingredients

2 large baking potatoes
½ small onion
1 large whole egg
½ teaspoon sea salt
¼ teaspoon freshly ground white pepper
⅛ teaspoon baking powder
Dash of Tabasco
1 teaspoon garlic purée
2 tablespoons parsley, minced
1 tablespoon all-purpose flour

½ cup Seasoned Oil *(see page 101)*

Who can resist a heaping platter of freshly made crispy edged, lightly seasoned potato pancakes? I've spruced up a basic recipe to impress any discerning palate, but the real trick to a good pancake is to use a cast iron griddle, not too much seasoned oil, and to work quickly to produce this Polish staple. Don't forget to pass around the applesauce and sour cream!

Chef's Tip!

Most people get freaked out that the minced potatoes turn brown so quickly, so let me give you a tip. Try adding a little bit of ground pure vitamin C powder to the potato mixture to avoid this problem.

Preparation

1. **Preheat the oven** to 400°F.

2. **Peel the potatoes,** rinse under cold water, and dry. Cut into medium sized pieces and set aside.

3. **Place the onion** into the work bowl of a food processor fitted with a steel blade, cover and process until finely chopped.

4. **Now add the potatoes** to the work bowl with the onions still in it, recover and pulse the potatoes until finely chopped. Remove the cover again, and using a plastic spatula, carefully push the potato onion mixture down off the sides of the bowl. Recover and pulse the mixture until slightly smooth.

5. **Place a medium-sized** fine mesh strainer over a large bowl, and using a plastic spatula scrape all of the potato onion purée into the strainer. Now very carefully using the spatula, lightly mix and push down on the purée to rid it of excess water, which will collect in the bottom of the bowl. When the purée looks slightly dry, it is ready. Put the purée aside.

6. **In a separate bowl,** whisk together the egg, salt, pepper, baking powder, tabasco, garlic purée, flour, and parsley. Now using the spatula, quickly combine the potato onion purée with the egg mixture until fully incorporated, and set aside.

7. **Heat a large griddle** over medium high heat until smoking, and pour in enough oil to thinly coat the bottom. Using a soupspoon, take about 2 tablespoons of the pancake mix and place on to the griddle. Lightly flatten the mixture with the back of the spoon and cook for a few minutes until golden brown. Using a spatula, flip the pancake over, lightly flatten, and brown the other side, and then remove to a paper-lined platter, and repeat the cooking process until done.

8. **Now place the browned** potato pancakes on to a nonstick sheet pan and cook in the oven to crisp for about 10 minutes.

Makes 12 to 16 pieces

Latkes with Chives and Parsley

The brother to the potato pancake, Latkes are grated coarsely to produce a slightly thicker and more textured pancake. The seasonings are similar, except for the addition of matzo meal and chives to the mix. You can get very creative with Latkes by shredding into the basic recipe zucchini, red peppers, or even cabbage. Use your imagination!

Chef's Tip!

People are in such a hurry to consume latkes that they forget all the basic rules of making them. It is vitally important that you have all your ingredients well blended, and your pots and pans ready to go. The trick to a good latke is to sear it quickly in the hot seasoned oil, then line the browned pancakes on a sheet pan and crisp all of them at the same time in the oven so that they are fully cooked. Cooking in too much oil will ruin your latkes.

Ingredients

2 large baking potatoes
1 large whole egg
$\frac{1}{2}$ teaspoon sea salt
$\frac{1}{4}$ teaspoon freshly ground white pepper
$\frac{1}{8}$ teaspoon baking powder
Dash of Tabasco
1 teaspoon garlic purée
1 tablespoon chives, minced
1 tablespoon parsley, minced
$\frac{1}{4}$ cup matzo meal

$\frac{1}{2}$ cup Seasoned Oil

Preparation

1. **Preheat the oven** to 400ºF.

2. **Peel the potatoes,** rinse under cold water, and dry.

3. **Using a hand grater,** grate the potatoes through the large hole into a large bowl. Now using your hands, pick up the grated potatoes and squeeze out as much excess water as you can, then set aside.

4. **In a separate bowl,** whisk together the egg, salt, pepper, baking powder, tabasco, garlic purée, chives, parsley, and matzo meal. Now using a plastic spatula, quickly combine the grated potatoes with the egg mixture until fully incorporated, and set aside.

5. **Heat a large griddle** over medium high heat until smoking, and pour in enough oil to thinly coat the bottom. Using a soupspoon, take about 2 tablespoons of the latke mix and place on to the griddle. Lightly flatten the mixture with the back of the spoon and cook for a few minutes until golden brown. Using a spatula, flip the latke over, lightly flatten, and brown the other side, and then remove to a paper-lined platter and repeat the cooking process until done.

6. **Now place the browned latkes** on to a nonstick sheet pan and cook in the oven to crisp for about 10 minutes.

Makes 12 to 16 pieces

Seasoned Oil

Ingredients

2 slices hickory smoked bacon, minced
3 large garlic cloves, chopped
6 black peppercorns, crushed
1 cup vegetable or canola oil

1. **In a small skillet** over medium high heat, sauté the bacon until it starts to render its fat and turn lightly golden brown. At this point, add the garlic and black peppercorns to the skillet and stir cook for exactly 1 minute.

2. **Now add the vegetable oil,** bring to a simmer, and then immediately remove the skillet from the fire. Let the mixture cool undisturbed for exactly 1 hour, then strain through a fine mesh sieve into a glass jar and refrigerate until needed.

Makes about 1 cup

Red Pepper, Zucchini, and Potato Cake

Ingredients

2 tablespoons unsalted butter
2 tablespoons olive oil
2 large garlic cloves, minced
1 medium onion, diced
1 large red pepper, diced
1 large zucchini, diced
1½ cups potatoes, boiled and diced
6 whole large eggs
¼ teaspoon sea salt
⅛ teaspoon freshly ground black pepper
Large pinch of nutmeg
⅓ cup Parmigiano-Reggiano cheese

Preparation

1. **Place a 12-inch** nonstick skillet over medium high heat, add the butter and oil and when hot, add the garlic and onion, then stir cook for exactly 2 minutes without browning.

2. **Now add the red pepper** and zucchini, and stir cook again for another 3 to 4 minutes until the peppers start to wilt. Add the potatoes and cook for 1 more minute.

3. **While the vegetables** are cooking, beat the eggs, salt, pepper, nutmeg, and cheese vigorously with a whip in a medium sized mixing bowl, then gently pour into the hot skillet. Using a plastic spatula, distribute the egg mixture evenly over the vegetables so as not to leave any open gaps in the skillet. Cook the cake slowly, undisturbed for 3 to 4 minutes until the edges begin to turn lightly brown.

4. **Now is the hard part.** Firmly grasp the pan's handle with your right hand, then cover the skillet with a flat topped pot cover using your left hand. Now push down with your left hand and then quickly, in one motion, flip the skillet over so that the cake falls onto the flat cover. Return the skillet back to the fire, then gently slide the vegetable cake back into the skillet, and cook for another 3 to 4 minutes uncovered. Slide onto a platter to serve.

Serves 4

Caramelized Onion and Ham Potato Cakes

Ingredients

1½ pound baking potatoes, peeled and cubed
½ teaspoon sea salt
¼ teaspoon freshly ground white pepper
Large dash nutmeg
Dash of cayenne
½ cup all-purpose flour
3 egg yolks
2 tablespoons unsalted butter, melted
2 large garlic cloves, minced
1 small onion, diced
½ cup smoked ham, diced
1 tablespoon parsley, chopped
1 tablespoon chives, chopped
¼ cup unsalted butter, melted

Preparation

1. **Put the potatoes** in a medium sized saucepot, cover with cold lightly salted water, and bring to a boil over high heat. Reduce to a simmer and cook for 18 to 20 minutes until fork tender. When the potatoes are cooked, drain thoroughly and return them to the pot. Over low heat, stir the potatoes for about 45 seconds to dry them out.

2. **Transfer the potatoes** to the bowl of a heavy-duty mixer and attach the paddle. Mash the potatoes on low speed until smooth, then add the salt, pepper, nutmeg, cayenne, and flour. Turn the machine off and let the mixture cool for exactly 5 to 7 minutes, then add the egg yolks one at a time until completely absorbed with the mixture.

3. **While the potatoes** are resting, heat the butter in a small skillet over medium heat, and sauté the garlic and onion until golden brown about 3 to 4 minutes. Do not burn the vegetables. Add the diced ham and cook for another 2 minutes, then remove the skillet from the fire. When the onion-ham mixture is cool, add it to the potatoes along with the parsley and chives, and paddle just until thoroughly mixed.

4. **Using floured hands,** gently form the potato mixture into golf ball size pieces, then place onto a parchment paper lined sheet pan. Flatten the balls slightly, cover with plastic wrap, then place the pan into the freezer for 1 hour to firm.

5. **After 45 minutes,** preheat the oven to 400°F. When ready to cook, heat a large nonstick skillet over medium high heat, add the reserved melted butter, and gently sauté the potato cakes for 2 minutes on each side until golden brown. Remove the browned potato cakes to a nonstick sheet pan and cook in the oven for 5 to 8 minutes until crisp.

Makes 24 pieces

Savory Stuffed Twice Baked Potatoes

Ingredients

4 large baking potatoes, cleaned and dried
3 strips hickory smoked bacon
6 tablespoons sour cream, full fat
2 tablespoons unsalted butter
2 tablespoons fresh chives, minced
$1/4$ teaspoon sea salt
$1/8$ teaspoon freshly ground black pepper
Dash of nutmeg
Dash of garlic powder
Dash of Tabasco
Sprinkling of paprika
$1/4$ cup grated Parmigiano-Reggiano cheese

Preparation

1. **Preheat the oven** to 375°. Using a kitchen fork, lightly pierce the tops of the potatoes, and bake on the middle rack of the preheated oven for about 1 hour or until the potatoes are tender. While the potatoes are cooking, brown the bacon in a sauté pan until crisp, drain on paper towels, cool, then finely chop and set aside.

2. **When the potatoes** are cooked, remove from the oven, cool slightly, carefully cut off the pierced tops, and using a soup spoon, scrape the soft potato pulp into a medium sized mixing bowl. (Be careful not to tear the potato skins while removing the pulp.)

3. **Now add to the pulp** the minced bacon, sour cream, butter, chives, salt, pepper, nutmeg, garlic powder, and Tabasco, and combine with a wooden spoon until evenly mixed. Taste the mixture, re-season if necessary, then evenly re-stuff the potato skins with the potato mixture mounding the filling slightly. Lightly sprinkle on the paprika and Parmesan cheese, place the potatoes onto a baking sheet, and re-bake in the hot oven for another 15 to 20 minutes.

Note: $1/2$ cup grated sharp cheddar cheese can be added to the seasoned pulp mixture if you like.

Serves 4

Cheesy Potato Gratinée

Ingredients

2 tablespoons unsalted butter, softened
2 large garlic cloves, minced
3 cups half and half
$1/2$ teaspoon sea salt
$1/4$ teaspoon freshly ground black pepper
$1/8$ teaspoon nutmeg
Large dash of cayenne pepper
Dash of garlic powder
Dash of Tabasco
$2^{1}/_{2}$ pounds Idaho potatoes
$1/2$ pound finely grated cheddar or Monterey Jack cheese

Preparation

1. **Preheat the oven** to 350°.

2. **Lightly butter** a medium sized oval earthenware casserole, then evenly sprinkle on the minced garlic.

3. **In a mixing bowl,** combine the half and half, salt, pepper, nutmeg, cayenne, garlic powder, and Tabasco. Peel the potatoes and slice them paper thin (a French tool called a Mandolin works great). As you're slicing the potatoes, place them into the mixing bowl un-rinsed. When all of the potatoes are sliced and placed into the bowl, add the grated cheese, combine with your hands until thoroughly mixed, then pour directly into the prepared casserole and bake for $1^{1}/_{2}$ to 2 hours until the top is golden brown.

Serves 4

n a l e s n i k i

*m*aster nalesniki batter recipe

*a*ssorted jam-filled for brunch

*s*weet cheese and white raisin with fresh fruit sauce

*f*laming "suzette"-style

*c*innamon apple with warm chocolate sauce

*c*aramelized banana with vanilla bean ice cream

*h*unter's-style with mushrooms

*p*olish ham and cheese

*s*avory seafood gratinée

*s*moky spinach and mushroom gratinée

*c*reamed chicken with broccoli and dill

Call it placinki, blinchiki, blini, or nalesniki; every ethnic group has their version of a savory stuffed crepe. I fell in love with the art of crepe making when I was a young cook working at a well-known Continental restaurant in the City. I was given the job of "flambé chef," where I would go into the dining room dressed up in a special chef's outfit and perform flaming dessert tableside for the amusement of the guests. By the time I was 20 years old, I had mastered all of the classical preparations such as crepes Suzette, cherries jubilee, and crepes praline. Yes, I singed a few eyebrows, and once torched a women's wig, but that was part of the show!

Through the years, I picked up more recipes that centered around crepes, and to my surprise, there was a whole other side to this thin pancake. Ukrainian cooks have a preference for stacking crepes like a cake or stuffing them with braised cabbage or lightly seasoned sauerkraut. The Hungarians like to fill their crepes with homemade poppy seed jam, pickled purple plum preserves, or a mixture of quark cheese and dill. Whereas the Russians in particular, prefer to stuff their crepes with assorted chopped meats, savory egg dishes, and even caviar that they consume in mass quantities at cocktail receptions with chilled vodka. When I visit Paris, there is a corner where a street vendor cooks crepes to order on a hot plate and slathers them with warm chocolate sauce as a quick dessert for passing patrons.

I guess any way you look at them; crepes can be served in a wide range of varieties both sweet and savory. I've served them either as an appetizer, main course, or dessert. Most Poles are accustomed to a nalesniki that is traditionally filled with sweetened farmer's cheese, sautéed mushrooms, fresh fruit jams or preserves, or even fresh fruits and homemade ice cream. I've always been an adventurous type so my fillings are more on the savory side. I always use a basic crepe batter that is not too sweet, but strong enough to hold up to any of the fillings. My personal favorites are the **Spinach and Mushroom** and the **Savory Seafood Gratinée.** I've successfully made them through the years for small lunch receptions or weddings, because the filling can be made in advance and cooled, and the nalesniki can be stuffed and rolled, and then refrigerated until needed. Along with an artfully arranged salad and a light dessert, the meal is complete without being too heavy.

Every once and awhile when I entertain and I'm not in the mood for making a heavy cake-like dessert, I borrow a restaurant's flambé kit and entertain my dinner guests with such beauties as **Cinnamon Apple Nalesniki** and **Caramelized Banana Nalesniki.** If you're lucky, most Polish restaurants feature some kind of crepe preparation that is usually accompanied by a fresh fruit or chocolate sauce. I urge you to give this classical presentation of the versatile and delicious crepe a try.

Master Nalesniki Batter Recipe

Ingredients

4 large whole eggs
¾ cup whole milk
½ cup water
4 tablespoons unsalted butter, melted
1 cup all-purpose flour
1 teaspoon sea salt
1 teaspoon sugar
½ teaspoon vanilla extract, optional
Dash of red or green food color, optional

½ cup unsalted butter, melted

Preparation

1. **In a mixing bowl,** whisk together the eggs, milk, water, butter, salt, and sugar for exactly one minute. Now add the optional ingredients and whisk together for another minute. Slowly whisk in the flour until the batter has no lumps and is perfectly smooth. Cover the bowl with plastic wrap and set aside to rest for 15 minutes.

2. **Take an 8-inch nonstick skillet,** and completely wipe out the interior with a paper towel, then place it over medium heat. Now add to the skillet about a teaspoon of the melted butter and using your wrist, grasp the handle and swirl the butter around the pan to evenly coat the bottom. Now ladle in about 2 tablespoons of the batter and again using your wrist, quickly lift the pan off the heat and swirl the skillet to evenly coat the bottom of the pan with the batter. Cook until the crepe is lightly golden brown on the bottom, then gently turn with a spatula and cook the other side. Remove to a platter and then repeat with the remaining batter.

Makes about 16 crepes

Assorted Jam-filled for Brunch

Ingredients

24 to 32 prepared Nalesniki crepes
2 tablespoons unsalted butter, melted
Assorted Polish fruit preserves for filling such as:
    raspberry, peach, bilberry, apricot, black currant,
    strawberry, blackberry, sour cherry, or gooseberry
1 recipe Sweet Whipped Cream *(see page 257)*
1 recipe Warm Chocolate Sauce *(see page 259)*
1 recipe Fresh Strawberry, Raspberry, or Blueberry Sauce
    (see page 253)
Powdered sugar for dusting

1 large sheet pan

Preparation

1. **Preheat the oven** to 350°.

2. **Ideally this is one** of those recipes that your guests can partake in the making of. If you have a lot of extra hands, place 2 small 8-inch non-stick skillets over medium heat and proceed in making the master Nalesniki recipe. When the crepes come off the fire, place them onto a clean serving platter, and have your guests spread on assorted Polish fruit preserves or even the warm chocolate sauce. When all of the Nalesniki are made, lightly butter the serving platter or use a sheet pan, and place the prepared crepes into the hot oven for 10 minutes to soften and warm the fruit fillings. After they are warmed, remove the platter from the oven and serve family style with the assorted garnishes.

3. **If you are stressed out** for time or just not an early riser, you can prepare the crepes the night before and refrigerate until needed. If this is more appealing to you, the next morning preheat the oven to 350° and start your coffee. Now to set the brunch table, remove the assorted jams to decorative serving bowls with small spoons, and then arrange onto a linen-lined table. Now prepare your sweet whipped cream, and warm chocolate sauce, and also place into decorative or crystal bowls. The fresh strawberry sauce should be prepared the night before. Now is a good time to add any fresh fruit or sweet rolls that you have on hand to your brunch table. (Fresh flowers are a nice added touch too.) When your guests awaken, remove the prepared Nalesniki crepes from the refrigerator, place onto a large sheet pan, and warm in the oven for 10 to 12 minutes then remove to a serving platter, and let your guests help themselves to the filling or garnishment of their choice.

Serves 4

Sweet Cheese and White Raisin with Fresh Fruit Sauce

Ingredients

12 to 16 prepared Nalesniki crepes
¼ cup unsalted butter, melted
2 tablespoons sugar
¼ cup white raisins
¼ teaspoon grated lemon rind
⅛ teaspoon sea salt
¾ teaspoon vanilla extract
1 cup farmer's or ricotta cheese
½ cup cream cheese
¼ cup sugar
1 egg yolk
1 recipe Fresh Strawberry, Raspberry, or Blueberry Sauce
  (see page 253)

1 medium sized oval earthenware casserole

Preparation

1. **Preheat the oven** to 350°.

2. **In a small mixing bowl,** combine the raisins, lemon rind, salt, and vanilla and gently stir with a soup spoon, and let marinate for 10 minutes.

3. **In another medium-sized** mixing bowl, combine the farmer's cheese, cream cheese, sugar, and yolk, and using a heavy wooden spoon beat vigorously until smooth.

4. **Now using a plastic** spatula, fold in the marinated raisins.

5. **Lay the crepes** onto a clean work surface, and using a table-spoon, evenly distribute the cheese and raisin mixture among all the crepes. Using the back of the spoon, carefully distribute the cheese mixture over the face of the crepe, then roll each crepe into a thick but tight cigar shape. Lightly butter the bottom of the casserole, sprinkle on a little of the sugar, then carefully arrange the rolled crepes on top of that being sure that they fit tightly next to each other.

6. **Pour the remaining butter** over all of the crepes, sprinkle on the remaining sugar, and then bake in the hot oven for about 20 to 30 minutes or until the Nalesniki are slightly puffy and golden brown. Remove the casserole from the oven, and carefully using a small spatula, divide the crepes among 4 dessert plates and serve with the fresh fruit sauce of your choice.

Serves 4

Flaming "Suzette"-style

Ingredients

12 to 16 prepared Nalesniki crepes
1 stick unsalted butter, softened
⅓ cup sugar
Grated rinds of 1 orange and 1 lemon
Juice of 1 orange and 1 lemon
6 tablespoons quality brandy
6 tablespoons Grand Marnier or orange-flavored liqueur

1 large non-stick skillet

Preparation

1. **Place the softened butter,** sugar, and grated rinds into a small mixing bowl, and using a wooden spoon, beat together until well blended.

2. **Measure out the rest** of the ingredients and place them in little containers next to the stove because the recipe goes very quickly.

3. **Before proceeding** with the recipe, lay each one of the crepes onto a clean work surface, fold each crepe over twice making them into a triangle shape, and then set onto a serving platter.

4. **Place the skillet** over medium high heat, add the sugar butter, and melt until it turns a slightly amber color but not totally caramelized. At this point, one by one using a kitchen tong, quickly pass each crepe through the syrup in the pan until each is completely coated. (It is imperative that you leave all of the crepes in the pan at the same time, just push the folded crepes to the edge of the pan until all are coated.)

5. **Now quickly add** the orange and lemon juice, and the brandy and Grand Marnier, and using a large fireplace match, ignite the contents of the pan. Carefully spoon the flaming liquid over each crepe. When the flame dies down, remove the skillet from the heat, and carefully place a few of the crepes onto dessert plates and serve.

Serves 4

Cinnamon Apple with Warm Chocolate Sauce

Ingredients

12 to 16 prepared Nalesniki crepes
2 tablespoons unsalted butter, melted (for casserole)
¼ cup Cinnamon Sugar *(see page 258)*
4 large granny smith apples, peeled and cored
1 tablespoon lemon juice
3 tablespoons unsalted butter, melted
2 tablespoons sugar
2 tablespoons brown sugar
½ teaspoon cinnamon
Dash of ground cloves
¼ cup water
1 tablespoon cornstarch
1 to 2 tablespoons rum
1 recipe Warm Chocolate Sauce *(see page 259)*
1 recipe Sweet Whipped Cream *(see page 257)*

1 medium sized oval earthenware casserole

Preparation

1. Preheat the oven to 400°.

2. On a clean work surface, using a sharp chef's knife, slice the apple halves into ¼-inch slices, then place into a medium sized mixing bowl and toss with the lemon juice.

3. Using a large nonstick skillet, heat the butter over medium high heat, add the apple slices and sauté for 2 to 3 minutes to release some of their juices. Now add the sugars, and cook stir for 3 to 4 minutes until the sugar starts to turn amber and caramelizes. Quickly dissolve the cornstarch into the water, and add it to the apples, then reduce the heat to a slow simmer. Sprinkle on the cinnamon, cloves, and the rum, and cook for another 2 to 3 minutes until the juices are thickened. Pour the hot apples into a small mixing bowl until needed.

4. Lay the crepes onto a clean work surface, and using a table-spoon, place a heaping tablespoon of the apple mixture onto the bottom half of each crepe. Now carefully fold the top half of the crepe over the apple mixture so that the ends meet, then grasp the right side of the crepe and fold it over to the left side so that you form a triangle. Repeat with the remaining crepes. Lightly butter the bottom of the casserole, sprinkle on a little of the cinnamon sugar, and then carefully arrange the folded crepes on top of that being sure that they fit tightly next to each other.

5. Lightly sprinkle a little more of the cinnamon sugar over the tops of the crepes, then bake in the hot oven for 12 to 15 minutes until the Nalesniki is slightly browned and caramelized. Immediately remove the casserole from the oven, and carefully using a small spatula, divide the crepes among 4 dessert plates, and serve with a dollop of sweet whipped cream and the warm chocolate sauce.

Serves 4

Caramelized Banana with Vanilla Bean Ice Cream

Ingredients

12 to 16 prepared Nalesniki crepes
2 tablespoons unsalted butter, melted (for casserole)
2 large bananas, peeled
6 tablespoons unsalted butter, melted
6 tablespoons brown sugar
½ teaspoon cinnamon
2 tablespoons banana liqueur
2 tablespoons rum
1 recipe Vanilla Bean Ice Cream *(see page 239)*
Powdered sugar for dusting

1 medium sized oval earthenware casserole

Preparation

1. Preheat the oven to 400°.

2. On a clean work surface, using a sharp chef's knife, slice the bananas diagonally in half, then cut each half again. Now cut the lengths into 3 equal pieces. (Each banana should yield 12 equal pieces.)

3. Using a medium nonstick skillet, heat the butter over medium high heat, add the banana slices and brown sugar and cook until the sugar starts to turn amber and caramelizes. Immediately lower the heat and sprinkle on the cinnamon and the liquors.

4. Very gently, using a soupspoon, flip the banana slices over and baste with the caramelized sugar. Remove the skillet from the heat until needed.

5. Lay the crepes onto a clean work surface, and using a table-spoon, evenly distribute the banana pieces among all the crepes, and carefully roll up each crepe into a thick but tight cigar shape. Lightly butter the bottom of the casserole, then arrange the rolled crepes on top of that being sure that they fit tightly next to each other.

6. Again using the soup spoon, stir any remaining sugar syrup that is left in the skillet, and then gently nap over the arranged crepes in the casserole, and bake in the hot oven for 12 to 15 minutes until the Nalesniki is slightly browned and caramelized. Remove the casserole from the oven, and carefully using a small spatula, divide the crepes among 4 dessert plates, sprinkle with powdered sugar and serve with a dollop of vanilla bean ice cream on top.

Serves 4

Hunter's-style with Mushrooms

Ingredients

12 to 16 prepared Nalesniki crepes
2 tablespoons unsalted butter, melted (for casserole)

4 tablespoons unsalted butter, melted
1/4 cup Pancetta ham, sliced thin and diced
2 pounds assorted field mushrooms, quartered,
  such as cepes, shitakes, oyster, or cremini
1/4 cup Madeira
1/2 cup chicken or veal stock
Pinch of sea salt
Pinch of freshly ground black pepper
Dash of Maggi
1 tablespoon fresh marjoram, chopped
1 tablespoon parsley, chopped
1/2 cup heavy cream

1 medium sized oval earthenware casserole

Preparation

1. **Preheat the oven** to 350°.

2. **Place a medium-sized** nonstick skillet over medium high heat, and when the pan turns white-hot, add the butter and pancetta, and cook for 1 minute. Add the mushrooms, and sauté quickly until the mushrooms start to release their liquid. When the liquid starts to dissipate, and the mushrooms start to brown at the edges, remove the pan from the heat, and pour in the Madeira. Return the pan back to the fire and tilt it slightly towards the flame so the Madeira will ignite. Shake the pan until the flames die down, then lower the heat to medium low.

3. **Now add the chicken** stock and cook stir for 1 minute until slightly reduced, then add the rest of the ingredients, and cook for 3 to 5 minutes until the sauce lightly coats the back of a spoon. Remove the skillet from the fire until needed.

4. **Lay the crepes** onto a clean work surface, and using a tablespoon, evenly distribute the mushroom mixture over the face of the crepe, then roll each crepe into a thick but tight cigar shape. Lightly butter the bottom of the casserole, and carefully arrange the rolled crepes on top of that being sure that they fit tightly next to each other.

5. **Pour the remaining butter** over all of the crepes, and bake in the hot oven for about 20 minutes until the Nalesniki are warmed through. Remove the casserole from the oven and serve immediately.

Serves 4

Polish Ham and Cheese

Ingredients

12 to 16 prepared Nalesniki crepes
2 tablespoons unsalted butter, melted (for casserole)

1/2 pound cooked Polish ham, off the bone
3 tablespoons unsalted butter, melted
3 tablespoons all-purpose flour
2 cups whole milk
1/8 teaspoon sea salt
1/8 teaspoon freshly ground black pepper
Pinch of nutmeg
Pinch of garlic powder
Dash of Tabasco
Heaping 2/3 cup grated Swiss or Gruyere cheese
2 tablespoons Parmigiano-Reggiano cheese

1 medium sized oval earthenware casserole

Preparation

1. **Preheat the oven** to 350°.

2. **Using a sharp** chef's knife, cut the pre-cooked smoked ham into medium sized diced pieces then set aside until needed.

3. **To prepare the sauce,** heat the butter in a medium sized saucepan over medium high heat, then add the flour and stir cook for exactly 1 minute until the flour is pale yellow and frothy. Now add the milk, and again stir cook until the sauce comes to a boil, then reduce the heat slightly, and continue to stir cook for another 3 to 4 minutes until the sauce resembles heavy cream. Season the sauce with the salt, pepper, nutmeg, garlic powder, and Tabasco, then add all of the grated Swiss cheese, stir cook for exactly 1 minute more and remove from the fire.

4. **Lay the crepes** onto a clean work surface, and evenly distribute the diced ham over the face of the crepes. Using a tablespoon, nap some of the cheese sauce over the diced ham, then quickly roll up each Nalesniki into a thick but tight cigar shape. Lightly butter the bottom of the casserole, and carefully arrange the rolled crepes on top of that being sure that they fit tightly next to each other.

5. **Carefully using** a ladle, spoon about half of the leftover cheese sauce over all of the crepes, (you will most definitely have extra sauce, however don't be tempted to drown the crepes). Sprinkle the Parmesan cheese over the top, and then bake in the hot oven for 20 to 30 minutes until the tops of the Nalesniki are golden and bubbly.

Serves 4

Savory Seafood Gratinée

Ingredients

12 to 16 prepared Nalesnike crepes
2 tablespoons unsalted butter, melted (for casserole)

3 tablespoons unsalted butter, melted
2 large garlic cloves, minced
1 cup domestic mushrooms, sliced
2 teaspoons lemon juice
$\frac{1}{2}$ pound lump crabmeat
$\frac{1}{2}$ pound bay scallops
3 tablespoons Cognac or brandy
1 cup heavy cream
$\frac{1}{8}$ teaspoon sea salt
$\frac{1}{8}$ teaspoon freshly ground black pepper
Pinch of cayenne
Pinch of nutmeg
$\frac{1}{3}$ cup Parmigiano-Reggiano cheese, grated
$\frac{1}{3}$ cup Swiss cheese, grated
$\frac{1}{4}$ cup parsley, chopped
$\frac{1}{2}$ cup heavy cream (reserved)

1 medium sized oval earthenware casserole

Preparation

1. **Preheat the oven** to 350°F.

2. **Heat the butter** in a medium-sized nonstick skillet over medium high heat, then add the garlic, mushrooms, and lemon juice, and cook stir until the mushrooms start to release their liquid. When the liquid evaporates, add the crabmeat and bay scallops, and gently cook for 1 minute, then add the Cognac, and tilt the pan until it flames. When the flame dies down, add to the pan 1 cup of heavy cream, salt, pepper, cayenne, nutmeg, 3 tablespoons Parmesan cheese, 3 tablespoons Swiss cheese, and the chopped parsley, lower the heat, and simmer until the sauce thinly coats the back of a spoon. Remove the pan from the fire.

3. **Using a pastry** brush, lightly coat the bottom of the oval earthenware casserole with the melted butter. Quickly but carefully, spoon about 2 tablespoons of seafood filling into each crepe, then roll up tightly and place into the buttered casserole. Repeat with the remaining crepes, then pour on top the reserved $\frac{1}{2}$ cup of heavy cream, and sprinkle on the remaining cheese.

4. **Immediately place** the casserole into the hot oven, and bake for 20 to 30 minutes until the tops of the Nalesniki are golden and bubbly.

Serves 4

Smoky Spinach and Mushroom Gratinée

Ingredients

12 to 16 prepared Nalesniki crepes
2 tablespoons unsalted butter, melted (for casserole)

2 pounds fresh spinach leaves, cleaned and pre-blanched
2 tablespoons unsalted butter, melted
1 slice hickory smoked bacon, minced
$\frac{1}{2}$ pound domestic mushrooms, sliced
3 large garlic cloves, minced
1 cup heavy cream
$\frac{1}{2}$ scant teaspoon sea salt
$\frac{1}{4}$ teaspoon freshly ground black pepper
$\frac{1}{8}$ teaspoon nutmeg
Large dash of Tabasco
Large dash of Maggi
1 tablespoon unsalted butter, chilled
$\frac{1}{2}$ cup heavy cream, reserved
$\frac{1}{2}$ cup grated Swiss or Gruyere cheese

1 medium sized oval earthenware casserole

Preparation

1. **Preheat the oven** to 350°.

2. **Place the blanched** spinach leaves onto a clean kitchen towel, and fold the long ends over each other. Now grasping both ends of the towel, twist to squeeze the excess liquid out of the spinach. Coarsely chop the spinach using a sharp kitchen knife, and set aside in a bowl until needed.

3. **Place a medium-sized** nonstick skillet over medium high heat, and when the pan turns white-hot, add the butter, bacon, mushrooms, and garlic, and sauté quickly until the mushrooms start to release their liquid. When the liquid starts to dissipate, add the heavy cream, salt, pepper, nutmeg, Tabasco, Maggi, and chopped spinach, and bring to the boil. Now reduce the heat, and simmer slowly until the cream thickly coats the back of a wooden spoon about 3 to 4 minutes.

4. **Remove the skillet** from the fire, re-season the mixture, and stir in the butter.

5. **Using a pastry brush,** lightly coat the bottom of the oval earthenware casserole with the melted butter. Quickly but carefully, spoon about 2 tablespoons of spinach filling into each crepe, then roll up tightly and place into the buttered casserole. Repeat with the remaining crepes, then pour on top the reserved $\frac{1}{2}$ cup of heavy cream, and sprinkle on the grated cheese.

6. **Immediately place** the casserole into the hot oven, and bake for 20 to 30 minutes until the tops of the Nalesniki are golden and bubbly.

Serves 4

Creamed Chicken
with Broccoli and Dill

I've always loved this continental favorite for its simplicity and excellent taste. Most Polish restaurants serve some type of meat filled crepe, but I often find that the fillings are too overpowering for the lightness of the crepes. Chicken breasts and broccoli are gently bathed with a lightly seasoned sauce, stuffed into the crepes, and then baked in the oven until golden perfection.

Chef's Tip!

If you like more sauce, ½ cup more of chicken stock can be added. Also, I like to sauté up ½ pound of sliced button mushrooms in butter and then add them to the chicken-broccoli filling.

Ingredients

Sauce

3 tablespoons unsalted butter, melted
3 tablespoons all-purpose flour
2 ½ cups chicken stock
½ heaping teaspoon Polish spice #1
    (see page 251)
Dash of Tabasco
2 dashes Maggi seasoning
¼ cup heavy cream, optional
¼ cup Parmagiano-Reggiano cheese or
    ½ cup shredded Colby cheese
2 tablespoons fresh dill, minced

Filling

2 tablespoons unsalted butter, melted
2 large garlic cloves, minced
¾ pound raw chicken breasts, cubed small
¾ pound small broccoli florets, pre-washed

12 to 16 prepared Nalesniki crepes

1 medium sized oval earthenware casserole

Preparation

1. **To prepare the sauce,** heat the butter in a medium sized non-stick saucepan over medium heat and when hot, add the flour, and stir cook for 1 to 2 minutes until the flour and butter are well incorporated. (Do not brown.) Immediately add the chicken stock and stir well with a whisk until the sauce thickens and comes to a boil.

2. **Reduce the heat** to medium low, add the Polish spice, Tabasco, and Maggi, and stir cook for at least 12 to 15 minutes until the sauce lightly thickens and takes on a good taste. Remove the saucepan from the fire and stir in the fresh dill and optional heavy cream.

3. **Place a medium sized** non-stick skillet over medium high heat, and when hot, add the butter and garlic, and stir cook for 1 minute. Now add the cubed chicken and broccoli to the skillet, and stir cook for exactly 2 to 3 minutes until the chicken turns slightly white opaque in color. Remove the skillet from the fire.

4. **Using a ladle,** spoon about 1½ cups of the sauce onto the chicken and broccoli, and carefully fold the two together until well combined. (At this point, I highly recommend that you let the remaining sauce and chicken mixture cool for about ½ hour for ease of preparation. It is difficult to roll the crepes when the mixture is hot.)

5. **Preheat the oven** to 350°.

6. **Lightly coat** the bottom of the oval earthenware casserole with some melted butter then quickly but carefully, spoon about 2 to 3 tablespoons of chicken-broccoli filling into each crepe, and then roll up tightly and place into the buttered casserole. Repeat with the remaining crepes, then gently ladle on top any reserved sauce, sprinkle on the cheese, and place the casserole into the hot oven, and bake for 20 to 30 minutes until the tops of the Nalesniki are golden and bubbly.

Serves 4

soups

*w*ild mushroom, barley, and dill

"*p*olish-style" creamed mushroom

*s*moky potato mushroom chowder with marjoram

*c*hicken kluski noodle

*t*urkey carcass matzo ball

*c*ream of whatever with rice

*c*hicago-style green split pea

*b*rown lentil and vegetable

*p*a's ham bone and bean

*a*utumn vegetable beef

*o*nion, garlic, and cheese crouton

*r*eal polish borscht

*f*lacki soup

*k*apusniak

*s*ummer tomato with basil

*c*hlodnik chilled soup

*c*hilled potato and leek with spinach

Without a doubt, to the Poles soup is at the very heart of basic family cooking; whether it is served as a snack, quick lunch, or at a sophisticated dinner party. Most people are surprised when I tell them that soup surpasses bread in the food chain of Polish culture. Our people regard soup as a "first course" to enhance the rest of the meal, irregardless of the time of day or season of the year. There are literally dozens of classical Polish soups of all tastes and textures, such as a chilled plum soup or a hearty oxtail, barley, and marjoram ragout. The spectrum is endless, and let's not forget the many garnishes that adorn all these beauties.

I've been fortunate in my career to learn the art of soup making from some really great chefs who were generous enough to share their secrets. In a French kitchen, I was known as the saucier, or the cook who makes soups, stocks, and sauces. This position, although respected, is often neglected because of the complexity of the art. As a young cook, you quickly learn that anyone can grill a steak, but the guy who can make a sauce or soup is the king. As you master the art, you develop an educated palate, or in layman's terms "you acquire good taste".

Soup making is a very easy process just as long as you follow two simple rules:

1. Use the best ingredients available.
2. Remember that the pot is not a garbage can for odd bits and pieces.

The key to making good soup is consistency, by that I mean the ingredients you use, the way you chop them, the seasoning you use, the way that the flavors are melded together with the other ingredients, and the time and temperature that the soup is allowed to simmer. When you read my recipes, the procedures and cooking times are very specific, because this allows the vegetables and herbs to release their fragrant oils, which in turn, produces a great soup that has a rich, clean, and identifiable taste.

I can personally attest to those rules, because it is exactly what my Aunt Minnie taught me on the farm some 30 years ago when we made **Chicken Noodle Soup** using ingredients that were pulled right from her garden. Catching the chicken was another matter, but a young cook has to start somewhere. I remember that my Aunt used to say, "From God to the ground to the pot to your heart." It's funny that I remember that after all of these years, but all in all, soup making is about comfort and security. You know that kind of warm fuzzy feeling that you would get from your mom when she used to make homemade soup for the family. We all have a memory of coming home from school and smelling that simmering pot which might have been short of meat or chicken at times, but was always made with an abundance of vegetables and a lot of love.

It's with those feelings that I am introducing you to the soups that I love. Through the years, fancy soups have come and gone, but this small collection has always brought a lot of comfort and happiness to my family. Nothing brings more joy to a chef's heart than to have his patrons or children compliment him on the quality of his soup. In my family, soup is a mainstay meal and is often the only course served. Of course, I embellish the soup with a lot of pasta, vegetables, bread, and a side salad, because I have three growing boys, but I also take comfort in the fact that the soup brings us closer together as a family. As we get older, our lives get busier and this gives us less of an opportunity to spend quality time together. Hopefully this collection of recipes will inspire you to adopt the tradition of making homemade soups, pass these onto your children, and leave them with so many wonderful memories. Don't worry if you don't see your favorite recipe in this book, it will be in the next.

Wild Mushroom, Barley, and Dill

Ingredients

2 tablespoons unsalted butter, melted
3 medium garlic cloves, minced
1 small onion, diced
1 large carrot, diced
1 large celery stalk, diced
1 pound sliced wild mushroom caps and stems,
    cleaned—such as cepes, shitakes, oyster, cremini,
    or a combination
    or
1 pound sliced domestic mushrooms and stems,
    cleaned
½ teaspoon dried thyme
1 bay leaf
2 tablespoons all-purpose flour
6 cups chicken stock
¼ teaspoon sea salt
⅛ teaspoon freshly ground black pepper
Dash of Tabasco
Dash of mushroom powder
2 dashes of Maggi seasoning
½ cup pearl barley, pre-cooked al dente
½ cup heavy cream
3 tablespoons fresh dill, minced

Easily the King of all Polish soups! My photographer Greg demanded that I didn't get skimpy on the mushrooms in my soups so check out the picture on the cover of the book. It's a Polish masterpiece. I've always loved mushroom barley soup for its pure taste and refinement. Recipes vary, but most chefs that I know prefer my recipe because it accentuates the heartiness of the mushrooms along with the subtle bite of the barley for garnish. Fresh dill and a splash of heavy cream really round out the taste and I know you'll enjoy it!

Chef's Tip!

Never soak mushrooms to clean; just give them a quick rinse under running water to remove excess dirt, then dry immediately with a paper towel. Also, I prefer to pre-cook the pearl barley because it removes a lot of the grit and starch that can cloud your soup.

Preparation

1. **Soak the pearl barley** in 2 cups hot water for at least 2 hours, then drain and rinse for 1 minute, and then cook in 4 cups of lightly salted water for 20 minutes or until slightly al dente. Drain, rinse and then rinse and drain again and set aside.

2. **Heat the butter** in a medium pot over medium heat and add the garlic, onion, carrots, and celery and cook stirring until slightly softened, about 2 minutes. Do not let the vegetables brown.

3. **Now raise the heat** to medium high and add the thyme, bay leaf and assorted mushrooms and cook, stirring until the mushrooms start to release their liquid, about 3 to 4 minutes. At this point, it is imperative to reduce the liquid in the pot to a syrup-like consistency.

4. **Add the flour** and cook exactly 1 minute.

5. **Now add the rest** of the ingredients, except the heavy cream and dill, and bring to a boil. Reduce the heat and simmer slowly for exactly 45 minutes until the mushrooms, vegetables, and barley are tender.

6. **Add the heavy cream** and fresh dill and cook stirring for another 5–7 minutes.

Serves 4

"Polish-style" Creamed Mushroom

Ingredients

2 tablespoons unsalted butter, melted
3 medium garlic cloves, minced
1 small onion, diced
1 large celery stalk, diced
1 leek, white and some of the green part, diced
1 pound sliced domestic mushrooms and stems, cleaned
½ teaspoon dried thyme
1 bay leaf
4 tablespoons all-purpose flour
6 cups chicken stock
¼ teaspoon sea salt
⅛ teaspoon freshly ground black pepper
Dash of Tabasco
2 dashes of Maggi seasoning
½ to 1 cup heavy cream
1 tablespoons fresh dill, chives, or parsley, minced
2 tablespoons dry sherry, optional

Great Polish cooks have handed down this recipe for generations. Each family has their own interpretation and varies the mushrooms that are used and the seasonings that are added. This is a Baruch family traditional recipe, which you can add to yours.

Chef's Tip!

Old Polish cooks sometimes add 6 to 8 dried mushrooms (pre-soaked in a little warm water) to the soup while it's cooking to give it a little more flavor.

Preparation

1. **Heat the butter** in a medium pot over medium heat and add the garlic, onion, celery, leek, and cook stirring until slightly softened, about 2 minutes. Do not let the vegetables brown.

2. **Now raise the heat** to medium high and add the thyme, bay leaf, and mushrooms and cook stirring until the mushrooms start to release their liquid, about 3 to 4 minutes. At this point, it is imperative to reduce the liquid in the pot to a syrup-like consistency.

3. **Add the flour** and cook exactly 1 minute.

4. **Now add the rest** of the ingredients except the heavy cream and dill and bring to a boil, and then reduce the heat and simmer slowly for exactly 40 minutes until the mushrooms and vegetables are tender.

5. **Remove the pot from the fire** and when it is cool enough to handle, either force the soup through a fine mesh sieve, or better yet, purée it in a food blender, then pass it through a fine mesh strainer into a clean pot.

6. **Return the pot to the fire** and add the heavy cream and fresh dill, and cook stirring for another 5 to 7 minutes.

Serves 4

Smoky Potato Mushroom Chowder with Marjoram

Technically speaking chowder is a one-pot dish, more of a stew than a soup. Ideally only the starch released from the potatoes should thicken "the stew," but the heavy cream brings a certain refinement to the dish.

Chef's Tip!

I recommend removing the fuzzy beard from the underside of the shitake mushrooms with a sharp paring knife before slicing.

Ingredients

2 tablespoons unsalted butter, melted
1/4 cup Polish oczek, pancetta, or hickory smoked bacon, finely diced
3 medium garlic cloves, minced
1 small onion, diced
1 large celery stalk, diced
1 leek, white and some of the green part, diced
1/2 pound shitake mushrooms, stemmed and thinly sliced
1/2 teaspoon fresh thyme
1 bay leaf
1 tablespoon all-purpose flour
5 cups chicken stock
1/4 teaspoon sea salt
1/8 teaspoon freshly ground black pepper
Large dash of nutmeg
Dash of Tabasco
2 dashes of Maggi seasoning
1 pound baby gold potatoes, cleaned and thinly sliced
1/2 cup heavy cream or sour cream, full fat
1 tablespoon parsley, chopped
1 tablespoon fresh marjoram, chopped

Preparation

1. **Heat the butter** in a medium pot over medium heat and add the Polish bacon. Cook stir with a wooden spoon until the bacon renders its fat and turns lightly brown, not crisp. Now add the garlic, onion, celery and leeks, and cook stirring until slightly softened, about 2 minutes. Do not let the vegetables brown.

2. **Now raise the heat** to medium high and add the mushrooms, thyme, and bay leaf, and cook stirring until the mushrooms start to release their liquid, about 3 to 4 minutes. At this point, it is imperative to reduce the liquid in the pot to a syrup-like consistency.

3. **Add the flour** and cook exactly 1 minute.

4. **Now add the rest** of the ingredients except the heavy cream, parsley, and marjoram and bring to a boil, and then reduce the heat and simmer slowly for exactly 30 minutes until the potatoes are al dente.

5. **Add the heavy cream,** parsley, and marjoram, and cook for another 10–12 minutes more.

Serves 4

Chicken Kluski Noodle

Ingredients

One plump 5–6 pound fresh chicken, excess fat
　　removed
10 cups cold water
3 large garlic cloves, sliced
1 large onion, chopped
2 large carrots, chopped
2 large celery stalks, chopped
1 leek, white and some of the green part, chopped
6 sprigs fresh thyme
6 sprigs parsley
2 whole cloves
2 bay leaves
¼ teaspoon sea salt
8 whole black peppercorns
¼ cup parsley, chopped
¼ cup dill, chopped
2 cups kluski noodles, pre-cooked

Everyone has their own special recipe for Grandma's chicken noodle soup, and I've never had one that I haven't liked. My earliest memories of cooking always take me back to Wausau, Wisconsin where my aunts on the farm prepared this recipe with ingredients pulled right from the ground. Catching the chicken was another adventure!

Chef's Tip!

If your soup seems too thin or lacking body, try adding a few cleaned chicken feet or a small calves foot to the pot while it's cooking. Also, always pre-cook the noodles in a separate pot to remove excess starch that would otherwise cloud the clear broth.

Preparation

1. **Rinse the chicken** under cold running water for 3 minutes and then put in a large stockpot. Add the water and set the pot over high heat. Bring to a boil then reduce the heat and simmer the soup for 10 minutes, skimming the surface carefully with a kitchen spoon to remove any impurities that rise to the top.

2. **Now add all the vegetables** and seasonings except the chopped parsley, dill, and noodles, and simmer slowly for 1½ hours.

3. **Remove the pot** from the fire and let it cool for 20 minutes.

4. **Now carefully using** a large slotted kitchen spoon, remove the chicken and vegetables to a large colander placed over a bowl (to collect all extra juices). And when cool enough to handle, place all of the cooked chicken meat and vegetables into a clean bowl, and return any of the extra juices back to the soup pot.

5. **Using a large ladle,** (trying not to agitate the sediment at the bottom of the pot) very carefully ladleful by ladleful pass the chicken soup through a fine mesh conical sieve into another bowl and cool it as quickly as possible.

6. **Refrigerate overnight** the chicken, vegetables and soup in their own bowls.

7. **The next day** remove any accumulated fat from the soup bowl surface and discard, and place the soup into a medium sized pot over medium heat, add the chopped parsley and dill, and bring the soup to a slow simmer. Cook for 10 minutes then add the reserved chicken, vegetables and kluski noodles and cook for 10 minutes more.

Serves 4

Turkey Carcass Matzo Ball

Ingredients

One cooked slightly meaty turkey carcass plus
   wings and thighs
12 cups cold water
6 large garlic cloves, sliced
1 large onion, chopped
3 large carrots, chopped
3 large celery stalks, chopped
1 leek, white and some of the green part, chopped
$\frac{1}{2}$ small head green cabbage, chopped
2 teaspoons dried thyme
1 teaspoon dried basil
1 teaspoon dried rosemary
2 bay leaves
$\frac{1}{4}$ teaspoon sea salt
8 whole black peppercorns
$\frac{1}{2}$ cup parsley, chopped
1$\frac{3}{4}$ cup diced tomatoes with a little juice
Dash of Tabasco
Dash of garlic powder

1 double recipe Matzo Balls

Preparation

1. **Preheat the oven** to 425°F.

2. **Place the carcass** and the bones into a large roasting pan, and roast for about 30 to 35 minutes until browned. Remove from the oven and transfer the carcass and the bones to a platter. Now take a large piece of cheesecloth, lay it out on the work surface, and place all of the roasted bones directly in the middle. Gather up all four corners and secure tightly with a piece of kitchen twine. (Cheesecloth is not absolutely necessary but it makes for a bone-free soup). Transfer the package to a large stockpot.

3. **Add the water** and set the pot over high heat. Bring to a boil then reduce the heat and simmer the soup for 10 minutes, skimming the surface carefully with a kitchen spoon to remove any impurities that rise to the top.

4. **Now add all the vegetables,** seasonings, and tomatoes except the matzo balls and simmer slowly for 2$\frac{1}{2}$ hours, slightly covered. Skim the surface every 20 minutes to remove any excess impurities.

5. **Now carefully using** a large slotted kitchen spoon, remove the turkey carcass package to a large colander placed over a bowl (to collect all extra juices).

6. **Skim the soup again,** and then, one by one, drop the matzo balls into the simmering soup. Recover the pot slightly and cook for exactly 20 to 25 minutes.

This is the perfect after the holiday soup recipe. Start the soup early so the pot simmers while the boys and girls are watching the game.

> **Chef's Tip!**
> Browning the carcass removes all excess fat, and enriches the color and the flavor of the soup.

Matzo Balls

Ingredients

2 large whole eggs
4 tablespoons olive oil or melted chicken fat
$\frac{3}{4}$ cup matzo meal
$\frac{1}{2}$ teaspoon baking soda
1 teaspoon sea salt
$\frac{1}{4}$ teaspoon freshly ground white pepper
$\frac{1}{4}$ teaspoon garlic powder
$\frac{1}{4}$ teaspoon onion powder
Large pinch of nutmeg

Preparation

1. **In a medium sized** mixing bowl, beat the egg and olive oil with a whisk until foamy. In another bowl, thoroughly combine all the other ingredients until well mixed, then carefully fold in the egg mixture until completely blended through. Cover the bowl with a piece of plastic wrap, and let the mixture rest in the refrigerator for 20 to 30 minutes.

2. **Using a tablespoon,** form the matzo mix into small balls about the size of a walnut and gently drop into the simmering soup.

Makes about 16 pieces

7. **While the matzo balls** are cooking, cut open the cheesecloth package and remove the bones to a sheet pan. Carefully pick off all excess meat and put it into a separate bowl.

8. **When the matzo balls** are cooked, return to the pot the picked over turkey meat and any extra accumulated juices. Simmer for 5 minutes more and serve.

Serves a small crowd

Cream of Whatever with Rice

Canned soups are good for an emergency meal, but the sodium content is just ridiculous! I've devised this recipe for any true cream soup lover. This is the deal; you can use any combination of vegetables you want, just as long as you follow the rest of the basic recipe. The trick is to cook the soup slowly so that the flavors meld together.

Chef's Tip!

If the soup seems too thick for your liking, just add ½ cup of stock to loosen it up a bit.

Ingredients

1½ pounds of your choice: broccoli, cauliflower, celery, leeks, mushrooms, or potatoes
4 tablespoons unsalted butter
4 large garlic cloves, chopped
1 small onion, chopped
1 medium carrot, chopped
2 medium celery stalks, chopped
1 leek, white and some of the green part, chopped
¼ cup parsley, chopped
1 bay leaf
1½ teaspoons dried thyme
10 whole black peppercorns
2 whole cloves
4 tablespoons all-purpose flour
7 cups chicken stock
2 dashes Tabasco
2 dashes Maggi
Dash of garlic powder
¼ teaspoon sea salt
½ cup long grain rice, pre-rinsed
½ cup heavy cream, optional

Preparation

1. **Prepare the vegetable** of your choice by chopping it into medium sized pieces, then set aside.

2. **Heat the butter** in a medium pot over medium heat; add the garlic, onion, carrots, celery, and leek, and cook stirring until slightly softened, about 2 minutes. Do not let the vegetables brown.

3. **Now add the bay leaf,** thyme, black peppercorns, cloves, and parsley, and cook for exactly 1 minute to release their oils.

4. **Add the flour** and cook for exactly 2 minutes more.

5. **Now add the chopped vegetables** and the rest of the ingredients except the rice and cream. Bring to a boil, and then reduce the heat and simmer slowly covered for exactly 40 minutes until the vegetables are extremely tender.

6. **At this point turn the heat off,** and remove the bay leaf and cloves from the pot, and purée the soup in batches in a food blender until completely smooth.

7. **Using a fine mesh,** conical sieve, strain the purred soup into a clean pot and bring back to a boil. Reduce the heat to a simmer, then add the rice and cream and cook stirring for another 10 minutes until the rice is tender. Re-season the soup and serve.

Serves 4

Chicago-Style Green Split Pea

Ingredients

1 small smoked hock or ham bone
2 tablespoons olive oil
3 medium garlic cloves, chopped
1 small onion, chopped
2 medium carrots, chopped
2 medium celery stalks, chopped
1 bay leaf
1½ teaspoons dried thyme
5 whole black peppercorns
1 cup green split peas, rinsed
6 cups chicken stock
Dash of Tabasco
Dash of garlic powder
¼ teaspoon sea salt

Often imitated but never duplicated, this is the real deal. I've made this soup for great chefs all over the world with rave reviews! The secret is to cook the soup slowly, purée, and then sieve through a fine mesh strainer to produce a creamy, smooth soup. In Chicago, the soup is then garnished with small bits of smoked ham and oyster crackers.

Chef's Tip!

Pushing this soup through a fine mesh strainer is a bit messy, but the end result is well worth it. Ask the Pope.

Preparation

1. Rinse the smoked hock or ham bone under cold running water for 1 minute and set aside.

2. Heat the oil in a medium pot over medium heat; add the garlic, onion, carrots, and celery, and cook stirring until slightly softened, about 3 minutes. Do not let the vegetables brown.

3. Now add the bay leaf, thyme, and black peppercorns and cook for exactly 1 minute to release their oils.

4. Add the rest of the ingredients to the pot and bring it to a boil, and then reduce the heat and simmer slowly for about 1½ hours until the split peas and vegetables are extremely tender.

5. At this point, turn the heat off and remove the bay leaf and hock or bone from the pot, and purée the soup in batches in a food blender until completely smooth.

6. Using a fine mesh conical sieve, strain the puréed soup into a clean pot and bring back to a quick boil. Simmer 2 minutes more and serve.

Serves 4

Brown Lentil and Vegetable

Ingredients

1 small smoked hock
2 tablespoons olive oil
3 medium garlic cloves, minced
1 small onion, diced
2 medium carrots, diced
2 medium celery stalks, diced
1 bay leaf
1 teaspoon dried thyme
¼ teaspoon dried oregano
¼ teaspoon caraway seeds, mortar crushed
1½ tablespoons tomato paste
½ cup brown lentils, rinsed
6 cups chicken stock
1 tablespoon red wine vinegar
2 dashes Tabasco
2 dashes Worcestershire sauce
¼ teaspoon sea salt
⅛ teaspoon freshly ground black pepper
¼ cup soup pasta (small shells, stars, or snails)

A Bavarian classic revisited without the hotdogs! I don't know a person who doesn't like lentil soup, but I often hear the complaint that it's mushy and overcooked in restaurants. So let me give you some advice—cook it very slowly in a nonstick pot and don't stir the soup, just swirl the pot once in awhile and the lentils will stay whole.

Chef's Tip!

Before cooking with dried beans, it's important to wash them thoroughly in a small strainer, then pick through to remove any pebbles or dirt.

Preparation

1. **Rinse the smoked hock** under cold running water for 1 minute and set aside.

2. **Heat the oil** in a medium pot over medium heat; add the garlic, onion, carrots, and celery, and cook stirring until slightly softened, about 3 minutes. Do not let the vegetables brown.

3. **Now add the bay leaf,** thyme, oregano, and caraway seeds and cook for exactly 1 minute to release their oils.

4. **Add the tomato paste** and brown lentils and cook for 30 seconds more.

5. **Now add the rest** of the ingredients, except the pasta, to the pot and bring it to a boil, and then reduce the heat and simmer slowly for about 1½ hours until the lentils and vegetables are tender.

6. **Remove the pot** from the heat and stir in the pasta, which will cook in about 20 minutes.

Serves 4

Pa's Ham Bone and Bean

Ingredients

3 cups canned Great Northern white beans
  (high-quality only)
1 small meaty ham bone or ham shank
  (about ¾ pound)
2 tablespoons olive oil
3 medium garlic cloves, minced
1 small onion, large diced
2 medium carrots, large diced
3 medium celery stalks, large diced
1 bay leaf
1 teaspoon dried thyme
1½ teaspoons dried basil
¼ teaspoon sea salt
⅛ teaspoon freshly ground black pepper
1 cup crushed tomatoes
Dash of Tabasco
6 cups chicken stock
1 large baking potato, large diced

Sometimes Pa needs to get into the kitchen to up his fiber, and reminisce about Busia's past bean soup recipe. So let him. I've greatly reduced the preparation time and gas-o-meter, so sleep easy tonight with the window open just a little bit.

Chef's Tip!

Depending on which beans you use, (some are saltier than others) taste the soup when it's almost done to determine whether or not to add the salt.

Preparation

1. **Place the white beans** into a colander and rinse under cold running water for 2 minutes to remove any residual cooking liquid. Drain well and set aside.

2. **Remove any excess fat** from the ham bone and rinse under cold running water for 1 minute, then set aside.

3. **Heat the oil** in a medium pot over medium heat; add the garlic, onion, carrots, and celery, and cook stirring until slightly softened, about 3 minutes. Do not let the vegetables brown.

4. **Now add the bay leaf,** thyme, and basil, and cook for exactly 1 minute to release their oils.

5. **Add the rest of the ingredients** to the pot, except the potatoes, and bring it to a boil, then reduce the heat and simmer slowly for about 1 hour.

6. **Now add the potatoes,** and simmer the soup for another 25 to 30 minutes.

7. **When the potatoes** are almost cooked, carefully using a ladle, remove about 2 to 3 cups of the soup to a blender, (beans, vegetables, potatoes, and liquid, not the bay leaf) and purée until smooth. Return the purée back to the pot, and simmer the soup about another 20 to 30 minutes until the beans are tender.

8. **Remove the ham bone** from the soup and cool. Remove any meat from the bone and return it to the pot.

Serves 4

Autumn Vegetable Beef

Ingredients

2 pounds meaty beef shanks or neck bones
2 tablespoons olive oil
3 large garlic cloves, minced
1 small onion, large diced
2 medium carrots, large diced
3 medium celery stalks, large diced
¼ head small green cabbage, large diced
1 bay leaf
1 teaspoon dried thyme
1½ teaspoons dried basil
¼ teaspoon sea salt
⅛ teaspoon freshly ground black pepper
1½ cups diced tomatoes
3 tablespoons tomato paste
Dash of Tabasco
Dash of Maggi
2 tablespoon Parmigiano-Reggiano cheese
8 cups beef stock
1 cup green beans, large diced
1 large potato, large diced
½ cup soup pasta (small shells, stars, or snails)

I f there were ever a time of the year in Chicago that I truly love, it would be late September and early October. The changing colors of the leaves, and the ever present light mist in the air always takes me back to my childhood and some fond memories. After trudging home from school on those misty and chilly rainy days, a bowl of this soup was a warm welcome.

Chef's Tip!

The key to making any vegetable soup is adding the vegetables in the proper order, harder vegetables first, followed by softer ones towards the end.

Preparation

1. **Heat a medium sized pot** over medium heat, add the olive oil, and sauté the beef shanks until golden brown on both sides, about 3 to 5 minutes. Remove the shanks to a platter, and discard all of the oil from the pot.

2. **Return the pot to the fire,** then add the new olive oil. Now add the garlic, onion, carrots, celery, and cabbage, and cook stirring until slightly softened, about 3 minutes. Do not let the vegetables brown.

3. **Now add the bay leaf,** thyme, and basil, and cook for exactly 1 minute to release their oils.

4. **Return the meat to the pot,** then add the rest of the ingredients, except the beans, potatoes, and pasta, bring it to a boil, then reduce the heat and simmer slowly for about 1½ hours. Add the potatoes and green beans, and cook for another ½ hour.

5. **Now add the pasta** and cook for a half hour more.

Serves 4

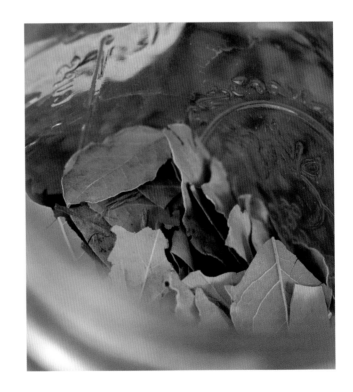

Onion, Garlic, and Cheese Crouton

Alright, it's French onion soup, but it's a great and easy recipe!

Chef's Tip!

To give your soup a richer broth, I always add a few browned meaty beef soup bones to the pot while it's cooking.

Ingredients

2 tablespoons unsalted butter, melted
2 large garlic cloves, thinly sliced
1½ pounds large onions
Pinch of sugar
¼ teaspoon sea salt
⅛ teaspoon freshly ground black pepper
8 cups beef stock
¼ cup dry white wine
2 teaspoons cornstarch
2 dashes Maggi
1 small bay leaf
Large pinch of thyme
12 thin slices French bread, toasted
½ pound thinly sliced Gruyere or Swiss cheese
¼ cup grated Parmigiano-Reggiano cheese

Preparation

1. **Peel the onions** and cut in half. Remove the hard toe, and using a sharp chef's knife, thinly slice the onions.

2. **Heat the butter** in a medium pot over medium heat, and add the garlic and onions, and cook stir until well browned. They should start to brown in about 10 minutes. Add the sugar, salt, and pepper, and cook for another 5 to 10 minutes. The onions should be a deep golden brown. Do not burn the onions.

3. **Add the beef stock,** white wine, cornstarch, Maggi, bay leaf, and thyme, bring it to the boil, then reduce the heat and simmer the soup for 1 hour.

4. **Preheat the oven** to 375°F.

5. **Place 4 earthenware** soup cups into a medium sized roasting pan filled with about ¼ inch of water. Ladle the hot soup into the cups, leaving about ¾ inch headroom between the soup and the rim of the cup. Quickly place 3 of the bread slices into each cup, lightly floating them on top of the soup. Now layer 2 slices of the cheese on top of the bread, and then sprinkle on the parmesan cheese.

6. **Immediately place the pan** into the hot oven on the middle rack, and bake until the tops are bubbly and golden brown.

Serves 4

Real Polish Borscht

Ingredients

2 tablespoons olive oil
3 duck legs with thigh attached
  or
2 pounds meaty beef bones or shanks
10 cups beef stock
5 medium garlic cloves, sliced
1 medium onion, chopped
4 medium celery stalks, chopped
1 leek, white and some of the green part, chopped
1 small fennel bulb, chopped
2 large beets, peeled and chopped
1 small parsnip, peeled and chopped
1 medium tomato, chopped
1 bay leaf
6 sprigs parsley
6 sprigs thyme
1 whole clove
¼ teaspoon sea salt
8 black peppercorns
3 tablespoons dill, chopped

1 recipe Mushroom Uszka, optional

Preparation

1. **Heat the oil** in a large skillet over medium high heat, add the beef bones or duck legs and sauté until the meat is well browned on all sides, about 5 minutes. Remove from the pot and place on to a paper towel lined platter to remove excess grease.

2. **Now place the meat** into a large stockpot, and add the beef stock. Over high heat, bring the stock to a boil then reduce the heat and slowly simmer the stock for 30 minutes, skimming the surface carefully with a kitchen spoon to remove any impurities that rise to the top.

3. **Now add all the vegetables** and seasonings except the chopped dill and simmer slowly for about another 2 hours.

4. **Strain the soup** through a fine mesh conical sieve into a clean saucepan and stir in the dill. Re-season the soup if needed, then gently ladle into four soup bowls. Garnish the soup with 3 praying monks and serve immediately.

Serves 4

P ure Polish Elixir.

Chef's Tip!

The trick to a great borscht is to shred the beets, and to cook the soup very slowly so that the liquid stays clear.

Mushroom Uszka

Ingredients

1 recipe Kluski noodle dough *(see page 99)*

2 tablespoons unsalted butter, melted
2 large garlic cloves, minced
1 small onion, finely diced
¼ cup pancetta ham, sliced thin and diced
2 pounds assorted field mushroom, finely diced
1 tablespoon parsley, chopped
1 tablespoon fresh marjoram, chopped
Dash of sea salt
Dash of freshly ground black pepper
1 large whole egg lightly beaten for sealing

Preparation

1. **Place a medium sized** nonstick skillet over medium high heat, and when the pan turns white-hot, add the butter, garlic, onion, and pancetta, and cook for 1 minute. Add the mushrooms, and sauté quickly until the mushrooms start to release their liquid. When the liquid starts to dissipate, and the mushrooms start to brown, season with the fresh herbs and a dash of salt and pepper, then remove from the fire.

2. **On a lightly floured** work surface, carefully roll out the pasta dough as thinly a possible (about ⅛-inch thick). Using a sharp knife, cut the dough into 1½-inch squares. Place a little of the cooled filling onto a square slightly off center, then fold in half to form a triangle, and pinch the edges together. Gently pull the 2 bottom corners together and join by pinching. Cook the uszka in lightly salted water for 2 to 4 minutes or until they float to the top. (If your uszka fall apart, try sealing the edges with a little beaten egg.)

Makes about 40 pieces

Flacki Soup

Ingredients

2½ to 3 pounds tripe, pre-blanched, rinsed, and
   cut into half inch strips
1 small smoked hock
2 thick slices hickory smoked bacon, diced
2 tablespoons olive oil
2 tablespoons all-purpose flour
3 large garlic cloves, minced
1 small onion, diced
2 medium carrots, diced
2 medium celery stalks, diced
1 leek, white and some of the green part, diced
1 large red or green pepper, diced
2 tablespoons parsley, chopped
1 bay leaf
⅛ teaspoon dried thyme
½ teaspoon dried marjoram
½ teaspoon dried oregano
1 teaspoon sweet paprika
⅛ teaspoon crushed red pepper flakes
¼ teaspoon freshly ground black pepper
1 cup diced tomatoes
8 cups chicken stock
Dash of Tabasco
2 dashes Maggi
Dash of mushroom powder
Scant ⅛ teaspoon each of cloves, ginger, and nutmeg

My hearty sweet and spicy version of classical Polish tripe soup!

Chef's Tip!

If you don't like your soup gamy, I highly recommend pre-blanching and rinsing the tripe at least 3 times before adding them to the soup.

Preparation

1. **Rinse the smoked hock** under cold running water for 1 minute, and then set aside.

2. **Heat a medium sized** pot over medium heat and add the diced bacon. Cook stir with a wooden spoon until the bacon renders its fat and turns lightly brown, not crisp. Pour the bacon into a small strainer set over a bowl to collect the excess fat. Cool the bacon and set aside with the tripe.

3. **Return the pot to the fire,** then add the olive oil and flour and cook stirring for 1 to 2 minutes until the flour has turned a light golden color and smells slightly nutty.

4. **Now add the garlic,** onion, celery, carrots, leeks, peppers, and parsley and cook stirring until slightly softened, about 2 minutes.

5. **Add the bay leaf,** thyme, marjoram, oregano, paprika, red pepper flakes, and pepper and stir cook for 1 minute to release their oils. Now add the rest of the ingredients, except the sweet spices, and lightly stir cook until the liquid comes to a boil, and then reduce the heat, and simmer slowly for about 1½ hours.

6. **Now add the sweet spices** to the pot and cook for another 15 minutes.

Serves 4

Kapusniak

Ingredients

2 pounds pork spare ribs or meaty pork neck bones

3 tablespoons olive oil

2 thick slices hickory smoked bacon, pre-blanched and diced

¾ pound smoked Polish sausage, pre-blanched and sliced

2 tablespoons sugar

4 medium garlic cloves, minced

1 medium onion, diced

1 large carrot, diced

1 large celery stalk, diced

½ pound green cabbage, shredded

1 pound sauerkraut, drained and rinsed, once

4 Polish dried mushrooms, sliced

2 tablespoons all-purpose flour

1 bay leaf

2½ teaspoons Polish spice #2 *(see page 251)*

1 tablespoon tomato paste

2 dashes Maggi seasoning

2 dashes Tabasco

7 cups beef or chicken stock

8 small red potatoes, quartered

O ften called "the bachelor party hangover soup," this hearty stew-like concoction will either cure ya or kill ya depending on how bad you feel. This old Polish peasant soup is usually made with pork hocks or feet, but I find that it makes it too greasy for my taste so I've refined the recipe. Slow cooking is an absolute must for this dish, so a crock-pot might be in order.

Chef's Tip!

If you're not partial to a sweet soup, just omit the sugar from the recipe. Old Poles like to add a small can of diced tomato with juice to the pot, and some substitute ½ cup quick cook well-rinsed pearl barley for the potatoes.

Preparation

1. **Remove any excess fat** and silver skin from the underside of the spare ribs, then cut the rack into four equal pieces.

2. **Heat 3 tablespoons** of the oil in a medium sized pot over medium heat, and working in batches to avoid overcrowding the pan, brown the spare ribs on both sides (about 3 minutes on each side). Remove the browned ribs to a serving platter, and brown the remaining ribs in the remaining olive oil.

3. **Discard the excess oil** from the pot, add the bacon and sausage, and cook stir over medium heat until the bacon renders its fat and turns lightly brown, not crisp. Carefully, using a slotted kitchen spoon, remove the bacon and sausage to the platter, and discard all of the bacon fat.

4. **Return the pot** to the fire and add the sugar and stir cook with a wooden spoon until it lightly caramelizes and turns amber brown, and then immediately add the garlic, onion, carrot, celery, green cabbage, sauerkraut, and mushrooms, and cook stirring until slightly softened, about 3 to 4 minutes. Do not let the vegetables brown.

5. **Sprinkle the flour** over the vegetables and cook for 1 minute more, then add the bay leaf, Polish spice, tomato paste, Maggi, Tabasco, and chicken stock and bring to a boil.

6. **Now add the spareribs,** bacon, and sausage back to the pot, reduce the heat, and simmer slowly for 2 hours.

7. **After 2 hours** have passed, add the quartered potatoes to the pot, and let the soup simmer for another 30 to 40 minutes until the spareribs are tender.

Serves 4

Summer Tomato Soup with Basil

Outside of Chicken Kluski soup, tomato soup reigns supreme as the ultimate comfort food. When I was a kid and I was home sick from school, my ma used to park me in front of the television in my footed pajamas and bring in a T.V. tray with a bowl of piping hot tomato soup with crackers and flat seven up to make me feel better. Although most people's experience has been out of a can, I wanted to give you a recipe that actually works with or without fresh tomatoes.

Chef's Tip!

If you prefer fresh, I highly recommend using late harvest plum tomatoes when they are at their peak ripeness. I also sometimes substitute fresh dill for the basil.

Ingredients

4 tablespoons unsalted butter
4 large garlic cloves, chopped
1 medium onion, chopped
1 medium carrot, chopped
2 medium celery stalks, chopped
1 leek, white and some of the green part, chopped
2 bay leaves
1½ teaspoons dried thyme
½ teaspoon sea salt
¼ teaspoon freshly ground black pepper
Dash of cayenne
2 whole cloves
2 tablespoons all-purpose flour
2 28 oz. cans whole plum tomatoes with juices
2 tablespoons tomato paste
4 cups chicken stock
3 dashes Tabasco
Dash of garlic powder
1 cup heavy cream
2 tablespoons fresh basil, minced

Preparation

1. **Heat the butter** in a medium pot over medium heat, add the garlic, onion, carrot, celery, and leek, and cook stirring until slightly softened, about 2 minutes. Do not let the vegetables brown.

2. **Add the bay leaves,** thyme, salt, black pepper, cayenne, cloves, and cook for exactly 1 minute to release their oils.

3. **Add the flour** and cook for exactly 2 minutes more.

4. **Now add the tomatoes,** tomato paste, stock, Tabasco, and garlic powder. Bring to a boil, reduce the heat, and simmer slowly for exactly 50 minutes until the vegetables are extremely tender.

5. **At this point,** turn the heat off and remove the bay leaves and cloves from the pot, and purée the soup in batches in a food blender until completely smooth.

6. **Using a fine mesh** conical sieve, strain the puréed soup into a clean pot and bring back to a boil. Reduce the heat to a simmer, then add the cream and the basil and cook stirring for another 15 minutes, re-season, and serve.

Serves 4

Chlodnik Chilled Soup

Ingredients

1 quart beet borscht, chilled
½ cup sour cream, full fat
2 tablespoons dill, chopped
Dash of sugar or vinegar, to taste
Cucumber
Radish
Dill pickle
Hard-boiled egg
Crayfish or shrimp
Mayonnaise
Dill
Chives
Lemon juice
Sea salt
Freshly ground white pepper

1 recipe Buckwheat Blini

Preparation

1. **Strain the chilled beet borscht** through a fine mesh conical sieve into a clean mixing bowl. Whisk in the sour cream until the soup is completely smooth, then strain the soup again through the sieve into another bowl. Add the dill, and the sugar or vinegar, if desired. Cover the bowl and refrigerate.

2. **To make the Chlodnik garnish,** combine the remaining ingredients in a mixing bowl, and gently fold together using a plastic spatula. Cover the bowl and refrigerate.

3. **To make the blini,** heat a large griddle over medium high heat, and pour in enough melted butter to thinly coat the bottom. Using a soupspoon, take about 2 tablespoons of the blini mix and place it onto the griddle. Cook for about 1 minute until golden brown. Using a spatula, flip the blini over and brown the other side, and then remove to a paper lined platter and repeat the cooking process until done.

4. **Remove the soup** and garnish from the refrigerator. Ladle the soup into small soup cups, and place about a tablespoon of the garnish on top of each of the blinis and serve on the side.

Serves 4

An old Eastern European favorite enriched with sour cream, and then classically garnished the old-fashioned way.

Chef's Tip!

It is important that you remove the fat layer that sometimes forms on top of the chilled clear beet borscht, or your soup will have a slightly greasy texture.

Buckwheat Blini

Ingredients

1¼ cups whole milk
1¼ teaspoons active dry yeast
2 large egg yolks
2 large egg whites
¼ teaspoon sea salt
½ teaspoon sugar
3 tablespoons unsalted butter, melted
1 cup buckwheat flour
1 cup all-purpose flour

¼ cup clarified butter for cooking

Preparation

1. **Place the milk** into a small saucepan, and over medium heat bring just to the boil, then remove and cool to lukewarm. Stir in the yeast until dissolved and then set aside.

2. **Beat the egg yolks,** salt, sugar, and butter until well combined and slightly thick then add it to the yeast mixture. Using a wire whisk, stir in the flours and mix thoroughly.

3. **Now in a separate bowl,** beat the egg whites until stiff and gently fold into the batter. Cover the bowl and let it rest for at least 30 minutes until the mixture gets slightly puffy.

4. **Preheat a heavy-duty** cast iron griddle over medium heat, and lightly brush with the melted butter. When hot, pour 1 tablespoon of batter onto the griddle and cook for about 1 minute or until golden brown. Now turn the blini and brown on the other side, then repeat until all of the batter is used.

Makes about 18 pieces

Chilled Potato and Leek with Spinach

Great for a light meal on a warm summer's day.

Chef's Tip!

Don't be tempted to add the spinach and chives to the soup while it is still warm, as this will cause the herbs to lose their nice green color. If you are not partial to spinach, 1 large bunch of fresh sorrel can be used in its place.

Ingredients

3 tablespoons unsalted butter, melted
3 large garlic cloves, minced
1 small onion, sliced
2 large leeks, white part only, sliced
1½ pounds potatoes, peeled and diced
5½ cups chicken stock
¼ teaspoon sea salt
⅛ teaspoon freshly ground white pepper
Dash of Tabasco
Dash of Worcestershire sauce
Dash of lemon juice
½ cup heavy cream
¾ pound fresh spinach leaves, stemmed, pre-blanched, drained, and chopped
1 tablespoon chives or parsley, minced

Preparation

1. **Heat the butter** in a medium pot over medium heat: add the garlic, onion, and leeks, and cook, stirring, until slightly softened, about 3 minutes. Do not let the vegetables brown.

2. **Now add the potatoes,** chicken stock, salt, pepper, tabasco, Worcestershire, and lemon juice, and bring to a boil, then reduce the heat and simmer slowly for exactly 40 minutes.

3. **At this point,** turn the heat off and purée the soup in batches in a food blender until completely smooth. Using a fine mesh conical sieve, strain the puréed soup into a clean pot and bring back to a quick boil, then reduce the heat to a simmer. Add the heavy cream and cook for another 5 minutes.

4. **Remove the pot** from the heat, and place it into a large bowl filled with ice cubes. Now using a wooden spoon, stir the soup until it is chilled, then add the chopped spinach and chives. Refrigerate the soup for at least 4 to 5 hours before serving.

Serves 4

one pot meals

*t*he best chicken and dumplings

*s*tuffed cabbage

zrazy ᶻ "pepper steak"

*o*ld-fashioned midwestern pot on the fire

*b*raised beef short ribs

*b*igos

*s*moked sausage garnished sauerkraut

*p*ork spare ribs and sauerkraut

*t*ripes warsaw-style

*v*eal goulash

*s*low-cooked beans with sausage, duck, and lamb

At one point in my career, a restaurateur on the west coast persuaded me to come out for a prominent chef's position at his infamous Italian restaurant. I arrived early Monday morning in Santa Monica to be greeted by the owner who was pleasant enough, but noticeably pre-occupied with business. The owner and myself sat at the bar, and had a cappuccino while he quickly glanced at my résumé. After a few minutes of small talk, he folded the résumé, and asked if I would have any objection in making lunch to show off my talents. I quickly agreed and was led to the restaurant's empty kitchen. He told me to make myself comfortable, as he would be back by noon. Since this was an Italian restaurant, I didn't think it was appropriate to whip the guy up a plate of pasta, but thought a more substantial braise or one pot meal would soul satisfy this Venetian owner.

Scouring the walk-in refrigerators, I realized there was no meat, fish, or fowl to be had, just the usual assorted vegetables and a few meaty oxtails and pigs trotters used for making stock. For a few frantic moments, I was panic-stricken and contemplated running out the back door. However, I composed myself and took a few deep breaths determined to make this work. I quickly began my preparation by browning the meat off with some aromatic vegetables, a sprinkling of fresh herbs, a little wine, and some stock. Braised oxtails are an old Eastern European dish and are cooked in a sealed tureen to retain all the beautiful juices. My plan was to let the tureen cook for a good 2½ hours until the meat literally falls off the bone, then I could serve the juices over some of the house homemade pasta.

A sole young Italian prep cook had just started his workday. As I don't speak the language, I tied an apron around the oven door to indicate "Do not touch" and went out to get some fresh air for a couple of hours. Upon returning, I found the kitchen buzzing with at least a dozen chefs all speaking some fast dialect of Italian, and giving me that evil eye look meaning "Who is this guy?" I'd worked in too many great restaurants to get spooked, but even I was relieved when the headwaiter Franco came out of nowhere to greet me. He told me the owner would be returning in 10 minutes and would be ready for his lunch. As I was introduced to some of the kitchen staff, it was noticeable that the beautiful perfume of my braised oxtails was emanating throughout the kitchen. I asked Franco to introduce me to the head chef, but it was apparent from the dagger looks he was throwing my way that it wasn't in the cards. No sooner had that thought crossed my mind, than the owner appeared in the doorway, grabbed a clean white napkin, tucked it into his collar, and asked for his lunch. Franco jumped to my defense rambling some Italian and was in turn told that the owner would taste the dish in the kitchen and not formally in the dining room, as I would've preferred. The kitchen got very quiet, and the owner pulled up a chair to the prep counter with knife and fork in hand. As I walked around the counter, I noticed someone had removed the apron from the oven door. I was so busy talking to Franco, I forgot to check it, but the fragrance reassured me that the dish was a success. As I opened the oven, and lifted the tureen to where the owner sat, the not-so-friendly chef got right in my face. For any uneasy second, our eyes met and I noticed he had a slight grin on his face, which sent a shiver down my spine. By this time, the entire kitchen staff was standing around anticipating the owner's reaction.

Franco my savior deftly removed the cover from the tureen and while a beautiful puff of steam emerged, the owner using his hand, gasped at the fragrance and smiled. When the steam cleared, he dipped a soupspoon into the tureen, took a sip of the juice, and then sopped some up with a piece of bread. Not a word was said! He manned himself with 2 forks, and started to remove the contents from the tureen into a soup bowl with a bewildered look on his face. To my amazement, all that was left in the tureen were oxtails bones and one picked over pigs hoof with absolutely no meat left on it. Someone in the kitchen had eaten the owner's lunch, and the not-so-friendly chef was the leading suspect. My heart was in my mouth, but what was I supposed to do? Italian eyes surrounded me. The owner, now mumbling something got up from his chair, removed his napkin, gave me a handshake without saying a word, and walked out of the kitchen. I was devastated. Even Franco turned on me!

So I returned to Chicago on the earliest flight I could get. Two weeks went by without a word, so I waited another week and then called about the position. When I got in touch with the owner, he was on his car phone in his Ferrari cruising the coast and I could hear the waves of the ocean. I pulled myself together and asked him the big question. ??? Dejectedly on a car phone long distance, I was told that I wasn't hired because my style of cooking was too rustic for the L.A. crowd, and bones and feet were not an appropriate dish to make for such a distinguished clientele. Ciao! Click!

The Best Chicken and Dumplings

Ingredients

¼ cup olive oil

One plump 5–6 pound fresh chicken, quartered, excess fat removed

¼ cup all-purpose flour

2 tablespoons unsalted butter, melted
6 tablespoons all-purpose flour
3 large garlic cloves, minced
1 small onion, julienne cut
2 medium carrots, julienne cut
2 medium celery stalks, julienne cut
1 leek, white and some of the green part, julienne cut
1 cup sliced domestic mushrooms
1¼ teaspoon Polish spice #1 *(see page 251)*
1 bay leaf
¼ cup dry white wine
5½ cups chicken stock
Dash of Tabasco
2 dashes of Maggi seasoning
¼ cup heavy cream (optional)

1 recipe Parsley Dumplings *(see page 94)*

Need I say more?!

Chef's Tip!

I highly recommend removing the skin from the chicken before sautéing so that your sauce and dumplings are not greasy. Also, after 45 minutes of cooking time, remove exactly ¾ cup of the cooking liquid, chill slightly in the freezer, and use to make your parsley dumplings instead of whole milk.

Preparation

1. Heat the oil in a medium pot over medium high heat.

2. Working quickly, lightly dredge half the chicken pieces into the flour, and then sauté in the hot oil for 3 to 5 minutes on each side until golden brown. Remove to a platter and do the same with the second half, then set aside.

3. When all the chicken is browned, pour off all but 2 tablespoons of excess oil from the pot, and then return the pot to the heat.

4. Again working quickly over medium heat, add the butter and 6 tablespoons of flour and cook stirring for 1 to 2 minutes until the flour has turned a light golden and smells slightly nutty.

5. Now add the garlic, onion, carrots, celery, leek, mushrooms, Polish spice and bay leaf, and cook stirring until slightly softened about 2 minutes.

6. Add the white wine, chicken stock, Tabasco, and Maggi spice and lightly stir cook until the liquid comes to a boil, and then reduce the heat, add the chicken and simmer slowly with the pot slightly covered for 1 hour.

7. After 45 minutes of simmering, start to prepare the parsley dumplings.

8. After 1 hour, remove the lid from the pot and turn the fire down to low. Pour in the heavy cream, and gently swirl it into the stew. Now very gently place the parsley dumplings one by one on top of the chicken, making sure to leave a little space between each dumpling.

9. Now cover the pot with the lid completely, and cook very slowly for another 25 minutes. Do not lift the lid until 25 minutes has passed.

Serves 4

Stuffed Cabbage

Ingredients

1 large head green cabbage
2 quarts water
1 tablespoon sea salt
2 tablespoons olive oil
3 large garlic cloves, minced
1 small onion, fine diced
½ pound 85% lean ground beef
¼ pound lean ground pork
½ cup long grain rice, pre-cooked and cooled
2 tablespoons parsley, minced
½ cup tomato sauce
1 large whole egg
1 teaspoon sea salt
⅛ teaspoon freshly ground black pepper
2 dashes Tabasco
1 dash Worcestershire sauce

1 recipe Spicy Tomato Sauce (*see page 253*)

All right for the last time, here's my personal favorite recipe for Golabki! Now don't ask me again, and don't let me catch you sneaking a can of tomato soup in there.

Chef's Tip!

Don't discard any leftover blanched cabbage leaves, just roll them up, and cook them along with the stuffed ones for a vegetarian treat.

Preparation

1. **In a large stockpot,** bring the water and salt to a rolling boil, then reduce the heat to a bubbling simmer.

2. **Working very carefully,** remove the core from the cabbage with a sharp paring knife, cutting out bit by bit in a circular motion around the core. Now insert a long handled two-prong roasting fork into the center of the cored cabbage (this will facilitate easier handling when moving the cabbage around).

3. **Immerse the cabbage** into the simmering salted water, and cook for 5 to 7 minutes until a few of the cabbage leaves start to separate from the cabbage head. Carefully with a kitchen tong, remove any of the cooked leaves to a colander to thoroughly drain, and continue the process until all the leaves are cooked. Drain and cool completely.

4. **Preheat the oven** to 350°F.

5. **Heat the oil** in a small skillet over medium heat, and add the garlic and onion and cook stirring until slightly softened and golden, about 3 to 4 minutes. Remove the vegetables to a small bowl, and place immediately into the freezer to quickly cool. After 5 minutes remove from the freezer and set aside.

6. **In a large mixing bowl,** combine all of the remaining ingredients (including the chilled vegetables) except the spicy tomato sauce.

Now gently using a heavy wooden spoon, blend the mixture thoroughly until evenly incorporated.

7. **Pick through** all the cabbage leaves, creating two piles. One for good equal sized leaves and the other for not so good leaves. Using a sharp paring knife, gently remove from the good cabbage leaves any hard leaf stems that will impair easy rolling, and then place flatly onto a clean work surface. Depending on leaf size, place 3 to 4 tablespoons of filling onto each cabbage leaf near their base. Fold the bottom of the leaf over the filling, then fold in the sides toward the center. Roll tightly into a bundle and place, seam side down into a medium sized shallow earthenware casserole. Repeat with the remaining cabbage leaves and filling, being careful to roll tightly and arranging them snugly in the casserole.

8. **Now gently ladle** the spicy tomato sauce over the cabbage rolls, and cover tightly with a piece of aluminum foil. Poke three small air holes down the center of the foil and bake for 1½ hours until cooked.

Serves 4

Zrazy ᶻ "Pepper Steak"

Ingredients

2 to 2½ pounds cubed steak, pounded
½ cup all-purpose flour
1 teaspoon dried thyme
1 teaspoon Hungarian sweet paprika
Large dash of sea salt
Large dash of freshly ground black pepper
Large dash of garlic powder
¼ cup olive oil
4 large garlic cloves, minced
1 medium onion, sliced
1 large red pepper, sliced
2 cups domestic mushrooms, sliced
1 bay leaf
1 teaspoon dried basil, marjoram, or rosemary
¼ teaspoon sea salt
⅛ teaspoon cayenne pepper
¼ cup dry red wine
1½ cups beef stock
1 cup tomato purée
1 teaspoon Worcestershire sauce
3 dashes of Maggi
3 dashes Tabasco

In its heyday, pepper steak was popular but fell out of fashion many years back. So here's some good news, I'm bringing it back big time due to the fact that meat is processed much leaner these days. Pounded steak is generously seasoned and simmered slowly with onion, peppers, mushrooms, marjoram, stock, and Worcestershire until the meat is fork tender and juicy. This is excellent with a side of Kluski noodles.

Chef's Tip!

If you can't find good cubed steak, buy a lean thin piece of beef round, loin, rib, or chuck steak and pound it out with a meat mallet yourself.

Preparation

1. **Preheat the oven** to 350°F.

2. **In a medium sized** mixing bowl, combine the flour, thyme, paprika, sea salt, pepper, and garlic powder, and reserve 1 table-spoon to thicken the sauce.

3. **Heat the oil** in a large skillet over high heat, and working in batches lightly dredge the cubed steak into the flour, and then sauté in the hot oil for 3 to 5 minutes on each side until golden brown. Remove the browned steaks to a medium sized earthenware casserole, and brown the remaining meat.

4. **When all the steaks** are browned, pour off all but 2 tablespoons of excess oil from the skillet, and then return the pan to the heat.

5. **Now add the garlic,** onion, peppers, and mushrooms, and cook stir until the vegetables are slightly softened, about 3 minutes.

6. **Add the bay leaf,** basil, and reserved tablespoon of flour, and cook for exactly 1 minute to release their oils.

7. **Now add the rest** of the ingredients to the skillet, and bring it to a boil.

8. **Pour the vegetables** and stock over the cubed steak, cover the casserole tightly, and cook in the oven for 1½ hours until the meat is fork tender.

Serves 4

Old-Fashioned Midwestern Pot on the Fire

Every ethnic group under the sun has their own version of "a boiled dinner." By the many variations of this dish I've researched, it is a very popular one-pot meal. Depending on where you live in the country, the ingredients might change slightly, but the main recipe is still the same. Feel free to add any combination of meat that suits your fancy.

Chef's Tip!

The secret to this dish is to use especially choice cuts of meat, and to use a large tall pot so that the ingredients are constantly under the water. If more water is needed, add enough just to cover the meats.

Ingredients

1 small fresh chicken about 2½ to 3 pounds, excess fat removed
2½ to 3 pounds beef brisket, chuck roast, or short ribs, excess fat removed
2 medium fresh ham hocks
1 small calves foot
4 beef marrowbones
2 teaspoons sea salt
3 quarts water, cold
6 large garlic cloves, peeled
1 small onion, peeled and studded with 3 whole cloves
2 medium onions, peeled and halved
3 medium carrots cut into 2-inch lengths
3 medium celery stalks, cut into 2-inch lengths
3 small leeks, including 3 inches of green, well washed and left whole
1 large parsnip, peeled and cut into 2-inch lengths
1 large turnip, peeled and quartered
12 small red potatoes
1 cup diced tomatoes
2 bay leaves
10 whole black peppercorns
4 large sprigs fresh thyme
1 large sprig rosemary
½ cup parsley, chopped

For Garnish: 1 recipe Whipped Horseradish Cream *(see page 252)*, coarse sea salt, freshly cracked black pepper, Polish gherkins, Polish grainy mustard, or Dijon

Preparation

1. **Rinse the chicken,** beef brisket, hocks, calves foot, and marrowbones under cold running water for 1 minute to remove any impurities. Put the chicken and marrowbones into a bowl and place in the refrigerator until needed. Now place the beef brisket, hocks, and calves foot into a very large stock pot, add the sea salt and the 3 quarts of cold water, and bring just to a simmer over high heat. (Do not let the water boil.) Reduce the heat to a slow simmer, and skim off any froth that has risen to the surface. Simmer the pot for 2 hours, skimming frequently until the meat is almost tender.

2. **Now add the rest** of the ingredients, including the reserved chicken and marrow bones taking care to push them down into the liquid, and simmer for another 1½ hours or until all the meat and vegetables are fork tender.

3. **Using a slotted** kitchen spoon, gently remove the meat and vegetables to a large serving platter and artfully arrange. (At this point, I recommend placing the platter into a preheated oven to keep warm.)

4. **Taste the broth,** and if it is weak, quickly boil over high heat to enhance the flavors, then strain through a fine mesh conical sieve into a soup tureen. Remove the platter from the oven and place in the middle of your table. Provide your guests with soup bowls and let them choose their own portion of meat and vegetables. Ladle on the hot broth and serve with the assorted garnish.

Serves 4 with leftovers

Braised Beef Short Ribs

Ingredients

2½ to 3 pounds meaty beef short ribs
¼ cup all-purpose flour
2 tablespoons olive oil
4 large garlic cloves, sliced
1 medium onion, large diced
2 large carrots, large diced
2 large celery stalks, large diced
2 cups domestic mushrooms, sliced
1 bay leaf
1 teaspoon dried thyme
1½ teaspoon dried marjoram or basil
2 tablespoons parsley, chopped
1 tablespoon all-purpose flour
¼ teaspoon sea salt
⅛ teaspoon freshly ground black pepper
Large dash of Tabasco
1 cup tomato purée
1 heaping tablespoon tomato paste
2¾ cups beef stock
½ cup dry red wine
16 small new potatoes

Man, when the digits fall in Chicago, short ribs take center stage as the popular lunchtime special at many restaurants around the city. Who can resist a bowl full of perfectly braised ribs surrounded by succulent onions, carrots, celery, and mushrooms, accompanied by steamy new red potatoes. In my opinion, the cut "short rib" produces the most flavorful braise due to the perfect ratio of fat to lean marbling.

Chef's Tip!

Short ribs with the bone still attached are an added treat, but are not necessary to this otherwise delicious stew.

Preparation

1. **Preheat the oven** to 350°F.

2. **Heat the oil** in a medium pot over medium high heat and working quickly, lightly dredge half the short ribs into the flour, and then sauté in the hot oil for 3 to 5 minutes on each side until golden brown. Remove the browned short ribs to a large earthenware casserole, and brown the remaining ribs.

3. **When all the short ribs** are browned, pour off all but 2 tablespoons of excess oil from the pot, and then return the pot to the heat.

4. **Now add the garlic,** onion, carrots, celery, and mushrooms. Cook stirring until the vegetables are slightly softened, about 3 minutes.

5. **Add the bay leaf,** thyme, marjoram, parsley, and flour, and cook for exactly 1 minute to release their oils.

6. **Now add the rest** of the ingredients to the pot except the potatoes, and bring it to a boil.

7. **Pour the vegetables** and stock over the short ribs, cover the casserole tightly, and cook in the oven for 1¾ hours. Add the potatoes to the covered casserole, and cook for another ½ hour.

Serves 4

Bigos

Hunter's stew has been a favorite national dish to the Poles for centuries, and most purists believe it should cook about that long to taste right. I say, "no way." I developed this recipe years ago and have demonstrated it for elk and moose lodges around the Midwest without a complaint yet. Get rid of your black caldron and make some Bigos today!

Chef's Tip!

If you like your Bigos on the sweet side, try adding some pitted dry prunes, diced green apples, and a dash of sugar to the simmering pot.

Ingredients

2 thick slices hickory smoked bacon, pre-blanched and diced
1 pound Polish sausage, pre-blanched and sliced
1 pound beef or pork stew meat, cubed
¼ cup all-purpose flour
3 large garlic cloves, minced
1 medium onion, diced
2 medium carrots, diced
1½ cups domestic mushrooms, sliced
4 cups green cabbage, shredded
1 pound sauerkraut, drained and rinsed twice
1 bay leaf
1 teaspoon dried basil
1 teaspoon dried marjoram
1 tablespoon sweet paprika
⅛ teaspoon caraway seeds, mortar crushed
¼ teaspoon sea salt
⅛ teaspoon freshly ground black pepper
Pinch of cayenne
Dash of Tabasco
Dash of Worcestershire sauce
2 dashes of Maggi seasoning
Dash of mushroom powder
¼ cup dry red wine
5 cups beef stock
2 tablespoons tomato paste
1 cup diced tomatoes

Preparation

1. **Preheat the oven** to 350°F.

2. **In a large pot** over medium high heat, cook the bacon until it renders its fat and turns lightly brown, not crisp. Carefully using a slotted kitchen spoon, remove the bacon to a large earthenware casserole.

3. **Now add the sliced** Polish sausage to the pot and cook stir until the sausage turns lightly brown, then using a slotted kitchen spoon, remove that to the casserole.

4. **Working quickly,** lightly dredge the cubed meat into the flour, and then sauté in the hot bacon and sausage fat for 3 to 4 minutes until golden brown. Again, using the slotted kitchen spoon, remove the meat to the casserole and discard all but 2 tablespoons of the bacon fat.

5. **Return the pot** with the bacon fat to the fire, and add the garlic, onion, carrots, mushrooms, green cabbage, and sauerkraut and cook stirring until slightly softened, about 3 to 4 minutes. Do not let the vegetables brown.

6. **Now add all** of the herb seasoning to the pot and cook for one minute more, then add the rest of the ingredients and lightly stir cook until the liquid comes to a boil.

7. **Pour the vegetables** and stock over the bacon, sausage, and meat, cover the casserole tightly and cook in the oven for 2½ to 3 hours until the meat is tender.

Serves 4

Smoked Sausage Garnished Sauerkraut

Ingredients

½ pound smoked pork butt
4 small smoked pork chops
4 Polish style veal wieners
1 pound smoked Polish sausage (kielbasa, mysliwska, or starowiejska)
12 small red potatoes
¼ cup parsley, chopped
2 thick slices hickory smoked bacon, pre-blanched and diced
4 medium cloves garlic, minced
1 medium onion, diced
1 large carrot, shredded
1 large celery stalk, shredded
½ pound green cabbage, shredded
2 pounds sauerkraut, drained and rinsed, twice
2 tablespoon all-purpose flour
1 bay leaf
2½ teaspoons Polish spice #2 *(see page 251)*
Pinch of sugar
1 tablespoon tomato paste
2 dashes Maggi seasoning
4 cups chicken stock

Chicago style Polish choucroute! This dish is the brother to pork ribs and sauerkraut, without the ribs. I've loaded this savory kraut dish up with more smoked pork products but feel free to choose whichever suits your fancy.

Chef's Tip!

Pre-blanching the sausages removes a lot of excess unwanted fat and salt from the dish.

Preparation

1. **Preheat the oven** to 350°F.

2. **In a large pot** over medium high heat, cook the bacon until it renders its fat and turns lightly brown, not crisp. Carefully using a kitchen spoon, remove all but 2 tablespoons of the bacon fat from the pot.

3. **Return the pot** with the bacon to the fire and add the garlic, onion, carrot, celery, green cabbage, and sauerkraut, and cook stirring until slightly softened, about 3 to 4 minutes. Do not let the vegetables brown.

4. **Sprinkle the flour** over the vegetables and cook for 1 minute more, then add the bay leaf, Polish spice, sugar, tomato paste, Maggi, and chicken stock and bring to the boil.

5. **Now carefully pour** all the ingredients from the pot into a large, oval earthenware casserole, cover tightly with a lid, and place in the hot oven. Cook for exactly 1 hour being sure to stir the pot every 15 minutes.

6. **While the sauerkraut** is cooking, pre-cook the potatoes in lightly salted water for about 10 to 15 minutes or until tender. When the potatoes are cooked, remove from the water and set aside. Cut the smoked sausage into 4-inch pieces, then blanch them in the potato water for 3 minutes to remove any excess fat. Discard the water and set the sausage aside.

7. **Remove the casserole** from the oven, uncover, and gently place the smoked pork butt into the middle of the sauerkraut. Now decoratively arrange the pork chops, veal wieners, cut sausage pieces, and potatoes in a circular fashion onto the remaining sauerkraut. (Lightly push the meat into the kraut so the flavors will meld together.) Recover the casserole and place it back into the oven for another 15 to 20 minutes or until the meats are hot.

8. **To serve,** spoon the sauerkraut into the center of a large platter, and arrange the sausages, potatoes, and pork chops around it. Slice the pork butt into ½-inch thick pieces and lay them on top of the arranged platter. Sprinkle with the chopped parsley and serve.

Serves 4

Pork Spare Ribs and Sauerkraut

Ingredients

2½ to 3 pounds pork spare ribs
¼ cup olive oil
2 thick slices hickory smoked bacon, pre-blanched
    and diced
4 medium cloves garlic, minced
1 medium onion, diced
1 large carrot, shredded
1 large celery stalk, shredded
½ pound domestic mushrooms, sliced
½ pound green cabbage, shredded
2 pounds sauerkraut, drained and rinsed, twice
2 tablespoon all-purpose flour
1 bay leaf
2½ teaspoons Polish spice #2 *(see page 251)*
Pinch of sugar
1 tablespoon tomato paste
2 dashes Maggi seasoning
4 cups chicken stock

Polish soul food at its best! My ma had a special, big, old, aluminum pot that she used specifically to cook this dish, which seemed to simmer away for hours. Every once in awhile, I'd sneak into the kitchen and nab a succulent rib out of the pot that would melt in your mouth.

Chef's Tip!

If the ribs at the butcher shop aren't meaty enough for your liking, try substituting boneless country pork ribletts instead.

Preparation

1. **Preheat the oven** to 350°F.

2. **Remove any excess fat** and silver skin from the underside of the spare ribs, then cut each rack into four equal pieces.

3. **Heat 2 tablespoons** of the oil in a large skillet over high heat, and working in batches to avoid overcrowding the pan, brown the spare ribs on both sides (about 3 minutes on each side). Remove the browned ribs to a large earthenware casserole, and brown the remaining ribs in the remaining olive oil.

4. **Discard the excess oil** from the skillet, add the bacon, and cook stir over medium heat until the bacon renders its fat and turns lightly brown, not crisp. Carefully, using a slotted kitchen spoon, remove the bacon to the casserole, and discard all but 2 tablespoons of the bacon fat.

5. **Return the skillet** with the bacon fat to the fire and add the garlic, onion, carrot, celery, mushrooms, green cabbage, and sauerkraut, and cook stirring until slightly softened, about 3 to 4 minutes. Do not let the vegetables brown.

6. **Sprinkle the flour** over the vegetables and cook for 1 minute more, then add the bay leaf, Polish spice, sugar, tomato paste, Maggi, and chicken stock and bring to the boil.

7. **Pour the vegetables** and stock over the bacon and spare ribs, cover the casserole tightly, and cook in the oven for 2 hours until the spare ribs are tender.

Serves 4

Tripes Warsaw Style

If you're not squeamish about tripe, you'll love my heartier and spicier version of this dish that is famous throughout Warsaw.

Chef's Tip!

Try tasting the tripe stew before adding the sweet spices at the end, as it is utterly delicious both ways.

Ingredients

2 tablespoons olive oil
1½ pounds beef short ribs

2½ to 3 pounds tripe, pre-blanched, rinsed, and cut into half inch strips
1 small smoked hock, rinsed
¼ cup olive oil
¼ cup all-purpose flour
3 large garlic cloves, minced
1 small onion, diced
2 large carrots, diced
1 large celery stalk, diced
1 leek, white and some of the green part, diced
1 small red pepper, diced
1 small green pepper, diced
¼ cup parsley, chopped
1 teaspoon sea salt
¾ teaspoon Polish spice #3 *(see page 251)*
1 bay leaf
¼ cup brandy
1 cup diced tomatoes
1 heaping tablespoon tomato paste
Dash of Tabasco
¾ teaspoon Worcestershire sauce
1½ teaspoons Maggi seasoning
8 cups beef stock
Scant ⅛ teaspoon of cloves, ginger, and nutmeg

Preparation

1. **Heat the oil** in a medium sized pot over medium high heat, and add the beef short ribs. Sauté in the hot oil until the meat is browned on all sides, about 3 to 5 minutes. Remove from the pot and pour off all the grease. Return the pot to the fire and reduce the heat to medium, then add the olive oil and flour and cook stirring for 1 to 2 minutes until the flour has turned a light golden and smells slightly nutty.

2. **Now add the garlic,** onion, celery, carrots, leeks, peppers, parsley, salt, and Polish spice, and cook stirring until slightly softened, about 2 minutes.

3. **Add the brandy** and cook for 30 seconds, then add the rest of the ingredients except the sweet spices, and lightly stir cook until the liquid comes to a boil, and then reduce the heat, and simmer slowly with the pot covered for about 1½ hours.

4. **Now add** the sweet spices to the pot, recover and cook for another 30 minutes.

Serves 4

Veal Goulash

Ingredients

2½ to 3 pounds cubed veal stew meat
¼ cup olive oil
3 large garlic cloves, minced
2 medium onions, thinly sliced
1 small red pepper, thinly sliced
1 large carrot, diced
1 large celery stalk, diced
2 cups domestic mushrooms, sliced
1 bay leaf
½ teaspoon dried thyme
½ teaspoon dried marjoram
1½ teaspoon caraway seeds, mortar crushed
2 tablespoons tomato paste
2 tablespoons Hungarian sweet paprika
2 tablespoons all-purpose flour
2 tablespoons red wine vinegar
½ cup dry white wine
3 cups beef stock
Dash of Tabasco
Dash of Worcestershire sauce
¼ teaspoon sea salt
⅛ teaspoon freshly ground black pepper

Thank God for Queen Jadwega of Poland, (a daughter of a Hungarian king), who decided that her childhood marriage wasn't suited to her lifestyle. History books tell the tale that she traveled with her personal Hungarian chef among the peasants spreading her wealth and sharing her food with those less fortunate. The Poles love for her earned her the name Saint Jadwega.

Chef's Tip!

Feel free to substitute beef or pork stew meat for the veal meat. Purists suggest that equal amounts of onions in weight equals the same amount of meat used. Also try adding a small whole red chili pod to the pot for a spicier stew.

Preparation

1. **In a large heavy pot,** heat the oil over medium high heat. Add half of the veal and sauté, stirring occasionally, until the meat is browned on all sides. Remove from the pot and repeat with the remaining veal until thoroughly browned, and then remove.

2. **Add to the pot** the garlic, onion, red pepper, carrot, celery, and mushrooms. Cook stirring until the vegetables are slightly softened, about 3 minutes.

3. **Now add the bay leaf,** thyme, marjoram, and caraway seeds and cook for exactly 1 minute to release their oils.

4. **Add the tomato paste,** paprika, and flour and cook for 30 seconds more.

5. **Now add the rest** of the ingredients to the pot and bring it to a boil, and then reduce the heat and simmer slowly covered, stirring occasionally for about 1½ to 2 hours until the veal is cooked through and extremely tender.

Serves 4

Veal Goulash

Slow Cooked Beans with Sausage, Duck, and Lamb

Ingredients

4 whole duck legs with thigh attached
2 tablespoons kosher salt
1/8 teaspoon freshly ground black pepper
1 bay leaf
6 sprigs fresh thyme
6 large garlic cloves, sliced
3 cups rendered duck fat or canola oil

1 pound dried Great Northern beans, rinsed

1 tablespoon duck fat
1/4 pound Polish-style bacon, diced
2 small smoked hocks, rinsed
1 pound smoked Polish sausage, blanched
   and sliced
1 pound lamb or pork stew meat, cubed
4 large garlic cloves, minced
1 large onion, diced
1/4 cup dry white wine
1 cup diced tomatoes
1 quart veal or beef stock
1/4 teaspoon sea salt
1/4 teaspoon freshly ground black pepper
2 bay leaves
1 dried red chili pepper
Dash of Tabasco
2 dashes of Maggi
1 tablespoon fresh thyme
1 tablespoon fresh rosemary, minced
2 tablespoons parsley, minced

Kielbasa Zapiekana Z Fasola dates back to the 1500s in Poland, where the bean was first introduced to Polish culture by an Italian princess. This dish was originally layered with all kinds of game meat, and simmered slowly in huge black caldrons with a sauce that consisted of newly acquired tomatoes, peppers, and herbs. I've stripped much of the fat out of the original recipe and formulated my own for the American palate.

Chef's Tip!

If you don't want to be bothered with the preserved duck legs, skip it. Just roast any game bird and add the diced meat to the rest of the recipe.

Preparation

1. At least 3 days before serving the dish, you have to preserve the duck legs. Place the duck legs into a large mixing bowl, and thickly season with the salt, pepper, bay leaf, thyme, and garlic cloves. Now using your hands, work the seasoning into the duck skin and meat. Cover the bowl and refrigerate for 48 hours.

2. When 2 days have passed, remove the duck legs from the bowl and gently, using your fingers only, remove as much seasoning as possible from the meat and skin.

3. Preheat the oven to 350°F.

4. Heat 4 tablespoons of rendered duck fat in a large nonstick skillet over medium high heat, then sear the duck legs on both sides until the skin is browned and crisp. Remove the browned legs to a high-sided earthenware casserole, and cover with the duck fat. Cover the casserole, place in the preheated oven, and cook for 2 to 3 hours until the meat is very tender. At this point, remove the casserole from the oven and very carefully, using a kitchen skimmer, lift the duck legs out of the pot and place on a platter to cool. When cool, place into a medium sized mixing bowl and cover with all of the reserved cooking fat. Cover the bowl tightly with plastic wrap and refrigerate for up to one week. (In European cooking terms, this technique is called confit. If stored properly, the meat will stay fresh for up to 1 year.)

5. The night before cooking this dish, you have to prepare the beans. Soak the rinsed beans for at least 2 hours in 1 quart of cold water. Drain and rinse twice, then cook in a pressure cooker for 10 to 12 minutes total, or cook in boiling salted water for exactly 40 minutes, then drain and rinse once more. Cover the beans with plastic wrap and refrigerate overnight.

6. The next day preheat the oven to 350°F. Remove the preserved duck from the refrigerator, and very gently using your fingers, remove the duck pieces from the chilled rendered fat being careful to scrape off as much excess as possible. Place the duck legs onto a small baking pan, then place the pan in the preheated oven for 15 minutes to warm through.

7. Heat 1 tablespoon of the preserved duck fat in a large heavy skillet over medium high heat, then add the bacon, and cook stir until the bacon renders its fat and turns lightly brown, not crisp. Carefully, using a slotted kitchen spoon, remove the bacon to a large earthenware casserole.

8. Return the skillet with the bacon fat to the fire, and add the Polish sausage, then cook stir for 2 minutes until the sausage renders its fat and turns lightly brown. Again, using a slotted kitchen spoon, remove the sausage to the casserole, then return the pan to the fire, and brown off the lamb or pork meat in the same fashion. While the meat is browning, add to the casserole the smoked hocks, heated duck legs, and the cooked beans, and gently distribute evenly.

9. Now discard all but 2 tablespoons of the remaining fat in the skillet, and sauté the garlic and onions for 2 to 3 minutes until slightly softened. Add the rest of the ingredients, and bring to a boil. Carefully pour the hot liquid into the casserole to cover the beans and meat, cover the casserole, then grasp the handles and give the pot a good swirl so the liquid is evenly distributed. Place the casserole in the oven, and cook slowly for 2 to 3 hours until the beans and meat are tender. (Be sure to swirl the casserole every half hour.)

Serves 4

fish

slow grilled salmon with pesto

father joe's comin' for dinner friday night salmon patties

grilled tuna and red pepper salad nicoise

crisp halibut in horseradish and fresh herbed crust

grandpa john gronek's smelts with spicy cocktail sauce

pan fried lake perch with tartare sauce

grilled lobster and fillet with herbed garlic butter

baked cod with tomato, zucchini, and peppers

northern pike "po polsku" style

seafood and kielbasa gumbo

What a thrill it must have been to live in Medieval Poland or Russia around the year 600 A.D. to have watched hundreds of men pull to shore gargantuan sturgeon that were hooked a few hundred yards offshore. History books recant the words "monsters of the sea," but cool, clean, and pristine waters have always been a haven for great fish. Feuding overlords kept the Poles from the Baltic for years, but to no dismay because fresh water and well-stocked streams provided ample varieties of tench, perch, carp, walleye, and pike. Herring, flounder, and cod were always available, but usually were heavily salted, pickled, or dried for preservation and transportation reasons. The monotony of the salted and dried food was enough to push any Pole to grab their fishing rig and head to the streams for a fresh catch.

Polish cookbooks have always portrayed the preparation of fish as an elegant or complex aspic coated delicacy that has never had a broad culinary appeal. As a classically trained chef, I've made dishes similar to this but have abandoned the practice some 20 odd years ago (too French, too European, too ostentatious) for Polish cooking. The famed Christmas Wigilia (or Christmas Eve) dinner features no less than 12 different fish preparations and is well known throughout the culinary world as a treasured and beloved ritual, but it is sad to say that even some of these preparations have come under scrutiny and should be revised.

Most Midwestern anglers that I know are more concerned with the freshness of the catch than they are with the complexity of the preparation. Depending on where you live on the great lakes, cooking styles vary. Fish cakes are popular in Minnesota, whereas Michigan is known for its fish boils, Wisconsin prefers to bread and fry, and the rest of the Midwest like to broil their catch. The people in these regions know their fish and I would be foolish to try and impress them.

Throughout my career, I've filleted a lot of fish, and have made a lot of trendy sauces to go with them, but most chefs agree that the simplest preparations are the ones that sell the best. A simple grill, quick pan sauté or broil with a sprinkling of seasoning, fresh herbs, a dash of white wine and lemon juice is all that is needed to enhance the flavor of a fresh catch. I know of a great Greek chef in New York City who has abandoned all of his complex fish presentations completely. His menu currently features 3 to 4 exceedingly fresh fish fillets that can be simply prepared in 3 to 4 different ways with 3 to 4 similar sauces. His business is very successful because he listened to his clientele and gave them what they wanted.

As I've stated throughout this book, I have to stay with my midwestern roots, because I feel it is a comfortable starting point for a series of cookbooks on the art of Polish cooking. The recipes that I have included in this chapter are most typical of what you would find in my neck of the woods and by no means represent the full gamut of fish cooking in general. I think that any non-fish eater would enjoy my **Grilled Salmon** with pesto because the fish isn't too gamy, whereas the true midwestern angler would delight in the taste of the **Pan Fried Perch** or **Grandpa John's Smelts**. Lately my kids have become connoisseurs of **Salmon Patties** and dinner guests have been requesting my recipe for **Baked Cod with Tomato, Zucchini, and Peppers**. For the more adventurous and health conscious fish eaters, I've included a few newer preparations such as **Tuna Salad Nicoise** and and **Seafood and Smoked Kielbasa Gumbo**.

People always ask me what's the best way to purchase fresh fish so here is the advice that I give: 1. Choose a market where you can actually examine the fish, and ideally you should only purchase fresh seafood on the day you plan to prepare it. 2. Smell the fish. It should have a fresh, clean aroma, without a fishy or ammonia like fragrance to the flesh. 3. Look at the eyes. They should be slightly bulging and crystal clear. Certain varieties of perch and pike have cloudy eyes so don't worry. 4. Feel the flesh. It should be slick and moist with firmly attached scales. Fins and tails should be soft and flexible, not brittle. Gills should also be moist with a good reddish color.

Slow Grilled Salmon with Pesto

Ingredients

2½ to 3 pounds center cut salmon, skin on
  and cleaned
4 tablespoons olive oil
½ teaspoon sea salt
¼ teaspoon freshly ground black pepper
½ cup pesto
1 large lemon, halved

The next time you go camping, and you just don't know what to do with the big one Pa caught, lather on the pesto and cook it real slow over a burning fire. The basil and the olive oil perfume the pink flesh beautifully, and I guarantee you will convert a few non-fish eaters!

Chef's Tip!

Stuck out in the woods with your pyromaniacal husband and no grill? Check this out. Gut and clean a whole salmon, lather on the pesto, and stuff the fish with a few red potatoes, carrots, or corn chunks, then lay on top of a big piece of aluminum foil and wrap it up tightly. Now throw the whole package onto the fire, and tell him in a half an hour that dinner is served! (What, no pesto? Stuff the fish with fresh pine needles, no joke!)

Preparation

1. **Place the salmon** onto a clean work surface, and using a sharp chef's knife, slit the skin, about ¼-inch deep. Make the cuts every inch on both sides of the fish. Rub the olive oil, salt, and pepper into the slits, then carefully work the pesto into the slits with your index finger. Put the fish into a Ziploc bag, sprinkle on the lemon juice, and refrigerate for at least 6 hours before grilling.

2. **Preheat the grill** to medium, then place the salmon into a grilling basket or directly onto the fire, and cook for 8 to 10 minutes on each side until the fish is cooked.

Serves 4

Pesto

Ingredients

2 cups fresh basil leaves
¼ cup fresh Italian parsley, stems removed
2 medium garlic cloves, peeled
¼ cup pine nuts or walnuts, lightly toasted
½ cup extra virgin olive oil
¼ teaspoon sea salt
¼ cup grated Parmigiano-Reggiano cheese

Preparation

1. **Place the basil,** parsley, garlic, and nuts into the work bowl of a food processor fitted with a metal blade, attach the lid, and pulse 5 to 6 times. Remove the lid, and scrape down the sides with a plastic spatula, then pulse again. Now with the machine running, add the rest of the ingredients in a slow steady stream until the pesto is smooth. Carefully remove to a clean glass mason jar and store in the refrigerator.

Makes about 1 cup

Father Joe's Comin' for Dinner
Friday Night Salmon Patties

Ingredients

1 pound boneless and skinless fresh salmon fillet
1 cup water
¼ cup dry white wine
Dash of lemon juice
Dash of sea salt
2 whole large eggs
2 tablespoons mayonnaise
1 teaspoon dry mustard
1 teaspoon Seafood Seasoning Spice *(see page 251)*
2 teaspoons Worcestershire sauce
2 teaspoons lemon juice
Large dash of Tabasco
2 tablespoons parsley or chives, minced
1 cups fresh breadcrumbs
4 tablespoons olive oil
2 tablespoons unsalted butter, melted

1 recipe Beet Horseradish Dressing

Every Polish kid dreads Friday night's mandatory fish dinner, because every Catholic knows that fish sticks don't count. When I was younger, I couldn't stand canned salmon because of the bones, but now that fresh salmon is readily available and economical, this is a great dish. Also, think about the fun you'll have yelling at your kids to "Be quiet and eat your patties and macaroni and cheese! Sorry, Father!"

Chef's Tip!

If you're having a cocktail party, try substituting fresh lump crabmeat for the salmon, or even a combination of the both is great! Just roll the patties into smaller sized portions, and top with a dollop of caviar and fresh horseradish.

Preparation

1. **Place the salmon** into a small saucepan with the water, white wine, lemon juice, and salt, and bring to a quick boil, then reduce to a slow simmer and cook for exactly 3 minutes. Remove the pan from the fire and let the salmon cool in the liquid for about 20 minutes, then carefully remove to a serving platter.

2. **In a large mixing** bowl, combine the eggs, mayonnaise, mustard, seafood spice, Worcestershire, lemon juice, Tabasco, and parsley, and using a heavy duty wooden spoon, combine the ingredients until well mixed.

3. **Now gently** using your hands, pick up the salmon piece and crumble it into the mixing bowl. Lightly stir with the wooden spoon until well combined, then pour on the fresh breadcrumbs.

4. **Again using** your hands, combine all the ingredients in the bowl until thoroughly blended, then carefully shape the mixture into 16 golf ball-size patties. Lightly flatten and then place onto a clean platter.

5. **Heat the olive oil** and melted butter in a large nonstick skillet over medium low heat, and add the patties one by one shaking the skillet often. Sauté for about 3 to 4 minutes on one side until lightly browned, then using a spatula, flip the patties over, cover the pan, and brown on the other side for 2 to 3 minutes. Remove the patties

to a serving platter and serve with the homemade beet horseradish dressing.

Serves 4

Beet Horseradish Dressing

Ingredients

1 cup mayonnaise, full fat
1½ to 2 tablespoons beet horseradish
2 teaspoons Dijon mustard
⅛ teaspoon celery salt
¼ teaspoon garlic powder
⅛ teaspoon freshly ground black pepper
Large dash of Worcestershire sauce
Large dash of Tabasco

Preparation

1. **At least 2 hours** before serving the dressing, place all the ingredients into a medium sized mixing bowl, and combine with a plastic spatula until well blended. Cover and refrigerate.

Makes about 1 cup

Grilled Tuna and Red Pepper Salad Nicoise

Poles I know have always been fond of fresh fish, so I've included this easy and refreshing salad that I've made through the years. Fresh tuna and red pepper are skewered, then lightly grilled to perfection, and adorned on a refreshing salad of assorted greens, eggs, potatoes, beans, and tomatoes then bathed in light vinaigrette.

Fancy Vinaigrette

Ingredients

3½ tablespoons red wine vinegar
2 teaspoons Dijon mustard
2 large garlic cloves, minced
Large dash sea salt
¼ teaspoon fresh ground black pepper
¾ cup extra virgin olive oil

Preparation

1. **In a small bowl or jar,** mix the vinegar, Dijon, garlic, salt and pepper until well combined. Now add the olive oil and mix with a small whisk until well blended and smooth. Store in a small jar until needed.

Makes about 1 cup

Ingredients

One 12-ounce fresh tuna steak, cut into
    1-inch cubed pieces
1 medium red pepper, cleaned, seeded,
    and cubed into 1-inch pieces
½ cup olive oil
¼ cup fresh lemon juice
2 large garlic cloves, minced
Dash of sea salt
Dash of freshly ground black pepper

4 large whole eggs
8 small Yukon gold potatoes, cleaned
¼ pound small string beans, ends trimmed
4 cups assorted field greens, washed and
    dried such as romaine, endive, radicchio,
    arugula, frisee, or watercress
16 red tear drop tomatoes, washed
16 Kalamata black olives
1 small red onion, thinly sliced
One 8 ounce jar artichoke hearts, well
    drained and quartered

1 recipe Fancy Vinaigrette

Preparation

1. **Carefully using four** 8-inch long wood skewers, skewer 4 to 5 pieces of tuna, alternating with 4 to 5 pieces of red pepper, or until it's all used up. Place the skewers side by side into a small earthenware casserole that will accommodate them snugly, then combine the olive oil, lemon juice, garlic, salt and pepper, and pour over the skewers. Tightly cover the casserole with plastic wrap and refrigerate for 4 to 6 hours.

2. **In a small saucepan,** cover the eggs with cold water, bring the water to a steady simmer, and cook the eggs for exactly 4 minutes. Turn the heat off and let the eggs cook for exactly another 4 minutes in the hot water. Now take the pan to the sink and let cool water run over the eggs until they are completely cold to the touch. Peel and clean the eggs.

3. **In another small saucepan,** cover the potatoes with cold water, bring the water to a steady simmer, and cook the potatoes for 12 minutes until tender. Fill a large bowl with ice cubes and cold water. Using a slotted kitchen spoon, carefully remove the potatoes

to the ice water to cool. Now cook the string beans in the potato water for 3 minutes, and then also remove to the ice water to chill. When the potatoes and string beans are cooled, remove to a paper towel lined plate and thoroughly dry.

4. **Go outside** and pre-heat your grill to medium high.

5. **When you are ready** to serve dinner, quarter the eggs and the potatoes. Place the assorted greens into a large mixing bowl and lightly bathe with some of the vinaigrette. Gently toss, and using a kitchen tong divide the salad equally among 4 dinner plates. Decoratively arrange around the salads, the quartered eggs, potatoes, string beans, tomatoes, black olives, onions, and artichoke hearts.

6. **Carefully grill** the skewered tuna and peppers on the hot grill for 2 to 3 minutes on each side, then place the skewers on top of the arranged salads, drizzle on more vinaigrette, and serve.

Serves 4

Crisp Halibut in Horseradish and Fresh Herbed Crust

Ingredients

Four 6 ounce halibut or snapper fillets
½ cup all-purpose flour
1 whole large egg
½ cup whole milk
1 cup fresh breadcrumbs
¼ cup freshly grated horseradish
1 heaping tablespoon finely minced fresh herbs
¼ cup vegetable oil

1 recipe Herbed Oil, optional

If you're from the Midwest, chances are that broiled halibut or snapper is more than likely on your favorite local restaurant menu. Both of these species of fish tend to be lean and pleasant tasting enough to impress any non-fish eater. As always, make sure that the crust is cooked crunchy, and that the fish is served immediately when it comes out of the oven.

Chef's Tip!

One heaping tablespoon of freshly grated orange rind can be added to the breadcrumb coating.

Preparation

1. **Preheat the oven** to 375°. Lay the clean fillets on a kitchen platter and lightly season with a little salt and pepper. Place the flour into a medium sized mixing bowl, then beat the eggs and milk, and place them into another medium sized mixing bowl. Now combine the fresh breadcrumbs, horseradish, and herbs into another medium sized mixing bowl and set aside.

2. **Heat the oil** in a large non-stick skillet over medium high heat, and when hot, dredge the fillets quickly into the flour then egg wash then breadcrumbs making sure that they are evenly coated.

3. **Carefully lay** the coated fillets into the hot oil, and sauté for 1 to 2 minutes until the crust is lightly browned Using a kitchen tong, flip the fillets over and place the pan into the preheated oven for 5 to 7 minutes to cook.

4. **When the fillets** are nicely browned and firm to the touch, gently remove to serving plates, drizzle the fresh herb oil around them, and serve.

Serves 4

Herbed Oil

Ingredients

6 tablespoons assorted fresh herbs, chopped, such as:
   rosemary, chives, sage, basil, or thyme
1½ cups olive oil
Sea salt
Freshly ground black pepper

Preparation

1. **Place all the ingredients** into a Ball mason jar, seal tightly, give a few shakes, and put into the warm sun for 1 hour so that the herbs release their fragrant oils.

Makes about 1½ cups

Grandpa John Gronek's Smelts with Spicy Cocktail Sauce

My Grandpa John Gronek, originally from Wausau, Wisconsin, used to own a company called "Land Em," one of the biggest manufacturers of the smelt net many years ago. Through the years, he taught me the fine art of smeltin, and we used to take our catch to a small fish house up on Montrose Ave. The Polish owner there used to quickly dredge the clean smelts into his famous batter and then fry those babies up just perfectly. Spicy cocktail sauce, French fries, and a cold beer was all that was needed to complete this truly simple dish.

Chef's Tip!

Smelts not to your liking? Try using "fresh only" and thoroughly dried clams, squid rings, shelled shrimps, or even scallops. I like to add in a couple of onion rings to boot!

Ingredients

2 to 2½ pounds fresh smelts, cleaned
2 teaspoons Seafood Seasoning Spice
   (see page 251)
2 whole large eggs
1 cup whole milk
1 cup all-purpose flour
2 tablespoons yellow cornmeal
1½ tablespoons cornstarch
1 tablespoon Seafood Seasoning Spice
   (see page 251)
1 quart canola oil or vegetable shortening
   for frying

Spicy Cocktail Sauce

1 cup ketchup
3 tablespoons prepared horseradish
2 large garlic cloves, minced
2 tablespoons parsley, minced
¾ teaspoon sea salt
¼ teaspoon freshly ground black pepper
2 tablespoons lemon juice
2 teaspoons Worcestershire sauce
½ teaspoon Tabasco
Large dash of celery salt
Large dash of garlic powder

Preparation

1. **At least 2 hours** before cooking the smelts, prepare the spicy cocktail sauce by placing all the ingredients into a medium sized mixing bowl, and combine with a whisk until well blended. Cover and refrigerate.

2. **Now grab your** smelt rig and go catch some smelts.

3. **To prepare the smelts,** spread a few layers of newspaper onto a work surface by the sink. Gently grasp the smelt in your hand, and using your thumb, tilt the head back until it comes off, then using your index finger, swipe out the stomach sac. Do this to all the fish, and then run them under cool running water for 1 minute to remove any impurities. Using a paper towel, remove any excess moisture from the fish, then place into a large mixing bowl. Season the smelts with 2 teaspoons of seafood seasoning, and using your hands, toss gently so the seasoning evenly coats the fish. Let the fish rest for 15 minutes.

4. **In another small bowl,** beat the eggs with the milk until frothy and then set aside. In another large mixing bowl, combine the flour,

cornmeal, cornstarch, and seafood seasoning until well mixed. Now place all 3 of the bowls on the counter next to your stove.

5. **Heat the oil** in a deep fat fryer or a medium sized heavy-duty soup pot until the temperature reaches 375°F. (I highly recommend using a frying thermometer to gage the temperature. It is imperative that the temperature remains in the 375°F range for proper cooking.)

6. **Pour the milk** egg mixture over the smelts and swirl the bowl until the smelts are evenly coated. Now working quickly, grasp a smelt by its tail and dredge into the flour mixture making sure it is evenly and thickly coated, then gently lower it into the hot oil. (I highly recommend working in batches, 7 to 8 pieces at a time, so that the oil temperature does not dip below 375°F.) Cook the smelts for about 2 to 3 minutes until the coating forms a deep brown color and they float to the top. It's a good idea to remove one and test it before removing all of them from the fryer.

7. **When the fish is cooked,** carefully remove it with a skimmer to a paper-lined basket, and serve with the cocktail sauce. Repeat with the remaining smelts

Serves 4

Pan-Fried Lake Perch with Tartare Sauce

Ingredients

2 to 2½ pounds fresh perch fillets, cleaned
2 teaspoons Seafood Seasoning Spice *(see page 251)*
2 whole large eggs
1 cup whole milk
1 cup all-purpose flour
1½ cups fresh breadcrumbs
1 tablespoon seafood seasoning spice
1 quart canola oil or vegetable shortening for frying

Tartare Sauce

¾ cup mayonnaise, full fat
1 tablespoon Dijon mustard
2 tablespoons green onion, minced
2 tablespoons Polish dill pickle, minced
2 tablespoons capers, minced
2 tablespoons parsley, minced
1 tablespoon lemon juice
⅛ teaspoon sea salt
¼ teaspoon freshly ground black pepper
2 dashes Worcestershire sauce
2 dashes of Tabasco
Dash of celery salt
Dash of garlic powder
2 hard boiled eggs, diced, optional

"**Y**a Hey Der," to all my Great Lakes fishing buddies. Sometimes in life it's best to leave well enough alone and this is one of those recipes. Fresh caught perch lightly breaded and fried until crisp and hot is the way to go! The savory and chunky tartare sauce is the perfect foil, so knock back a few cold ones and tell Ma about the big one that got away.

Chef's Tip!

If you don't have any yellow perch fillets handy, try using cod or tilapia fillets. Also, another cool trick is to replace the breadcrumbs with dried potato flakes.

Preparation

1. **At least 2 hours** before cooking the perch, prepare the tartare sauce by placing all the ingredients into a medium sized mixing bowl, and combine with a plastic spatula until well blended. Cover and refrigerate.

2. **Now grab your fishing pole** and go catch some perch.

3. **To prepare the perch,** spread a few layers of newspaper onto a work surface by the sink. Gently grasp the perch by the tail, and using a sharp boning knife, remove the fillets. Do this to all the fish, and then quickly run the fillets under cool running water to remove any impurities. Using a paper towel, remove any excess moisture from the fish, then place into a large mixing bowl. Season the fillets with 2 teaspoons of seafood seasoning, and using your hands, toss gently so the seasoning evenly coats the fish. Let the fish rest for 15 minutes.

4. **In another small bowl,** beat the eggs with the milk until frothy and then set aside. Place the flour into a medium sized mixing bowl, and then in another large mixing bowl, combine the fresh breadcrumbs with the remaining seafood seasoning until well mixed. Now place all 4 of the bowls on the counter next to your stove.

5. **Heat the oil** in a deep fat fryer or a medium sized heavy-duty soup pot until the temperature reaches 375°F. (I highly recommend using a frying thermometer to gauge the temperature. It is imperative that the temperature remains in the 375°F range for proper cooking.)

6. **Combine the seasoned** fillets with the flour and toss until well coated. Grasping a floured fillet by it's tail, carefully dip it into the egg wash, and then working quickly, dredge it into the breadcrumbs making sure that it is evenly and thickly coated. Now gently lower it into the hot oil. (I highly recommend working in batches, 4 to 5 pieces at a time, so that the oil temperature does not dip below 375°F.) Cook the perch for about 3 to 4 minutes until the coating forms a deep brown color and they float to the top. It's a good idea to remove one and test it before removing all of them from the fryer.

7. **When the fish is cooked,** carefully remove it with a skimmer to a paper-lined basket, and serve with the tartare sauce. Repeat with the remaining fillets.

Serves 4

Pan-Fries Lake Perch
with Tartare Sauce

Grilled Lobster and Fillet with Herbed Garlic Butter

Ingredients

Four 1½-pound lobsters
Four small fillet steaks, 4 to 6 ounces each

Herbed Garlic Butter

½ small head garlic cloves, peeled
1 tablespoon dry white wine
1 teaspoon brandy
1 teaspoon lemon juice
1 teaspoon sea salt
⅛ teaspoon freshly ground white pepper
Pinch of nutmeg
Pinch of cayenne
Dash of Tabasco
½ cup parsley, chopped
1 pound unsalted butter, chilled

All right, this is my interpretation of the classic surf and turf, but more upscale. Boiling a lobster actually renders the meat tasteless, but grilling imparts a wonderful and intense flavor. You can omit the steak if you'd like, and try substituting some slow grilled vegetables such as, asparagus, baby leeks, zucchini, or summer corn.

Chef's Tip!

If lobsters are too expensive, try using whole jumbo shrimps in the shell. Just flip them over a few times while grilling until the shells turn a deep reddish color.

Preparation

1. **Light the fire** on your grill and let the embers burn down to a medium heat.

2. **Place all of the** ingredients for the herbed butter into the work bowl of a food processor, attach the lid, then pulse 4 to 5 times. Remove the cover, scrape down the sides of the bowl with a plastic spatula, recover, and pulse again until the mixture is smooth. Remove the butter to a small bowl and set aside.

3. **Using a sharp** chef's knife, cut the lobsters in half lengthwise through the center of the head and tail, and remove the grainy stomach sac and the pinkish coral. Very carefully, using the back of the kitchen knife, crack the claws on the side facing up. Lightly brush the shell and tail meat with olive oil, then season with a little salt and pepper, and place the lobsters on a serving platter. (If using fillets, season in the same fashion.)

4. **Place about half** of the garlic butter into a small saucepan, and warm over low heat just until melted. (Do not burn the butter.)

5. **Clean the grill** grate with a wire brush, then place fillets onto the grate. Liberally brush the meat with the melted garlic butter, then cover the grill, and cook for 3 to 4 minutes. Remove the cover, flip the fillets over, and then place the lobsters, shell side down onto to the grate surrounding the fillets. Liberally brush the claw, body, and tail meat with the melted garlic butter, then recover the grill, and cook the lobsters and fillets for about 5 minutes more, or until the lobster meat is firm and white. When the lobsters and fillets are cooked, re-brush with the melted butter, then remove to a platter to serve. Pass around the remaining melted butter.

Serves 4

Baked Cod with Tomato, Zucchini, and Peppers

If you are looking for a healthy alternative to cooking fish, this is a great and easy recipe to prepare. Fresh cod is simmered slowly in a slightly spicy Mediterranean style sauce. A great dish for a casual dinner party.

Chef's Tip!

Be sure to use only exceedingly fresh fish fillets for this dish. I do not recommend using any of the oily fish specimens as they have a tendency to give the sauce a fishy taste.

Ingredients

Four 6 ounce fillets of cod or halibut, deboned
¼ cup all-purpose flour
2 tablespoons olive oil
1 large zucchini, sliced

Spicy Tomato Sauce

2 tablespoons olive oil
2 large garlic cloves, minced
1 medium onion, sliced
1 medium red or green pepper, sliced
¾ teaspoon dried thyme
1 bay leaf
3 tablespoons tomato paste
1½ cups tomato sauce
1½ cups beef or chicken stock
¼ cup dry white wine
Dash of cayenne pepper
Dash of Tabasco
Dash of Worcestershire sauce
¼ teaspoon sea salt
Freshly ground black pepper

Preparation

1. **Preheat the oven** to 375°F.

2. **To make the sauce,** heat the oil in a medium pot over medium heat, add the garlic, onion, and peppers and cook, stirring until softened, about 3 minutes. Do not let the vegetables brown.

3. **Now add** the bay leaf and thyme and cook for exactly 1 minute to release their oils.

4. **Add the rest** of the ingredients to the pot and bring it to a boil, and then reduce the heat and simmer slowly for about 20 minutes.

5. **While the sauce** is simmering, place a medium sized skillet over medium heat; add the olive oil and when hot, quickly dredge the cod fillets into the flour, and then sauté in the hot oil for 1 to 2 minutes on each side until lightly browned. Remove the fillets to a shallow earthenware casserole.

6. **Now add the sliced** zucchini to the skillet, and stir cook for about 1 to 2 minutes, then pour over and around the cod fillets.

7. **Gently ladle** about half of the sauce over the cod and zucchini, and bake, uncovered for about 20 minutes.

Serves 4

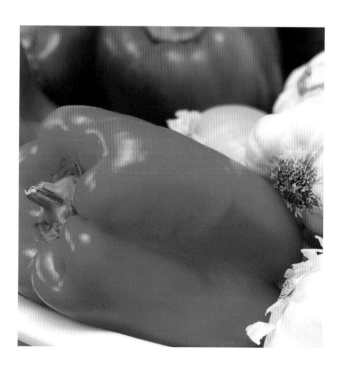

Northern Pike "Po Polsku" Style

Ingredients

1 whole cleaned and dressed Northern pike
(about 2½ to 3 pounds)
2 tablespoons olive oil
2 slices bacon, finely diced
2 large garlic cloves, minced
½ pound chanterelle mushrooms, sliced
1 medium carrot, cut julienne
1 large celery stalk, cut julienne
1 medium leek, white part only, cut julienne
1 pound red potatoes, peeled then sliced
¼-inch thick
¼ teaspoon sea salt
⅛ teaspoon freshly ground black pepper
2½ cups chicken stock

Topping

¼ cup breadcrumbs
2 tablespoons unsalted butter
2 hard boiled eggs, minced
Dash of lemon juice
1 tablespoon chopped parsley and dill

Here is a beautiful and fairly simple autumn dish that pays tribute to my early training in French kitchens! This classic combination of vegetables, potatoes, stock, and fish is as timeless as it is flawless. This dish can be found in most classical cookbooks under the heading "slow braise," and it really pays tribute to the old Polish style of "haute cuisine."

Chef's Tip!

You can substitute any other white fish fillets for this dish and feel free to use any mushroom that you like. Also, 1 or 2 tablespoons of butter and a splash of white wine really kick this dish up a notch!

Preparation

1. **Preheat the oven** to 375°. In a medium sized skillet, heat the olive oil over medium heat, add the minced bacon, and cook until it renders its fat and turns lightly brown. Now add the garlic, mushrooms, and julienne vegetables, and sauté for exactly 2 minutes then remove from the fire.

2. **Layer the bottom** of a medium sized oval earthenware casserole with the cut potato slices, then place the pike on top of them. (The casserole should just be big enough to accommodate the length of the fish.) Season the potatoes and fish with the salt and pepper, then cover the potatoes all around with the sautéed vegetable mixture. Now pour on the chicken stock, cover the casserole tightly with aluminum foil, and bake in the hot oven for 30 to 40 minutes or until the potatoes are tender and have absorbed the stock.

3. **While the fish** is baking, heat the butter in a small skillet until melted, then add the rest of the topping ingredients and sauté for 1 minute.

4. **After 30 minutes,** remove the foil and check the potatoes, and if cooked, remove the entire casserole to the dinner table, sprinkle on the topping and serve.

Serves 4

Seafood and Kielbasa Gumbo

When I was an apprentice cook, I worked under a great Creole French chef at Lake Point Tower Club in Chicago, where I learned the art of fine Creole cooking. Gumbos have always been one of my favorite dishes because of the variety of the ingredients used, and for the way the spices meld together to create a pure taste sensation. Poles have always had a spicy side to their cooking so I've included this dish for your enjoyment.

Chef's Tip!

The trick to a really great gumbo is to use exceedingly fresh seafood, a well-seasoned stock, and a slightly heavy hand on the spices. ½ pound of sliced okra can be added to the simmering gumbo, and I usually serve the gumbo over some white rice.

Creole Spice

Ingredients

1 tablespoon sea salt
1 tablespoon onion powder
1 tablespoon garlic powder
1½ teaspoons oregano
1½ teaspoons basil

1 teaspoon thyme
1½ teaspoons black pepper
1 teaspoon cayenne
1½ teaspoons paprika

Preparation

1. **Place all of the ingredients** in a small mixing bowl, and stir with a fork to combine. Store in a small glass jar.

Makes about ¼ cup

Ingredients

2½ pounds skinless chicken thighs
1 to 2 teaspoons Creole Spice
3 tablespoons olive oil

1 pound smoked kielbasa, pre-blanched and
    sliced ½-inch thick

⅓ cup olive oil
⅓ cup all-purpose flour
4 large garlic cloves, minced
1 medium onion, diced
2 large celery stalks, diced
1 medium red pepper, diced
1 medium green pepper, diced
¼ cup parsley, chopped
½ teaspoon dried oregano
½ teaspoon dried basil
2 small bay leaves
¼ teaspoon freshly ground black pepper
2 pinches cayenne
7 cups chicken stock
2 dashes Tabasco
2 dashes Maggi
1 cup diced tomatoes with juice
1 tablespoon tomato paste

1 pound small shrimp, peeled and de-veined
1 pound small blue crab claws, cleaned
½ pound crayfish tail meat, cleaned
8 shucked oysters, optional
½ teaspoon gumbo filé powder

Preparation

1. **Liberally sprinkle** the seafood seasoning onto the chicken thighs, and let them rest for ½ hour.

2. **Heat the olive oil** in a medium sized heavy-duty pot over medium high heat and add the seasoned chicken. Sauté in the hot oil until the meat is browned on all sides, about 3 to 5 minutes. Remove from the pot to a serving platter, add the sliced kielbasa to the pot, and lightly brown that for 3 to 4 minutes. Remove from the pot, and pour off all of the grease. Return the pot to the fire, reduce the heat to medium, then add the olive oil and flour, and cook stirring for 3 to 5 minutes until the flour has turned a dark golden and smells slightly nutty.

3. **Now add the garlic,** onion, celery, peppers, parsley, and dried spices, and cook stirring until slightly softened, about 2 minutes. Add the chicken stock, Tabasco, Maggi, tomatoes, and tomato paste, and lightly stir cook until the liquid comes to a boil, then reduce the heat, add the chicken and sausage, and simmer slowly for about 1 hour and 15 minutes.

4. **After that time,** add the shrimps and crabs and let them cook in the gumbo for 3 to 4 minutes, then add the crayfish meat, oysters, and gumbo filé, stir the pot, and then immediately remove it from the fire. Re-season the gumbo if necessary and serve.

Serves 4

*m*eat, poultry, and game

grilled butt steak with black peppercorns and cognac

beef tips with wild mushrooms and pickles

perfect veal schnitzel

veal with lemon and capers

honey mustard pork shoulder with caraway potatoes

ma's sunday dinner ham

grilled pork chops with mustard and pickles

chef walter's apricot stuffed pork loin

"don't kiss me tonight" garlic chicken

diabelski red chicken

chicken and potatoes greek style

orange duck

roast pheasant salad with apple, honey, and rosemary sauce

minnie's holiday turkey with sage stuffing

ursula's christmas goose

If you're in Chicago and want to see a truly beautiful sight, visit any sausage or meat shop on a Saturday morning and watch some power meat shoppers go to town. Everyone knows Chicago for being a meat eaters and purveyors goldmine, but it's the true neighborhood butcher that makes the reputation of the City. There are small storefronts with their black and white tiled floors, meat cases lined with fanciful prime cuts, and the ominous scale awaiting your order. These generations of butchers love to show off rows of beef, pork, veal, offal, fowl, and game, which are artfully arranged and masterfully cut.

The medieval ages were lean times for the Poles—meat consumption was left for the aristocratic set whereas the peasants usually had to poach what they could off the land with the constant fear of being caught by the feudal lords. At that time, pork was plentiful for sausage making or other charcuterie, but prime cuts and joints of meat were really prized for special occasions only. It is worthy to note that salt, pepper, juniper, and sweet spices were used heavily around this time for curing and preserving.

It would be difficult to jump through history and say that Poles just out of the blue started eating prime steaks and chops. Their cooking evolution is based more on a traditional rustic peasant style of home cooking, but the new world has brought them new hope, new found wealth, and an appetite for quality carnivorous food products. When I was researching this book, I kept hearing the same complaint over and over again about how much meat has influenced the art of Polish cuisine, and how can we avoid that heavier side of the food? This is a good question. To put it simply, Poles rejected the new found vegetables that were being introduced by their Italian queen at the time. Historically, people in all Eastern European countries had three sides to their meat consumption: 1. Charcuterie and sausage making. 2. The slow pot cooking method. 3. The more recent refinement of a quick sauté or a grill. Since there was no modern refrigeration, the art of charcuterie and sausage making was the most prevalent as a way of preserving the meats. Conventional cooking utensils weren't available until the 17th century; so stewed dishes were the second most popular method of preparing meats. Subsequent invasions of Poland brought a cooking refinement and the ability to quick sauté and grill. I would be hard pressed to have written a book about vegetarian Polish cuisine. Eastern European cooking has always had a heartier side to it, but in a more health conscious society, it's really up to the individual to curtail their portion size and meat intake. Polish cuisine is what it is!

When I was younger, Sunday dinners in my home always included a meat dish as the main course; whether it was pork roast with rosemary potatoes, a beef rump roast au jus, or a lightly smoked Sunday dinner ham with sweet potatoes. On special holidays, my mom was known for knocking out a crispy duck or goose like no one's business. It wasn't so much as to what we ate but it was the fact that it was the only day our whole extended family could get together and enjoy each other's company. It was always a nice occasion because everyone helped set the table, my mom would arrange the food artfully onto serving platters, and we would all sit down at the same time and give thanks for the feast. As I get older, my mind gravitates back to those times, and I miss them dearly.

Meat, poultry, and game have always played an important role in the art of Polish cuisine, and I feel that if you look through this voluminous book you should be able to find a recipe that is familiar to your past and to your liking. **"Don't Kiss Me Tonight" Garlic Chicken** is a great dish if you are entertaining close friends and want to share a salad and a couple of bottles of wine, whereas **Perfect Veal Schnitzel** and **Ma's Sunday Dinner Ham** are Polish staples that this book would be incomplete without. **Chef Walter's Apricot Stuffed Pork Loin** works well if you are having an elegant dinner party, but don't discount the **Roast Pheasant Salad** or the **Orange Duck** if you are trying to impress the boss.

Grilled Butt Steak with Black Peppercorns and Cognac

Ingredients

4 Sirloin Butt steaks (5 to 6 ounces each)
1 tablespoon whole black peppercorns
¼ teaspoon sea salt
2 large garlic cloves, minced
¼ cup cognac
1 cup veal or beef stock
¼ cup heavy cream or sour cream
2 tablespoons unsalted butter, cold

If you're at your local butcher and he has a sale on butt steaks, buy them. This is an excellent, but sometimes overlooked cut of meat for the grill. Slightly marbled with just the right amount of fat, the meat grills beautifully, and the black peppercorn and cognac sauce are a perfect compliment for the dish.

Chef's Tip!

Any high quality filet steak can be substituted. Also, for an interesting variation, try using assorted color peppercorns that come pre-packaged in fancy food stores.

Preparation

1. **Coarsely crack** the black peppercorns on a wooden work surface with a kitchen mallet or with the bottom of a heavy-duty pot. Do not grind finely.

2. **Now sprinkle the salt,** crushed peppercorns, and garlic equally over one side of the steaks, and using your hand press the seasoning in so it adheres to the steak. Set aside for 30 minutes to lightly marinate.

3. **Heat a cast iron** stovetop griddle or heavy high-sided skillet over medium high heat until white hot, and then lightly brush with olive oil. Immediately place the steaks on the griddle peppercorn side down and grill for 3 to 4 minutes on each side until medium rare.

4. **Remove the steaks** to a platter and pour off all the grease in a pan, being careful to retain any crushed peppercorns, and return the pan to the fire. Lower the heat and carefully add the cognac to the pan, which will ignite. When the flame dies out, add the veal stock and heavy cream and bring it to a slow boil. Using a wooden spoon, lightly swirl the sauce and reduce until slightly thickened or until it coats the back of the spoon. At this point, swirl in the whole butter until incorporated into the sauce and then pour over the steaks.

Serves 4

Beef Tips with Wild Mushrooms and Pickles

I've always loved this continental favorite, and have prepared it tableside for many a gourmet in my career. Old classics never die; they just get reinvented for new generations to enjoy.

Chef's Tip!

This dish sautés up very quickly so it is vitally important that all of the ingredients (meat and mushrooms) are cut up into equal sized pieces. Also, don't be tempted to use a cheaper cut of meat as beef tenderloin works the best.

Ingredients

1½ pounds beef tenderloin tips
2 tablespoons unsalted butter
1 small onion, diced
1 large garlic clove, minced
1 medium sized dill pickle, diced
¾ pound assorted wild mushrooms, cleaned and quartered (such as cepes, shitakes, oyster, or cremini)
Dash of Hungarian paprika
Dash of sea salt
Dash of freshly ground black pepper
⅓ cup dry red wine
1½ cups veal or beef stock
2 tablespoons sour cream
Dash of Tabasco

Preparation

1. **Place the tenderloin tips** between 2 sheets of parchment paper and slightly flatten with a meat mallet.

2. **Using a large heavy-duty** non-stick skillet, heat the butter over high heat until smoking hot, then quickly sauté the beef tips for about 1 to 2 minutes until both sides are lightly browned. Using a kitchen tong, remove the meat to a platter.

3. **To the reserved** cooking juices in the pan, add the onion, garlic, dill pickle, and mushrooms and sauté for about 2 minutes until the mushrooms start to give off some of their liquid. Reduce the liquid to a syrup-like consistency, then sprinkle on the paprika, salt, and pepper, and then add the red wine and let that reduce by half. Now add the veal stock and simmer until the stock is reduced by half.

4. **Return the meat** to the skillet to re-warm, then add the sour cream and Tabasco, and swirl the pan until the sauce is slightly thickened and smooth.

Serves 4

Perfect Veal Schnitzel

Ingredients

Four boneless veal cutlets (4 to 6 ounces each)
½ cup all-purpose flour
2 large whole eggs
1 cup fresh breadcrumbs
2 tablespoons Parmigiano-Reggiano cheese
1½ teaspoons dried oregano
1½ teaspoons dried basil
¼ teaspoon Hungarian sweet paprika
¼ teaspoon sea salt
⅛ teaspoon freshly ground black pepper

1 cup light olive oil or canola oil

Everyone loves a good schnitzel whether it is made of veal, pork, chicken, or even turkey breast. The secret lies in using an old-fashioned cast iron skillet, and well-seasoned fresh breadcrumbs. I think you'll enjoy it!

Chef's Tip!

Schnitzel is one of those meals that stands best on its own. A side dish of sautéed potatoes or baked apple is all that is needed to complement this rustic fare.

Preparation

1. **Preheat the oven** to 400°F.

2. **Remove the veal** from the refrigerator, and using a sharp kitchen knife, trim away any excess fat. Place a piece of parchment paper or plastic wrap onto a clean, flat work surface, and lay the cutlets on top of the paper equally spaced apart. Cover with another piece of paper, then using a meat mallet, pound the cutlets until they are about ¼-inch thick. Discard the paper and place the veal onto a serving platter.

3. **Place the flour** into a medium sized mixing bowl, then put the eggs into another medium sized bowl and beat with a whisk until frothy. Now put the breadcrumbs and the rest of the seasoning into another bowl, and mix with a fork to combine. Move all of the bowls to the counter next to your stove.

4. **Heat half the oil** over medium high heat in a large caste iron skillet. (Make sure that the skillet will accommodate 2 schnitzels at a time with room to spare. If not, you'll have to sauté them one at a time.)

5. **When the oil is hot,** but not smoking, quickly dredge 2 of the veal pieces into the flour, then egg, then seasoned breadcrumbs, and place into the hot pan. Make sure that there is plenty of space between the 2 cutlets so that the hot oil can crisp the coating. Let the veal cook on one side for about two minutes, then using a kitchen tong, grasp the cutlet and flip the meat over, being careful not to disturb the breading. Now let it cook on the other side for a two minutes. When the coating is nicely browned on both sides, remove the schnitzel to a paper towel lined platter for 5 seconds, then place them onto a nonstick baking pan.

6. **Repeat the process** with the other 2 schnitzels, then place the pan into the preheated oven for 5 minutes to warm and serve.

Serves 4

Veal with Lemon and Capers

Ingredients

Four 4 to 5 ounce veal cutlets
$^1\!/_2$ cup all-purpose flour
$^1\!/_4$ teaspoon sea salt
$^1\!/_8$ teaspoon freshly ground black pepper
2 tablespoons olive oil
2 tablespoons unsalted butter

$^1\!/_3$ cup dry white wine
1 cup chicken stock
$^1\!/_4$ cup fresh lemon juice
2 tablespoons capers, rinsed
2 tablespoons parsley, chopped

My Sicilian mother-in-law Geri DeCarl and her twin sister, Fran, are easily the best Italian cooks in the city of Chicago. Through the years, my sons and I have enjoyed many of their delicacies and have had some of our best meals at their tables. Veal with Lemon and Capers is a beautifully simple dish that I learned from the girls and their recipe is foolproof.

Chef's Tip!

The true secret to good Veal with Lemon and Capers is to use prime veal cutlets and fresh lemon juice only.

Preparation

1. **Remove the veal** from the refrigerator then place a piece of parchment paper or plastic wrap onto a clean, flat work surface, and lay the cutlets on top of the paper equally spaced apart. Cover with another piece of paper, then using a meat mallet, pound the cutlets until they are about $^1\!/_4$-inch thick. Discard the paper and place the veal onto a serving platter.

2. **Place the flour,** salt, and pepper into a medium sized mixing bowl and stir together until well combined. Move the bowl and the platter of cutlets to the counter next to your stove.

3. **Heat the oil** and butter in a large heavy-duty non-stick skillet over medium high heat. When the butter starts to sizzle, quickly dredge the veal cutlets into the flour, and then place into the hot skillet. Sauté the cutlets for 2 minutes on each side or until they are nicely browned. Using a kitchen tong, remove the veal to a platter and set aside until needed.

4. **Discard any** of the excess oil from the pan and then return the skillet to the fire. Now add the wine to the pan and let it reduce by half, then pour in the chicken stock and boil for 4 to 5 minutes until the liquid is again reduced and slightly thickened. Add the lemon juice and capers, and cook stir for 1 minute more.

5. **Return the cutlets** to the pan to re-warm for another 30 seconds. Sprinkle with the chopped parsley and serve immediately.

Serves 4

Honey Mustard Pork Shoulder
with Caraway Potatoes

Whenever I entertain, I cook buffet style only so I can enjoy the party and not break the bank either. Pork shoulder is an economical and savory cut of meat. The pork is stuffed and rolled with a sweet and sour honey mustard filling, then roasted with caraway potatoes until golden brown. The meat is then sliced thin and arranged on platters with the potatoes to be passed around. (Don't be afraid to ask your butcher to butterfly the meat for you.)

Chef's Tip!

The rolled shoulder sometimes has a tendency to fall apart when sliced. That's okay, just arrange the pieces neatly onto a serving platter and be sure to use a sharp chef's knife.

Ingredients

3–5 pounds boneless pork shoulder, butterfly cut
5 tablespoons Dijon mustard
5 tablespoons honey
3 large garlic cloves, minced
$\frac{1}{4}$ teaspoon sea salt
$\frac{1}{4}$ teaspoon freshly ground black pepper
$\frac{1}{2}$ cup bread crumbs
2 tablespoons olive oil

6 medium sized potatoes, skinned and quartered
2 teaspoons caraway seeds
$\frac{1}{4}$ teaspoon sea salt
$\frac{1}{8}$ teaspoon freshly ground black pepper
$\frac{1}{4}$ teaspoon garlic powder
$\frac{1}{4}$ teaspoon Hungarian sweet paprika

$\frac{1}{2}$ cup fresh bread crumbs
4 tablespoons parsley, chopped

$\frac{1}{4}$ cup dry white wine
1 cup chicken or beef stock

Preparation

1. **Preheat the oven** to 400°F.

2. **Place the butterflied** pork shoulder onto a clean cutting board, cut side up, and using a sharp chef's knife, lightly score the meat about $\frac{1}{4}$-inch deep.

3. **In a small bowl,** combine the Dijon mustard, honey, and garlic until well blended. Lightly season the meat with half of the salt and pepper, and using a soupspoon, spread half of the mustard mixture onto the scored meat, being sure to work it in to the cuts. Now sprinkle on the breadcrumbs, and gently roll the meat back into a tight sausage shape. Using kitchen twine, secure the meat every inch along the width to hold the filling in. Season the outside of the meat with the remaining salt and pepper.

4. **In a medium-sized skillet,** heat the olive oil over medium high heat, then add the rolled pork and sauté on all sides until lightly browned.

5. **While the meat** is browning, place the quartered potatoes into a large mixing bowl, and season with the olive oil, caraway seeds, sea salt, pepper, garlic powder, and paprika, and using your hands, toss to coat thoroughly. Pour the potatoes into a large, nonstick roasting pan, then shake the pan so that the potatoes are evenly distributed.

6. **When the meat** is thoroughly browned on all sides, remove it from the skillet and place it directly onto the potatoes, and pour any excess pan juices from the skillet over the potatoes. Place the pan into the preheated oven and cook for exactly 30 minutes, then remove the pan and quickly spread the remaining mustard mixture onto the top of the meat. Now sprinkle the breadcrumbs and parsley on top of that, and return to the oven to cook for another 20 minutes.

7. **After 20 minutes,** remove the meat to a serving platter, then pour the white wine and stock over the potatoes. Return the pan to the oven, and let the potatoes cook for another 20 minutes until brown and tender.

8. **Carefully remove** the string from the roast, and using a sharp chef's knife, cut the meat into thin slices. Serve with the roasted potatoes.

Serves 4

Ma's Sunday Dinner Ham

Ingredients

One 10 to 12 pound lightly smoked ready-to-eat
   ham, bone-in
3 large garlic cloves, minced
One 9 oz. jar Major Grey's mango chutney or
   bitter orange marmalade
¼ cup Dijon mustard
½ cup light brown sugar
½ cup fresh orange juice
¼ teaspoon freshly ground black pepper
12 whole cloves, optional

Not only is this a great Sunday staple, but it is also a beautiful center-piece for any buffet table. The combination of mango chutney, Dijon mustard, brown sugar, and orange juice are the perfect sweet and sour foil to the smokiness of the ham. This is also a great dish for a picnic or tailgate party, just be sure to bring the rye bread, horseradish, mustard and pickles.

Chef's Tip!

If you're intimidated by carving a ham in front of your dinner guests, feel free to substitute a pre-sliced spiral cut ready-to-eat ham. Also, be sure to work some of the glaze into the cuts of the ham to keep it nice and moist.

Preparation

1. **The night before** cooking the ham, prepare the baste. Place the garlic, chutney, Dijon mustard, brown sugar, orange juice, and black pepper into a medium sized mixing bowl, and whisk until smooth. Cover the bowl with plastic wrap and refrigerate. Rinse the smoked ham under cold running water for 1 minute, then dry with a paper towel. Using a sharp chef's knife, peel the skin from the ham and trim the fat, leaving a ¼-inch layer. Using the tip of a sharp knife, score the fat in a diamond pattern. Insert the cloves in the crossed points of each diamond. Place the ham onto a rack set over a roasting pan, cover with plastic, and refrigerate overnight.

2. **The next day** take the ham and baste out of the refrigerator at least 1 hour before cooking.

3. **Preheat the oven** to 350°F. (I recommend cooking the ham 10 to 12 minutes per pound, so set your clock accordingly.)

4. **Place the ham into the hot oven** and cook for exactly 30 minutes. After 30 minutes, remove the ham from the oven, and baste it with the chutney glaze. Return the pan to the oven and bake, basting frequently with the rest of the glaze for another 1½ hours. When the ham is cooked, remove it from the oven and let it rest 15 minutes before carving.

Serves 4 with leftovers

Grilled Pork Chops with Mustard and Pickles

Ingredients

4 center cut pork chops at least 1-inch thick,
   6 to 8 ounces each
3 tablespoons olive oil
Sea salt
Freshly ground black pepper

2 tablespoons unsalted butter, melted
1 large garlic clove, minced
¼ cup onion, minced
½ cup dry white wine
1½ cup veal or beef stock
1 tablespoon Dijon mustard
1 tablespoon chives, chopped
5 Polish gherkins cut into thin strips
Sea salt
Freshly ground black pepper
Dash of Tabasco

I've eaten this dish many a time at the famed Hotel Bristol in Poland, and have always been amazed at how a simple Polish country dish can be elevated to haute cuisine!

Chef's Tip!

Be sure to pre-season your chops at least 20 minutes before grilling. The pork will be more succulent if cooked over a medium high heat slowly.

Preparation

1. **Preheat the grill,** then rub the pork chops with the olive oil, salt, and pepper and set aside.

2. **While the grill** is heating, prepare the sauce. Heat 2 tablespoons of the butter in a medium sized sauce pot over medium high heat, then add the garlic and onion, and cook stir for 2 minutes until the vegetable have softened. Add the white wine and reduce until 2 to 3 tablespoons remain. Now add the veal stock and cook gently until it is thick enough to coat the back of a spoon. Add the rest of the ingredients and cook for 1 to 2 minutes until the sauce has good taste, then set aside.

3. **Now clean your grill** with a brush, then lightly oil with cooking spray. Grill the pork for 4 minutes on each side or until cooked to your liking.

4. **Remove the pork chops** to serving plates, then spoon the sauce over them.

Serves 4

Chef Walter's Apricot Stuffed Pork Loin

Ingredients

2½ to 3 pound whole pork loin, boneless
¾ pound dried apricot halves
1 cup apple juice
½ cup chicken stock
½ teaspoon ground ginger
3 medium garlic cloves, minced
1 tablespoon lemon juice
¼ teaspoon sea salt
⅛ teaspoon freshly ground black pepper
2 large sprigs fresh sage or rosemary, minced

4 tablespoons olive oil
¼ teaspoon sea salt
⅛ teaspoon freshly ground black pepper
2 large sprigs each of rosemary, thyme, parsley,
    and sage

2 large garlic cloves, chopped
1 medium onion, chopped
1 medium carrot, chopped
1 medium celery stalk, chopped
½ cup dry white wine
2 cups veal stock

I learned how to make this dish over 20 years ago by master chef Walter Piasecki of the Starlight Inn, when I was an apprentice cook. Walter made this dish so popular, it has been served to mayors, governors, and dignitaries from all around the world. Over the last few years, I have seen a resurgence of this dish in different forms, but nothing compares to the master's recipe.

Chef's Tip!

Any left over apricot stuffing can be added to the simmering sauce to give it a nice sweet and fruity flavor.

Preparation

1. **The night before** preparing the pork, combine the apricots, apple juice, stock, ginger, garlic, lemon juice, salt, pepper, sage, and rosemary in a medium sized saucepan. Cook over medium heat for 20 to 25 minutes until the apricots have plumped and the liquid is reduced by half. Pour the apricots into the work bowl of a food processor fitted with a metal blade, then puree until thick and smooth. Remove the puree to a small mixing bowl, cover with plastic wrap, and refrigerate overnight.

2. **The next day,** using a sharp boning knife, trim the pork loin of any excess fat, then using a sharpening steel, make a hole in the center of the loin, all the way through from one end to the other. Now widen the hole using the backside of a wooden spoon or a turkey baster.

3. **Now very carefully,** using a small spoon or better yet, a pastry bag fitted with a large open metal tip, stuff the loin on each side until all of the filling is used. (If using the pastry bag, fill the bag with the mixture, then pipe one end until full and then the other.) Lay the pork loin out onto a clean surface, and lightly brush all around with 2 tablespoons of the olive oil. Season with the salt and pepper, then lay the fresh herbs on top of the loin. Carefully, using kitchen twine, tie the stuffed loin at 2-inch intervals so as to secure the herbs on top of the loin.

4. **Preheat the oven** to 375°F.

5. **Heat the remaining** 2 tablespoons of olive oil in a large nonstick skillet over medium high heat, and sear the pork loin on all sides until golden brown. While the meat is searing, place the remaining vegetables onto a small baking pan, and when the meat is brown, transfer it to the top of the vegetables. Place the pan into the hot oven, and roast the stuffed pork loin for 45 to 50 minutes or until a meat thermometer registers 160°F.

6. **Remove the pan** from the oven, and place the pork loin onto a serving platter to rest. Quickly pour the vegetables into a medium sized saucepan over medium high heat, then add the white wine and reduce by half. Now add the veal stock and cook for 20 minutes until the sauce lightly coats the back of a spoon. Re-season and strain the sauce through a fine mesh conical sieve into a sauceboat, then serve with the pork.

Serves 4

"Don't Kiss Me Tonight" Garlic Chicken

Ingredients

2 small fresh chickens (about 3 pounds each),
  left whole
4 tablespoons olive oil
1 teaspoon sea salt
¼ teaspoon freshly ground black pepper
2 teaspoons fresh thyme, minced
2 teaspoons fresh rosemary, minced

24 medium sized garlic cloves, peeled
1 cup lightly salted water

2 tablespoons unsalted butter, melted
½ pound domestic mushrooms, quartered
½ cup dry white wine
2 cups chicken stock
2 teaspoons cornstarch, dissolved
1 tablespoon tomato paste
2 tablespoons parsley, chopped
1 teaspoon fresh thyme
1 teaspoon fresh rosemary
Sea salt
Freshly ground black pepper
2 large dashes of Tabasco
2 large dashes of Maggi

Please don't be put off by the amount of garlic in this dish. The pre-blanching and subsequent roasting renders the garlic jewels sweet and succulent!

Chef's Tip!

Feel free to cut up the chickens before cooking if you are nervous about carving. Also, the pre-blanching of the garlic really removes the heartburn effect associated with it.

Preparation

1. **Preheat the oven** to 400°F.

2. **Place the chickens** onto a clean work surface, and using a sharp boning knife, trim away any excess fat. Rinse the chickens under cold running water for 1 minute, then dry with paper towels. Using kitchen twine, truss the birds, then rub all over with the olive oil. Now season the birds inside and out with the salt, pepper, thyme, and rosemary. Place the chickens into a medium sized nonstick roasting pan, and put in the hot oven to cook for 45 minutes.

3. **While the chickens** are cooking, place the garlic cloves and water into a small saucepan, and bring to a boil over medium high heat. Reduce the heat to a simmer, and cook the garlic cloves for exactly 2 minutes, then drain into a colander. Now repeat the process, then drain again in a small colander. Remove the garlic cloves to a small bowl, sprinkle on 2 tablespoons of olive oil, then toss to coat.

4. **After 1 hour,** remove the roasting pan from the oven, then sprinkle the garlic cloves over the chickens and return the pan to cook for another 20 minutes.

5. **When the chickens** are cooked, remove the pan from the oven, and carefully using a kitchen fork, transfer the chickens to a serving platter.

6. **Pour off all** the chicken fat from the roasting pan, then place the pan with the garlic cloves over medium high heat on the stove. Add the melted butter and mushrooms to the pan, and using a wooden spoon, scrape the bottom of the pan to release any accumulated juices. (The brown morsels that are stuck to the bottom of the pan.) After 1 minute of stirring, add the white wine, and let it reduce until syrupy. Now add the rest of the ingredients, bring to a boil, then reduce the heat, and simmer slowly for about 10 minutes. When the sauce has good taste, spoon it over the chickens.

Serves 4

Diabelski Red Chicken

I dedicate this devil dish to Bona Sforza (1518–1557), an Italian princess who married Sigismund I of Poland. The princess introduced the tomato to Polish culture and rumor has it that when Sig got a taste of this dish, he coined the famous phrase "Hey Mama, that's a spicy sauce!"

Chef's Tip!

This dish is excellent if served with a crusty rustic loaf, a simple green salad, and a side of rice or thin linguine noodles. A nice Chianti goes great with this meal, too.

Ingredients

¼ cup olive oil
One plump 5 to 6 pound fresh chicken, quartered, excess fat removed
¼ cup all-purpose flour

Spicy Tomato Sauce

2 tablespoons olive oil
2 large garlic cloves, minced
1 medium onion, sliced
1 medium red or green pepper, sliced
1 cup domestic mushrooms, sliced
¾ teaspoon dried thyme
1 bay leaf
3 tablespoons tomato paste
1½ cups tomato sauce
1½ cups beef or chicken stock
¼ cup dry white wine
Dash of cayenne pepper
Dash of Tabasco
Dash of Worcestershire sauce
¼ teaspoon sea salt
Freshly ground black pepper
1 large dried red pepper pod

Preparation

1. **Preheat the oven** to 350°F.

2. **Heat the oil** in a medium pot over medium heat; add the garlic, onion, peppers, and mushrooms, and cook stirring until softened, about 3 minutes. Do not let the vegetables brown.

3. **Now add** the bay leaf and thyme and cook for exactly 1 minute to release their oils.

4. **Add the rest** of the ingredients to the pot and bring it to a boil, and then reduce the heat and simmer slowly for about 10 minutes.

5. **While the sauce** is simmering, place a large sized skillet over medium heat; add the olive oil and when hot, quickly dredge the chicken pieces into the flour, and then sauté in the hot oil for 3 to 5 minutes on each side until golden brown. Remove to a medium sized earthenware casserole.

6. **Now gently** ladle all of the spicy tomato sauce over the chicken, cover tightly, and bake for 1½ hours until cooked.

Serves 4

Chicken and Potatoes Greek Style

Ingredients

5 large potatoes, peeled and quartered
½ teaspoon sea salt
¼ teaspoon freshly ground black pepper
½ teaspoon garlic salt
2 teaspoons dried oregano
½ cup fresh lemon juice
2 tablespoons olive oil
1 teaspoon Hungarian sweet paprika

2 small fresh chickens (about 3 pounds each),
    quartered
2 large cloves garlic, minced
½ teaspoon sea salt
¼ teaspoon freshly ground black pepper
1 teaspoon dried oregano
½ teaspoon garlic salt
¼ cup olive oil
⅓ cup fresh lemon juice

¼ cup dry white wine
2 cups chicken stock
1 teaspoon cornstarch, dissolved
3 large dashes Tabasco
3 large dashes Maggi
¼ cup parsley, chopped

As early as the 1300s, the Byzantine's had begun trade relations with the Polish Empire, introducing to Polish culture lemons, oregano, and olive oil. These exciting food products have inevitably left their mark on Polish cuisine. Chicken and potatoes is a simple dish, but the addition of lemon, oregano, and olive oil really kick it up a notch!

Chef's Tip!

This is an excellent dish that reheats well or can be served at a summertime picnic in the woods.

Preparation

1. **Bring a medium-sized** pot of salted water to a boil, add the potatoes, and cook for exactly 3 minutes. Drain and cool in a colander. When the potatoes are cool, place them into a large mixing bowl, and sprinkle on the salt, pepper, garlic salt, oregano, lemon juice, olive oil, and paprika, and using your hands, gently toss until well coated. Cover with plastic wrap, and let the potatoes marinate for at least 1 hour.

2. **Place the chicken** pieces onto a clean work surface, and using a sharp boning knife, trim away any excess fat. Rinse the chicken under cold running water for 1 minute, then dry with paper towels, and place the pieces into a large Ziploc bag. In a small bowl, combine the garlic, salt, pepper, oregano, garlic salt, olive oil, and lemon juice, then pour into the Ziploc bag over the chicken. Seal the bag, and using your hands, flip the bag a few times to distribute the marinade evenly into the pieces. Let the chicken marinate for at least 1 hour.

3. **Preheat the oven** to 375°F.

4. **Give the potatoes** a quick toss in the bowl, then pour directly into a medium sized nonstick roasting pan, and place in the hot oven to cook for 30 minutes.

5. **Carefully remove** the chicken from the bag, and reserve the excess marinade for basting. Take the roasting pan out of the oven, and carefully using a kitchen tong, flip the potatoes over. Now place the chicken pieces directly on top of the potatoes, add the white wine, and put the pan back in the oven to roast another 30 minutes. Remove the pan from the oven again, and baste the chicken with the reserved marinade. Now add the chicken stock, cornstarch, Tabasco, Maggi, and parsley to the roasting pan, and roast for another 30 minutes.

6. **After 1½ hours,** remove the pan from the oven and carefully arrange the chicken pieces and potatoes decoratively onto a serving platter.

Serves 4

Orange Duck

Ingredients

One 5-pound duck
¼ teaspoon sea salt
⅛ teaspoon freshly ground black pepper
¼ teaspoon dried thyme
1 bay leaf

1 tablespoon olive oil
Reserved neck and wings
4 tablespoons sugar
3 tablespoons red wine vinegar
¾ cup fresh orange juice
3 cups veal stock
Zest of 2 oranges, blanched
Sea salt
Freshly ground black pepper
3 medium sized thin skinned oranges, peeled
   and sectioned

I have at least 100 recipes to prepare duck, but when I get a hankering for a succulent bird, I always go back to this classical preparation. It's true that ducks can be fatty, but if you follow the directions and cook it to its proper crispness, you'll become a true believer. The caramelized orange sauce is the perfect compliment to any game bird.

Chef's Tip!

Professional chefs prepare roast duck the day before as to facilitate de-boning and carving. The next day, when needed, we reheat the duck in a hot oven until crisp then serve it with the freshly prepared sauce.

Preparation

1. **Preheat the oven** to 400°F.

2. **Clip the wing tips** off the bird, and remove the neck, then rinse the duck under cold running water for 1 minute, then dry with a paper towel inside and out. Using a sharp kitchen knife, remove any excess fat from around the neck and the butt. Season the inside and outside of the bird with the salt, pepper, and thyme, and place the bay leaf inside. Truss the legs with kitchen twine and secure the remaining neck skin to the back with a bamboo skewer, and twist the wings behind the back. Using a kitchen fork, gently prick the skin all over. (This helps remove excess fat during cooking.)

3. **Place the duck** onto a roasting rack set over a roasting pan, and pour about ¼-inch of water into the pan. Place the pan in the hot oven and roast for 1 hour. After 1 hour of roasting, remove all of the fat that has accumulated in the pan and discard. Continue roasting for another 45 minutes until the bird is crisp. (Be sure to baste the bird every 15 minutes in the last part of the roasting with the accumulated juices.)

4. **While the duck** is cooking, prepare the sauce. Heat 1 tablespoon of olive oil in a medium sized saucepan over medium high heat. Add the reserved wings and neck, and stir cook for about 5 minutes until they become dark golden brown. Now tilt the saucepan and remove any excess grease from the pan, return it to the fire, then add the sugar and vinegar, and stir cook with a heavy wooden spoon until it turns to a deep golden caramel color. Immediately pour in the veal stock and orange juice and bring to a boil, then lower the heat and simmer the sauce for 20 to 25 minutes until it lightly coats the back of a spoon. (It is important to skim off any impurities that rise to the surface of the sauce while cooking.) Now strain the sauce through a fine mesh conical sieve into a clean saucepan, season with salt and pepper, and add the reserved orange sections. Re-taste the sauce, and if needed, reduce it a little more over low heat, then set aside until needed.

5. **When the duck** is cooked, carefully remove it from the roasting rack and place it onto a platter. Very carefully remove the kitchen twine from the duck legs, and let it rest for at least 10 minutes before carving. Gently reheat the sauce, add the orange zests, and pour into a sauceboat to serve with the duck.

Serves 4

Roast Pheasant Salad with Apple, Honey, and Rosemary Sauce

Ingredients

Two 2½ pound pheasants
Sea salt
Freshly ground black pepper
2 tablespoons olive oil

2 slices thick cut hickory smoked bacon,
    pre-cooked and crumbled
⅓ cup walnut pieces, lightly toasted
4 cups assorted field greens, washed and dried
    such as Belgian endive, baby oak leaf, watercress,
    radicchio, limestone lettuce, or red leaf
1 cup thin green beans, pre-cooked al dente
1 cup red cabbage, thinly shredded

½ cup Sherry Wine Vinaigrette

1 recipe Apple, Honey, and Rosemary Sauce
    (see page 253)

This is really an upscale dish if you are having an elegant sit-down dinner. Domestic pheasants are available in most markets these days, and when roasted to perfection, their succulent white-fleshed meat provides the perfect background for a cool, colorful, and healthy salad. The sweet and sour sauce can be prepared well in advance, and the rest of the dish comes together in a snap.

Chef's Tip!

Depending on where you live, pheasants might come at a premium price so I like to substitute semi-boneless quail. The quail are small in size so I recommend 2 per person and, if used, just reduce all of the cooking times by half. Also, serve the quails whole!

Preparation

1. **Preheat the oven** to 425°F.

2. **Season the pheasants** inside and out with salt and pepper, then using kitchen twine, truss the birds. Heat the olive oil in a large ovenproof sauté pan over medium high heat, then brown the pheasants on each side in the hot oil for 5 to 7 minutes. Pour off any excess grease from the pan, then arrange the birds, breast-side up, and roast in the oven for 12 to 15 minutes or until the juices run clear. (This might seem like a short cooking time, but nothing is worse than an over-cooked pheasant.)

3. **Remove the pan** from the oven, and allow the birds to rest for at least 10 to 15 minutes before carving.

4. **Gently reheat** the sauce in a small saucepan and keep warm.

5. **In a large mixing bowl,** combine the assorted greens, green beans, cabbage, bacon, and walnuts, and toss gently with the vinaigrette.

6. **Quickly using** a sharp kitchen knife, remove the thighs and legs from the pheasants, and then remove the breast meat. Divide the salad mixture evenly onto 4 dinner plates, and place one leg on top of each salad. Now thinly slice the breast meat against the grain, and decoratively arrange the slices in a circular pattern around the leg meat.

7. **Carefully ladle** the warm sauce over the breast pieces and serve immediately.

Serves 4

Sherry Wine Vinaigrette

Ingredients

¾ cup extra virgin olive oil
¼ cup sherry wine vinegar
Dash of sea salt
Dash of freshly ground black pepper

Preparation

1. **Place all the ingredients** into a small mason jar and mix together until well combined. Set aside until needed.

Makes about 1 cup

Roast Quail Salad with Apple, Honey, and Rosemary Sauce

Minnie's Holiday Turkey with Sage Stuffing

Ingredients

One 10 to 12 pound all-natural fresh turkey
   with gizzards

Stuffing

2 tablespoons unsalted butter
2 large garlic cloves, minced
$\frac{1}{2}$ cup onion finely diced
$\frac{1}{2}$ cup celery, finely diced
1 large bay leaf
1 teaspoon dried thyme
1$\frac{1}{2}$ teaspoons ground sage
$\frac{1}{4}$ teaspoon sea salt
$\frac{1}{8}$ teaspoon freshly ground black pepper
Whole turkey hearts, gizzards, and livers, cleaned
5 cups chicken stock
2 dashes Tabasco

1 extra large loaf white bread, cubed
2 whole large eggs

1 large roasting pan with rack

Preparation

1. **The day before cooking** the bird remove it from its package, and thoroughly rinse under cold running water for at least 3 to 4 minutes to remove any impurities. Also rinse off the neck, heart, gizzards, and livers, and reserve until needed. Dry the bird with paper towels, and season the inside and out with some sea salt and pepper, then place the bird into a plastic bag and refrigerate until the next day.

2. **Also the day before** cooking the turkey, prepare the stuffing ingredients. Preheat the oven to 400°, and when hot, toast the cubed white bread on a large baking sheet until golden brown. Do not burn.

3. **To prepare the stock** for the stuffing, heat the butter in a medium sized saucepan until melted, then add the garlic, onion, and celery, and stir cook for exactly 2 to 3 minutes. Now add the bay leaf, thyme, sage, sea salt, and pepper, and stir cook for 1 minute more to release their oils. Add the chicken stock, Tabasco, and the reserved heart, gizzards, and livers, bring the stock to a boil, and then reduce the heat and simmer slowly for exactly 15 minutes. Remove from the fire, and when cool, pour into another container and refrigerate over night. Place the cooled toasted cubes into a large mixing bowl and cover with plastic wrap.

4. **The next day preheat** the oven to 350°, and remove the bird and stock from the refrigerator. Place the turkey onto a large clean

Turkey Gravy

Ingredients

$\frac{1}{2}$ cup dry white wine
3 tablespoons turkey pan drippings
3 tablespoons all-purpose flour
3 cups chicken stock
$\frac{1}{4}$ teaspoon sea salt
$\frac{1}{8}$ teaspoon freshly ground black pepper
Large dash of garlic powder, sage, and Tabasco

Preparation

1. **After the turkey is roasted,** pour all of the pan drippings into a pyrex cup. Place the roasting pan onto the stove set at medium heat, add the white wine, and using a wooden spoon, scrape up any residue that is left on the pan. Remove the pan from the fire, and place a medium sized saucepan onto the fire. Pour in 3 tablespoons of turkey drippings, and the flour, and stir cook for exactly 2 to 3 minutes until nutty brown. Now add the stock, salt, pepper, seasonings, and pan residue, bring the sauce to a quick boil, lower the heat, and simmer for 20 to 25 minutes until the sauce has good taste. Strain into a sauceboat.

Makes about 2$\frac{1}{2}$ cups

baking pan so it won't move around when being stuffed. Carefully using a kitchen tong, remove the bay leaf, heart, gizzards, and livers from the stock, taste the stock, and re-season if needed. Beat the eggs in a small bowl, and pour directly on top of the cubed bread. Now using a ladle, ladle the stock and vegetables, one scoop at a time, onto the stuffing and thoroughly combine with your hands until the liquid is well incorporated into the bread. (Do not add all the stock at one time because you will only need about 4 to 4$\frac{1}{2}$ cups.)

5. **When the stuffing** is well moistened, stuff the cavity and neck of the bird in the traditional fashion, and secure the legs with kitchen twine. Carefully tuck the wings under, and then place the bird onto the baking rack set over a roasting pan. Place the neck into the bottom of the pan, and then massage 3 tablespoons of olive oil into the turkey. Pour 2 cups of water into the bottom of the pan, and roast and baste the bird for 4 hours or until there is an internal temperature of 180° to 185°.

Serves a small crowd

Ursula's Christmas Goose

Every Christmas my Grandpa John would show up with a bottle of Scotch and a freshly butchered goose, head and all, wrapped up in old newspaper. We would all stand around, sip the Scotch, marvel at this majestic bird, and ponder great thoughts as to the most appropriate cooking technique. My mother Ursula, who was a great Polish cook, would quickly clean and stuff the bird, then roast it for a few hours until it was delectably crisp and ready to devour. In honor of this Polish family tradition, I give you Ursula's Christmas Goose!

Chef's Tip!

I recommend doubling all the ingredients for the sauce, and also be sure to save the carcass from the goose to make a really good stock for czarnina soup!

Ingredients

One dressed goose about 8–10 pound avg.
1 medium onion, chopped
6 to 8 small tart apples, deseeded and
    chopped
$\frac{1}{2}$ teaspoon sea salt
$\frac{1}{8}$ teaspoon freshly ground black pepper
$1\frac{1}{2}$ teaspoons dried marjoram

2 tablespoons goose fat
Reserved neck, giblets, and wings, rinsed
2 large garlic cloves, minced
1 small carrot, diced
1 medium celery stalk, diced
1 bay leaf
$\frac{1}{4}$ teaspoon dried thyme
3 cups chicken stock
3 teaspoons cornstarch
Large pinch of sugar
Sea salt
Freshly ground black pepper
Dash of Maggi

Preparation

1. **Preheat the oven** to 425°F.

2. **Clip the wing tips** off the bird, remove the giblet sack and neck, and rinse the goose under cold running water for 1 minute, then dry with a paper towel inside and out. Using a sharp kitchen knife, remove any excess fat from around the neck and the butt. Season the inside and outside of the bird with the salt and pepper. In a bowl, combine the onions, apples, and marjoram, then stuff it into the cavity of the goose. Truss the legs with kitchen twine and secure the remaining neck skin to the back with a bamboo skewer, and twist the wings behind the back. Using a kitchen fork, gently prick the skin all over. (This helps remove excess fat during cooking.)

3. **Place the stuffed goose** onto a roasting rack set over a roasting pan, and pour about $\frac{1}{4}$-inch of water into the pan. Place the pan in the hot oven and cook for about 45 minutes. Turn the oven temperature down to 375°F and continue roasting for another $1\frac{1}{2}$ hours. (I recommend cooking the bird 20 minutes per pound, being sure to baste the bird every 20 minutes with the accumulated juices.)

4. **When the goose** is cooked, carefully remove it from the roasting rack and place onto a platter.

5. **Pour off all** but 2 tablespoons of goose fat from the roasting pan, then place the pan over medium high heat on the stove. Add to the pan, the reserved neck, giblets, and wings, and stir cook about 3 to 4 minutes until they turn lightly brown. Now add the garlic, carrot, celery, bay leaf, thyme, and cook stir for about 2 to 3 minutes more until the vegetables are slightly softened. Add the chicken stock and cornstarch, bring it to a boil, then reduce the heat and simmer slowly.

6. **Very carefully,** remove the kitchen twine from the goose legs, and using a long handled kitchen spoon, remove the onion, apple, and marjoram mix and add it to the simmering sauce. Season the sauce with the sugar, salt, pepper, and Maggi, and cook for about 15 to 20 minutes until the sauce is slightly reduced and has a good taste.

7. **Strain the sauce** through a fine mesh conical sieve into a decorative sauceboat and serve with the goose.

Serves 4

pastry shop

breakfast buchty

heavenly walnut coffee cake

cinnamon and raisin cat's eyes

strawberry and cheese squirrel's tail

buttery kolaczki with
polish fruit preserves

busia's rum raisin babka

lemon babka

chocolate glazed pachki

bismark twist (a.k.a. longjohns)

crisp chrusciki

festive rosettes

low lemon cheesecake

praline cheesecake

chocolate swirl cheesecake

high soufflé vanilla cheesecake

pick me up!

biscuit chopin

chocolate raspberry torte

strawberry layer cake

bittersweet chocolate tart

hot apple tart with
vanilla bean ice cream

red fruits in flaky pastry

profiteroles with chocolate sauce

vanilla bean ice cream

chocolate almond ice cream

pistachio ice cream

caramel strawberry ice cream

orange honey roof tiles

candied grapefruit peel

chocolate-dipped strawberries

easy almond brittle

mushroom meringues

polish kolaczki light and flaky

dainty lemon squares

apricot rugelach

wedding cookies

oatmeal chocolate chip cookies

pecan crescents

lemon sables

Polish Trivia: A Pole by the name of Kulczynski had set up Vienna's first pastry and coffee house in 1683. King Stanislaw Leszczynski introduced the French to the babka in the year 1700.

Of all the chapters in this book, this one was undoubtedly the hardest to write. Polish pastry covers such a wide arena that I could have easily written a whole book on the subject, but it wouldn't have done justice to all of the local bakeries around the country who toil and strain daily to produce delectable baked products more consistently than I could have written recipes about. Cookbooks are about balance so I'll give you my interpretations and highlights.

Polish pastry making has always been a very elusive subject for home cooks because it has been classified as labor intensive, time consuming, and better left for the local bakers. Those statements are true in the fact that 75% of Polish baked goods usually contain yeast, which scares people off. I've been making pastry for at least 25 years, and I know of a few busias who can put my babka or churst to shame. Some people have a magic touch for making pastry while others find it to be a difficult task. Practice makes perfect, and a good recipe always helps. Poland's turbulent past has undoubtedly left some deep scars on the country, but the flip side is that different occupants have contributed to the fine art of Polish pastry.

Polish pastry has been classified into three different categories: Babkas, Mazurkas, and Tortes. Everything else beyond these is self-explanatory.

Babka is a term that is loosely used to describe any product that is yeast raised and slightly sweetened, whether it is a Kolach, Strucla, Placek, coffee cake, or Danish. In Poland, the word babka also describes other kinds of cakes that might not be yeast raised but this creates too much confusion. When I mention the word babka, it is most definitely sweet or rich dough that contains yeast.

Mazurkas is a notably Polish Easter time favorite that contains a base of seasoned flaky pastry dough that is pre-baked in a rectangular pan then topped with a savory filling and re-baked again. Most traditional Mazurkas are kept under one and a half inches in height and usually filled with such delicacies as fresh raspberries, apricots and walnuts, or chocolate.

Tortes—a German word meaning any savory cake batter that is baked into a round shape, chilled then split into equal sections to be filled or iced. The word torte is a standard culinary term that is used to describe any fanciful decorated cake that is layered, filled and cut into serving size pieces.

I've been lucky in my career to work at a few well-known Polish and German bakeries on the northwest side of the City, and to say who invented pastry or who makes the best would start a huge culinary debate. I've traveled throughout Eastern Europe and there is a substantial similarity between their pastry making. Technique never changes among chefs but maybe a special ingredient that is indigenous to the area might be added to distinguish its origin. In Medieval times, honey was the primary ingredient of pastry along with poppy seeds. And even though a Pole opened the first coffee shop in Vienna, the Poles in general feasted on apples, pears, cherries, peaches, raisins, figs, and an assortment of wild berries that were preserved for the winter months as their dessert course. The fields of grain in Poland dictated a diet of baked goods that were concentrated around the addition of yeast.

Since this is the first volume in a series on Polish cooking, I was faced with the task of including pastries that were readily identifiable to the average home cook. My personal view about Polish pastry has always been that it can be excessively heavy when combined with traditional Polish food. Most well known Polish pastries are baked as seasonal items to compliment a holiday, but I never thought a fruit filled babka went with a hearty bigos. Chefs have to provide balance among all their dishes and pastry is no exception. I've therefore divided my pastry section in this book into seven sections. They are yeast raised, bronzed, layered, cheese, new world, lody, and coffee treats. Some of the recipes are at least 20 years old, whereas others are fashionably new. All of the desserts in this chapter are based on my lifetime of accumulated cooking experience and the recipes reflect that.

Breakfast Buchty

Ingredients

8 tablespoons sugar
½ teaspoon sea salt
6 tablespoons unsalted butter, softened
1 teaspoon ground cardamon
1 whole large egg plus 1 yolk
¾ cup warm half and half (about 110 degrees)
3 cups all-purpose flour
¾ cup cake flour
3 teaspoons active dry yeast
4 tablespoon unsalted butter, melted

Egg wash

1 egg, well beaten, with a little water

1 recipe Streusel (*see page 258*)
1 recipe Butter Cream Icing, optional
 (*see page 259*)

Translated, it means to "puff up." This is a truly delicious and easy Polish coffee cake to make. A cardamon scented sweet dough is molded into a free-form coffee cake pan, drizzled with melted sweet butter, sugary streusel, and baked until golden brown and puffy. The finished cake is then bathed in butter cream icing and pulled apart with your fingers. Does Burny Brothers Bakery ring a bell?

Chef's Tip!

Golden raisins steeped in a little warm Spiritus or rum for 15 minutes then drained can be added to the mixed dough.

Preparation

1. **Thoroughly combine** the flour and yeast in a medium sized mixing bowl, and then set aside.

2. **To mix the dough** in a heavy-duty mixer, place the sugar, salt, butter, and cardamon in the mixer bowl, attach the paddle and mix on low speed for 1 minute to blend the ingredients. Add the eggs, one by one, until they are absorbed, then add the half and half and mix briefly.

3. **Now slowly add** all of the flour until the dough forms a mass around the paddle. Turn the machine off, remove the paddle and replace with the dough hook. Knead the dough on medium low speed for about 4 minutes, or until the dough is smooth and elastic. If the dough is excessively soft and sticky, add 1 to 2 tablespoons more flour, one at a time, and knead a little longer.

4. **Place the dough** in a large oiled bowl and turn to coat all sides. Cover the bowl tightly with plastic wrap, and allow the dough to rise in a warm place until doubled in bulk, about 1½ hours.

5. **While the dough is rising,** prepare a 9-inch spring form pan by placing a piece of parchment paper into the bottom of the pan, then paint the interior of the pan with some of the reserved melted butter. Mix the excess butter in with the egg wash, then set aside.

6. **Turn the risen dough** out onto a lightly floured work surface, and flip it over. Now very carefully, using your hands, push out the dough into an 8 by 8-inch square, then cut the dough into 16 equal pieces. Using lightly floured hands, form each piece of the cut dough into a tight ball, by tucking the ends under the bottom. Place each rounded piece into the prepared pan so that they fit snugly. (I recommend starting in the middle and working your way to the outer edges leaving a ½-inch gap between the pan and the dough.)

7. **Using a pastry brush,** lightly paint the tops of the formed balls with the egg wash mixture, sprinkle on the streusel topping, then cover the Buchty loosely with plastic wrap, and let it rest undisturbed for about 1 hour until almost doubled.

8. **Preheat the oven** to 350°F. When the oven is hot, uncover the cake, and bake on the middle rack for about 25 to 35 minutes until it is a deep golden color. When thoroughly baked, remove from the oven and let it rest 5 minutes in the pan. Now unhook the spring and carefully, using a kitchen spatula, remove the cake while still on the parchment paper onto a rack to cool.

9. **Re-warm the icing,** and using a kitchen fork, liberally drizzle onto the cooled cake.

Makes one 9-inch cake

Heavenly Walnut Coffee Cake

It wasn't until I moved a few years ago to the West coast that I realized how many things I miss about Chicago. The two that come to mind are hotdogs and fresh coffee cake. Bakeries on the Northwest side easily make the most delicious coffee cakes I've ever had. Their beautiful cakes are sold in a large, flat shape, lightly braided and stuffed with a sweet Walnut filling, topped with a fresh sugary streusel then baked and drizzled with a warm butter cream icing. It seemed that every Sunday after Church, we would head right to a bakery to receive our second blessing. It took me years to duplicate the original, but I think I've got it!

Chef's Tip!

If you are not partial to walnuts, sliced blanched almonds can be substituted.

Ingredients

6 tablespoons sugar
1 teaspoon sea salt
8 tablespoons unsalted butter, softened
1 teaspoon vanilla extract
$\frac{1}{2}$ teaspoon ground cardamon
2 whole large eggs
1 cup half and half (about 110 degrees)
$3\frac{1}{2}$ cups all-purpose flour
1 cup cake flour
4 teaspoons active dry yeast
1 recipe Walnut Filling (*see page 257*)

Egg wash

1 egg well-beaten with a little milk

1 recipe Clear Glaze (*see page 259*)
1 recipe Butter Cream Icing (*see page 259*)

Preparation

1. **Thoroughly combine** the flours and yeast in a medium-sized mixing bowl, and then set aside.

2. **To mix the dough** in a heavy-duty mixer, place the sugar, salt, butter, vanilla, and cardamon in the mixer bowl, attach the paddle and mix on low speed for 1 minute to blend the ingredients. Add the eggs, one by one, until they are absorbed, then add the half and half and mix briefly.

3. **Now slowly add** all of the flour until the dough forms a mass around the paddle. Turn the machine off, remove the paddle and replace with the dough hook. Knead the dough on medium low speed for about 5 minutes, or until the dough is smooth and elastic. If the dough is excessively soft and sticky, add 1 to 2 tablespoons more flour, one at a time, and knead a little longer.

4. **Place the dough** in a large oiled bowl and turn to coat all sides. Cover the bowl tightly with plastic wrap, and allow the dough to rise in a warm place until doubled in bulk, about 1 hour.

5. **Turn the risen dough** out onto a lightly floured work surface, and cut it in half. (Tightly wrap and freeze half of the dough for another day's coffee cake.) Now very carefully, using a rolling pin, roll out the dough into an 8 by 15-inch oblong. Brush off any excess flour, and place the piece onto a parchment lined heavy-duty sheet pan. Place the long end of the sheet pan in front of you, and using a 12-inch ruler, lightly mark but don't cut the dough into 3 equal sections, working your way from the bottom to the top. You should now have 3 sections that are 3-inches each, a left side, middle, and right side. Using a rolling cutter, cut through the two outer most sections of the dough, diagonally downward at $\frac{3}{4}$-inch intervals.

6. **Evenly spread** half of the walnut filling down the center (unslashed sections), then fold the slashes, one at a time, over the center filled section, alternating a strip of dough from one side then the other. Brush the loaf with the egg wash, heavily sprinkle on the remaining walnut filling, then cover the coffee cake loosely with plastic wrap, and let it rest undisturbed for about 1 hour until almost doubled.

7. **Preheat the oven** to 350°F. When the oven is hot, uncover the coffee cake, and bake on the middle rack for about 25 to 35 minutes until it is a deep golden color. When thoroughly baked, slide the coffee cake, still on the parchment paper, onto a rack to cool. Let cool for 5 minutes, then carefully brush the entire loaf with the clear glaze.

8. **When the cake** is completely cool, re-warm the butter cream icing, and using a kitchen fork, liberally drizzle onto the cake.

Makes one cake

Cinnamon and Raisin Cat's Eyes

Ingredients

1 recipe Danish Dough (*see page 256*)
1 recipe Cinnamon Filling (*see page 258*)
½ cup raisins

Egg glaze

1 large egg
2 tablespoons whole milk

1 recipe Streusel (*see page 258*)
1 recipe Clear Glaze (*see page 259*)
Powdered sugar

Cinnamon swirls are probably the most popular breakfast Danish eaten around the world. The delectable combination of buttery Danish dough along with a savory cinnamon filling and a streusel topping are a real morning eye opener. I like to make my cat's eyes on the larger side, but sometimes I make them smaller and bake them in well-buttered cupcake tins sprinkled with extra streusel.

Chef's Tip!

It might seem like the recipe makes a lot of pastry, but don't worry. After you roll out the dough and apply the cinnamon filling and re-roll, you can freeze any portion you don't want to use and bake at a later date.

Preparation

1. **Line 2 baking** sheets with parchment paper.

2. **Lightly flour** a work surface, and roll out the dough to measure a 24 by 10-inch rectangle.

3. **Using an offset spatula,** spread the cinnamon filling over the entire surface leaving a 1 inch border all the way around. Evenly sprinkle on the raisins over the cinnamon filling.

4. **Now carefully** using both hands, tightly roll up the dough starting at the bottom and working your way to the top.

5. **Now using a sharp** chef's knife, cut the roll into 10 to 12 equal pieces, then place them cut side down onto the baking sheets leaving enough room between each one for them to double in size. Using the palm of your hand, lightly flatten each roll to about 1 inch thick.

6. **In a small bowl,** whisk together the egg and the milk, and using a pastry brush, coat each pastry with the egg glaze. Sprinkle the streusel over each pastry, then cover the pans with plastic wrap, and let rise for about 30 minutes.

7. **While the cat's eyes** are rising, preheat the oven to 350°F., and when ready, bake for about 20 minutes until golden brown. Remove the pans from the oven and let the pastry cool for 5 minutes, then brush with the clear glaze. When completely cool, sprinkle on the powdered sugar.

Makes about 12 pieces

Strawberry and Cheese Squirrel's Tail

I guess some bakers just can't leave well enough alone when it comes to making Danish. When I invented this recipe, I took a thin rope of Danish and twisted it to resemble a large number six, then I filled the center with sweetened cheese and strawberry preserves (utterly delicious)! Think of the tail part as something to hold onto when you dip your Danish into a hot cup of coffee or tea.

Chef's Tip!

Sometimes I replace the cheese filling with freshly made lemon curd, or I'll just fold 2 to 3 tablespoons into the cheese mixture and then stuff it into the tail. Also, please feel free to substitute any other Polish jam that strikes your fancy.

Ingredients

1 recipe Danish Dough *(see page 256)*

Egg Glaze

1 large egg
2 tablespoons whole milk

1 recipe Cheese Filling for Danish
    (see page 257)
¾ cup Polish strawberry jam
1 recipe Streusel *(see page 258)*
1 recipe Clear Glaze *(see page 259)*
1 recipe Butter Cream Icing *(see page 259)*

Preparation

1. **Line 2 baking sheets** with parchment paper.

2. **Lightly flour** a work surface, and roll out the dough to measure 12 by 12 by ½-inch thick. Using a pastry cutter, cut the dough into 12 equal strips.

3. **Place one strip** in front of you horizontally on a clean work surface, grasp each end lightly, and begin to roll in opposite directions until the strip is twisted from end to end. You should have about a 12 to 14-inch long twisted piece. Pinch one end of the dough onto the work surface, and lift the other end of the dough up and start to circle it around the pinched end in a spiral motion keeping the dough flat on the work surface. You should now have a form that resembles a tight number 6. Repeat with the remaining dough, then transfer to the baking sheets leaving enough room between each one for them to double in size.

4. **In a small bowl** whisk together the egg and the milk, and using a pastry brush, coat each pastry with the egg glaze.

5. **Using your index finger,** push down into the center of the tight circle to form a pocket, then using a soupspoon place about a heaping tablespoon of cheese filling into the pocket. Using another soupspoon, place about a tablespoon of strawberry jam over the cheese filling, then sprinkle the streusel over the entire pastry.

Repeat with the remaining pastry, cover with plastic wrap, and let rise for about 1 hour until doubled in size.

6. **When the squirrel's tails** are almost doubled, preheat the oven to 350°F., and when ready, bake for about 15 to 20 minutes until golden brown. Remove the pans from the oven and let the pastry cool for 5 minute, then brush with the clear glaze. When completely cooled, using a fork, drizzle on the butter cream icing in a decorative fashion.

Makes about 12 pieces

Buttery Kolaczki with Polish Fruit Preserves

If you're a semi-experienced baker and a kolaczki connoisseur, this is the recipe for you. I've been making this recipe for at least 22 years and people just love them. Your basic kolaczki dough is lightly sweetened, then given special treatment with butter, eggs, buttermilk, and yeast to give it that extra lift. The next day the dough is cut and allowed to rise before filling and baking. I guarantee that these Polish treats will be gone before the sun sets!

Chef's Tip!

If you're having a hard time rolling out the dough, don't get frustrated, just break off walnut size pieces, roll into a ball, place onto the baking sheets, lightly flatten, and then let the shaped pieces rise before filling.

Ingredients

1½ cups all-purpose flour
2 cups cake flour
3 tablespoons sugar
1 teaspoon sea salt
1 teaspoon baking powder
¾ pound unsalted butter, softened
½ cup buttermilk
3 egg yolks
2½ teaspoons active dry yeast

Egg glaze

1 large egg, 2 tablespoons whole milk

1 recipe Streusel (*see page 258*)
Assorted Polish fruit preserves for filling, such as raspberry, peach, bilberry, apricot, black currant, strawberry, blackberry, sour cherry, plum, or gooseberry

Powdered sugar for dusting

Preparation

1. **The night before** preparing the Kolaczki, make the dough. Place the bread flour, cake flour, sugar, salt, and baking powder into a medium sized mixing bowl and stir to combine. Now pour the contents of the bowl through a sifter, and sift into another large mixing bowl.

2. **Combine the butter** into a small pile, and using your hands, pinch off little pieces directly into the bowl with the sifted flours. Working quickly but gently cut the butter into the flour mixture with a pastry blender until the mixture is evenly distributed.

3. **Place the buttermilk** into a small saucepan and heat over a low fire until luke warm, not hot. Let the buttermilk cool for a minute, then whisk in the egg yolks and yeast until completely dissolved.

4. **Now very carefully** using both hands pour the buttermilk around the inside edges of the flour bowl, and gently knead the dough until it just comes together to form a semi-shaggy mass. Lightly flour your work surface, and pour the dough on top of it. Gently knead in a little bit more flour just until you feel comfortable in handling the dough. (Do not over mix. At this point, the dough will be crumbly but that's the way it should be.) Carefully place the dough into a Ziploc bag and refrigerate overnight.

5. **The next morning,** remove the dough from the refrigerator to a clean work surface, and let it come to room temperature. After about 1 hour or so, check the dough and if it gives a little with the push of your finger, it is ready to be kneaded. Lightly flour a clean work surface, and place the dough on top. Gently knead the dough with the flour until you have a smooth elastic but soft dough, then cut it into 2 pieces. Again lightly flour the work surface, and using a rolling pin, roll out the dough to a ¼-inch thickness. Brush off any excess flour, then cut the dough using a 2-inch round pastry cutter. Carefully using an icing spatula, transfer the circles to parchment lined sheet pans. Repeat with the remaining dough. (Don't throw out the scraps, just combine them together and refrigerate for 1 hour before re-rolling.) Now cover the baking pans with plastic wrap and let the Kolaczki rise until doubled.

6. **Preheat the oven** to 375°F.

7. **In a small bowl,** whisk together the egg and the milk, and using a pastry brush, coat each Kolazcki with the egg glaze. Sprinkle the streusel over each Kolaczki, then very carefully using your index finger, indent the center of the each circle. Using a baby spoon, scoop the preserves into the indent of each Kolaczki.

8. **Place the pans** into the preheated oven, and cook for 12 to 15 minutes until the pastries are light golden brown. When cooked, remove the pans, and let the Kolaczkis cool on baker's racks. Sprinkle on the powdered sugar.

Makes about 40 to 50 pieces

Busia's Rum Raisin Babka

Around the holidays, Busia used to go into her secret hiding place and pull out a jar of Polish rum marinated raisins that she would use exclusively for this special babka. Sometimes Busia would seem especially happy when making this holiday treat and we could never figure out why!

Chef's Tip!

Don't be tempted into adding any more rum as 2 tablespoons is plenty for this recipe. Also one whole stick of butter can be omitted from this recipe if you are on a strict diet. Babka pans are hard to come by so please feel free to use a non-stick fluted Bundt pan, unbuttered.

Ingredients

Sponge

1 cup half and half (about 110 degrees)
2¼ cups bread flour
4 teaspoons active dry yeast

½ pound unsalted butter, softened
10 tablespoons sugar
1 teaspoon sea salt
¾ teaspoon vanilla extract
½ teaspoon cardamom
2 whole large eggs plus 1 yolk
2¼ cups all-purpose flour
¾ cup white raisins marinated in
   2 tablespoons rum
1 recipe Butter Cream Icing *(see page 259)*

1 babka pan, well buttered

Preparation

1. **To make the sponge,** place the half and half in a mixing bowl and whisk in the yeast. Stir in the flour until smooth, then cover with plastic wrap and let the sponge rise until doubled in volume, about 1 hour.

2. **To mix the dough** in a heavy-duty mixer, place the butter, sugar, salt, vanilla, and cardamom in the mixer bowl, attach the paddle, and mix on low speed for 1 minute to blend the ingredients. Add the eggs, one by one until they are absorbed, then add the sponge, remaining flour, and raisins, and mix the dough for 2 minutes until the dough forms a mass around the paddle. Turn the machine off, remove the paddle, and replace with the dough hook. Knead the dough on medium low speed for 2 to 3 minutes, or until the dough is smooth and elastic. If the dough is excessively soft and sticky, add1 to 2 tablespoons more flour, one at a time, and knead a little longer.

3. **Place the dough** into a large bowl, then cover the bowl tightly with plastic wrap, and allow the dough to rise in the refrigerator for at least 2 to 4 hours. (This chilling time is imperative so that the butter doesn't seep out of the dough.)

4. **After a couple of hours** or overnight, turn the risen dough out onto a lightly floured work surface, and gently punch it down. Using floured hands, roll the dough into a fat cigar shape about 12 to 14 inches long. Now form the dough into a small tire, and pinch together the open ends. Place the dough into the buttered babka pan, cover tightly with plastic wrap, and let rise slowly in a warm place until doubled.

5. **Preheat the oven** to 350°, and when the babka is risen, place into the hot oven and cook for 40 to 45 minutes until golden brown. Remove the pan from the oven, and carefully remove the babka to a cooling rack. When completely cool, drizzle with butter cream icing.

Makes one cake

Lemon Babka

Ingredients

10 tablespoons sugar
1 teaspoon sea salt
½ pound unsalted butter, softened
1 teaspoon lemon extract
½ teaspoon vanilla extract
2 teaspoons grated lemon zest
3 whole large eggs
1 cup half and half (about 110 degrees)
2¼ cups bread flour
2¼ cups all-purpose flour
4 teaspoons active dry yeast
Powdered sugar for dusting

1 nonstick fluted Bundt pan, unbuttered

I love just plain cake, the simpler the better. This recipe produces a slightly lemony, fine grained, but utterly moist and delicious babka. Many cooks need to abandon the notion that more eggs, sugar, and butter makes a better cake. This recipe is proof that less is more, and I recommend serving it with freshly whipped cream, and a homemade summer fruit salad.

Chef's Tip!

Babkas need a lot of love and care when making them. It is important that the dough is allowed to chill out in the refrigerator for a while to relax the gluten and let the flavors meld together.

Preparation

1. **Thoroughly combine** the flours and yeast in a medium sized mixing bowl, and then set aside.

2. **To mix the dough** in a heavy-duty mixer, place the sugar, salt, butter, lemon, and vanilla extract, and grated zest in the mixer bowl, attach the paddle and mix on low speed for 1 minute to blend the ingredients. Add the eggs, one by one, until they are absorbed, then add the half and half and mix briefly.

3. **Now slowly add** all of the flour until the dough forms a mass around the paddle. Turn the machine off, remove the paddle and replace with the dough hook. Knead the dough on medium low speed for about 5 minutes, or until the dough is smooth and elastic. If the dough is excessively soft and sticky, add 1 to 2 tablespoons more flour, one at a time, and knead a little longer.

4. **Place the dough** into a large bowl, then cover the bowl tightly with plastic wrap, and allow the dough to rise in the refrigerator for at least 2 to 4 hours. (This chilling time is imperative so that the butter doesn't seep out of the dough.)

5. **After a couple of hours** or overnight, turn the risen dough out onto a lightly floured work surface, and gently punch it down. Using floured hands, roll the dough into a fat cigar shape about 12 to 14 inches long. Now form the dough into a small tire, and pinch together the open ends. Place the dough into the unbuttered bundt pan, cover tightly with plastic wrap, and let rise slowly in a warm place until doubled.

6. **Preheat the oven** to 350°F., and when the Babka is risen, place into the hot oven and cook for 35 to 45 minutes until golden brown. Remove the pan from the oven, and carefully remove the Babka to a cooling rack. When completely cool, heavily dust with powdered sugar.

Makes one cake

Chocolate Glazed Pachki

Ingredients

5 tablespoons sugar
¾ teaspoon sea salt
3 tablespoons shortening
½ teaspoon vanilla extract
1 heaping teaspoon grated lemon or orange zest
2 large egg yolks
1 scant cup whole milk (about 110 degrees)
1¾ cups all-purpose flour
1¾ cups cake flour
4 teaspoons active dry yeast
1 tablespoon baking powder
2 tablespoons Spiritus or rum, optional

1 recipe Chocolate Glaze *(see page 259)*

Shortening for frying

Over the last few years, Pachki, or Polish doughnuts, have become the breadwinners at ethnic bakeries around the country, but sadly most are being made from a commercial mix. I wanted to give you an original Polish Pachki recipe that contains no preservatives, and is lighter and healthier. Lemon and vanilla scented sweet dough is lightly bronzed, then dipped into a warm bath of chocolate glaze to create a breakfast lover's treat!

Chef's Tip!

Traditionally, Pachki are filled with a Polish jam called Rosa Rugosa before frying. Polish cooks like to fry the doughnuts in a combination of ⅔ part Crisco to ⅓ part lard for extra taste.

Preparation

1. **Thoroughly combine** the flours, yeast, and baking powder in a medium sized mixing bowl, and then set aside.

2. **To mix the dough** in a heavy-duty mixer, place the sugar, salt, shortening, vanilla, and zest in the mixer bowl, attach the paddle and mix on low speed for 1 minute to blend the ingredients. Add the yolks until they are absorbed, then add the whole milk and liquor, and mix briefly.

3. **Now slowly add** all of the flour until the dough forms a mass around the paddle. Turn the machine off, remove the paddle and replace with the dough hook. Knead the dough on medium low speed for about 5 minutes, or until the dough is smooth and elastic. If the dough is excessively soft and sticky, add 1 to 2 tablespoons more flour, one at a time, and knead a little longer.

4. **Place the dough** in a large oiled bowl and turn to coat all sides. Cover the bowl tightly with plastic wrap, and allow the dough to rise in a warm place for 20 minutes.

5. **Turn the dough** out onto a lightly floured work surface, and carefully using your hands, pat down the dough until it is exactly ½-inch thick. Cover the dough with a piece of plastic wrap, and let it rest for exactly 15 minutes. After 15 minutes, cut the dough, using a 2½ or 3-inch round pastry cutter, making sure you cut completely through the dough. Carefully, lift up any excess dough

around the cut circles, and place in a mixing bowl. Cover the cut rounds with plastic wrap, and let them rest undisturbed for 20 minutes, or until they are ¾ risen.

6. **Using your hands,** thoroughly combine the excess dough to form a ball and let rest for 15 minutes, then roll out like in step #5.

7. **Heat a good amount** of shortening in a medium sized heavy-duty pot until it reaches 375°F to 385°F. After the doughnuts have rested, fry 1 or 2 at a time in the hot fat, for about 1½ to 2 minutes until golden brown on each side. Drain the Pachki on brown paper bags, then transfer to a cooling rack.

8. **Dip the slightly cooled** Pachkis into the chocolate glaze.

Makes about 14 to 16 doughnuts

Bismark Twist (a.k.a. Longjohns)

Ingredients

7 tablespoons sugar
¾ teaspoon sea salt
6 tablespoons shortening or margarine
1 teaspoon vanilla or lemon extract
Large dash of mace
1 heaping teaspoon grated lemon or orange zest
2 whole large eggs
1 cup warm whole milk (about 110 degrees)
4¼ cups bread flour
1½ tablespoons baking powder
4 teaspoons active dry yeast

1 recipe Cinnamon Sugar (*see page 258*)
   or
1 recipe Chocolate Glaze (*see page 259*)

Shortening for frying

I don't know anyone who doesn't like Bismark twists. Depending on where you live in the country, this breakfast treat falls under the name cinnamon longjohns, sugar mice, or Sophie's braids. The end result is still the same, as these tiny tasty treats disappear quickly with a cup of coffee or a glass of milk.

Chef's Tip!

The cut out squares can be lightly rolled and twisted into the traditional Bismark shape with a little care and practice.

Preparation

1. **Thoroughly combine** the flour, baking powder, and yeast in a medium sized mixing bowl, and then set aside.

2. **To mix the dough** in a heavy-duty mixer, place the sugar, salt, shortening, vanilla, mace, and zest in the mixer bowl, attach the paddle and mix on low speed for 1 minute to blend the ingredients. Add the eggs, one by one, until they are absorbed, then add the milk and mix briefly.

3. **Now slowly** add all of the flour until the dough forms a mass around the paddle. Turn the machine off, remove the paddle and replace with the dough hook. Knead the dough on medium low speed for about 5 minutes, or until the dough is smooth and elastic. If the dough is excessively soft and sticky, add 1 to 2 tablespoons more flour, one at a time, and knead a little longer.

4. **Place the dough** in a large oiled bowl and turn to coat all sides. Cover the bowl tightly with plastic wrap, and allow the dough to rise in a warm place until doubled in bulk, about 1½ hours.

5. **Turn the risen dough** out onto a lightly floured work surface, and flip it over (it is very important not to punch the dough down.) Now very carefully, using a rolling pin, roll out the dough into a 10 by 20-inch oblong, exactly ½-inch thick. Cut the dough into 1½ by 1½-inch squares using a rolling cutter, making sure you cut completely through the dough. Cover the cut pieces with plastic wrap, and let them rest undisturbed for 20 minutes.

6. **Heat a good amount** of shortening in a medium sized heavy-duty pot until it reaches 375°F to 385°F. After the Bismarks have rested, fry 3 to 4 at a time in the hot fat, for about 1½ to 2 minutes until golden brown on each side. Drain the Bismarks on brown paper bags, then transfer to a cooling rack.

7. **Roll the cooked dough** into the cinnamon sugar or dip into the chocolate glaze.

Makes about 50 bite-size pieces

Crisp Chrusciki

It seems that every ethnic group has their own favorite recipe for Chrust-Faworki, or "angel wings." A slightly sweetened dough is thinly rolled out, cut into a shape to form angel wings, gently fried, and then dusted with powdered sugar. These delicate treats are often served around religious holidays, or are even stacked to act as sweet table centerpieces at wedding receptions.

Chef's Tip!

The secret to a great "angel wing" is to let the dough rest a while, then roll it out until you can just see the counter top through the dough.

Ingredients

2 egg yolks
1 whole large egg
5 tablespoons sugar
¼ cup heavy cream
1 teaspoon orange, lemon, or vanilla extract
1⅓ cups all-purpose flour
Pinch of sea salt

Preparation

1. **In a large mixing bowl,** lightly whisk the eggs for 1 minute. Add the sugar, heavy cream, vanilla, and salt, and whisk until fully incorporated.

2. **Now using a heavy** wooden spoon, stir in the flour, then beat vigorously until a raggedy ball forms. (At this point, the dough will be soft and sticky. If it is too sticky to handle, add 1 to 2 more tablespoons of flour, one at a time, and knead in with your hands until the dough is manageable.)

3. **Lightly flour** a work surface, and place the dough on top of it. Using floured hands, gently knead the dough until it is smooth, elastic, and not at all sticky. Place the ball into a Ziploc bag, and let rest at room temperature for 40 minutes.

4. **Remove the dough** from the bag, lightly flatten with the back of your hand, and cut into 2 equal pieces. Place one of the pieces back into the Ziploc bag and set aside. Now on a lightly floured work surface, using a rolling pin, roll half of the dough into a long strip, about 5-inches wide by 30-inches long. You should be able to see the table surface underneath the dough. Brush off any excess flour.

5. **Using a rolling cutter,** cut the dough into strips about 4-inches long and 1½-inches wide. Slit each piece in the center, and pull one end through the slit. Place the cut pieces on a parchment lined baking sheet, and cover with another piece of parchment paper. Repeat with the remaining dough.

6. **Heat a good amount** of shortening in a medium sized heavy duty pot until it reaches 375°F, then fry the dough strips, a few at a time, until lightly browned on both sides, about 1 minute.

7. **Drain the Chrusciki** on brown paper bags, then transfer to a cooling rack and sprinkle with powdered sugar.

Makes about 75 pieces

Festive Rosettes

Ingredients

2 whole large eggs
1 egg yolk
⅓ cup sugar
1 cup all-purpose flour
⅔ cup heavy cream

Shortening for frying
One set rosette molds

Powdered sugar for dusting

A long time ago, when I was an alter boy, some of the local church ladies used to decorate the Nativity scene Christmas tree with fanciful colored cookies. The other boys and I used to sneak down to the rectory kitchen and watch the women color and deep fry all shapes and sizes imaginable. There were rosettes in the shapes of Christmas trees, bells, and stars that were beautiful to look at and even better to eat!

Chef's Tip!

The trick to a great rosette is to use a good set of broken-in irons, and to use a quality shortening, such as Crisco, for frying.

Preparation

1. **In a medium-sized mixing bowl,** beat the eggs, egg yolk, sugar, and cream together until well combined. Now add the flour and stir until well blended. Let the batter rest for at least 1 hour.

2. **After 1 hour,** place the shortening into a deep fat frying pot and heat until a thermometer registers 365° to 375°.

3. **Place the rosette iron** into the hot fat for 2 minutes to heat up, remove, pat once on a paper towel, and dip into the well- stirred batter. (Make sure you do not submerge the iron completely into the batter so that the rosette can release itself from the mold.)

4. **Now gently dip** the coated mold into the hot shortening and leave it there until the crisp shell falls off the iron. Remove the bronzed rosette with a kitchen tong to a paper towel lined sheet pan, and repeat the process until all of the batter is used. When the rosettes are cool, sprinkle on powdered sugar and store in an airtight container.

Makes about 30 pieces

Low Lemon Cheesecake

This is the perfect cake if you're having a small, elegant dinner party. The lemon-flavored cheese is baked into a sweet pastry crust, which gives the chilled cake a perfect crisp background for the smoothness of the cheese. A thin apricot glaze coats the top and gives it a European flavor.

Chef's Tip!

If your apricot jam seems too thick to brush on top of the chilled cake, just re-heat it again with a little bit more water, and then pass it through a fine strainer directly over the cake.

Ingredients

1 recipe Sweet Pastry Dough

12 ounces cream cheese
4 tablespoons unsalted butter, softened
6 tablespoons sugar
1 teaspoon vanilla extract
1 whole large egg plus 1 yolk
1 tablespoon lemon juice

$^1/_2$ cup apricot jam
2 tablespoons water

Preparation

1. **Preheat the oven** to 350°F.

2. **Place the dough** on a lightly floured work surface, and using a rolling pin, roll out the dough into a 12-inch circle, $^1/_8$-inch thick. Now carefully fit the dough into a 9-inch fluted tart pan with a removable bottom, and trim away the excess.

3. **Place the cream cheese** and butter into a work bowl of an electric mixer, and using the paddle attachment, beat on low until smooth. With the machine running, add the sugar and vanilla in a slow stream. Turn the machine off, and using a plastic spatula, scrape down the sides of the bowl. Turn the machine back on low, and add one egg at a time until fully incorporated. Now add the lemon juice.

4. **Turn the machine off,** remove the bowl and paddle from the machine, and using a plastic spatula, scrape off any excess filling that is stuck to the paddle. Lightly stir it into the mix, then gently pour the filling into the prepared pastry lined tart pan. Bake the tart on the middle rack for about 40 minutes, until the filling is set and the crust is golden brown. Remove the cheesecake from the oven, and cool on a wire rack.

5. **Put the apricot jam** and water into a small sauce pan and bring to a boil, then lower the heat and simmer slowly until the glaze coats the back of a spoon. Cool slightly, then using a soft pastry brush, paint the top of the cooled cheesecake lightly.

Makes one 9" cake

Sweet Pastry Dough

Ingredients

1 cup plus 2 tablespoons unsalted butter, softened
$^3/_4$ cup plus 2 tablespoons sugar
1 teaspoon vanilla extract
2 whole large eggs, beaten
$3^1/_2$ cups all-purpose flour
$^1/_4$ teaspoon sea salt

Preparation

1. **Using an electric mixer,** beat the butter, sugar, and vanilla together in a bowl until smooth and creamy.

2. **With the beaters** running on a slow speed, gradually add the beaten eggs until well incorporated.

3. **Sift the flour** and salt together, and with the mixer set on the slowest speed, gradually add the flour until the mixture just comes together and forms a shaggy mass. Now turn the mixer off, pour the dough out onto a clean work surface, and then gently knead with your hands until the dough is smooth, about 1 to 2 minutes. (Don't over knead the pastry.)

4. **Divide the dough** into 2 to 3 batches, tightly cover them with plastic wrap, and then refrigerate for at least 2 hours before using.

Makes enough for 2 to 3 9-inch shells

Praline Cheesecake

Ingredients

Praline

¹⁄₂ cup sugar
2 tablespoons water
Dash of lemon juice
²⁄₃ cup almonds, hazelnuts, or pecans

2 pounds cream cheese
1¹⁄₄ cups sugar
2 teaspoons vanilla extract
4 large whole eggs
1 tablespoon lemon juice

6 whole graham crackers, finely crushed
2 teaspoons sugar
4 tablespoons unsalted butter, melted

Simple, easy, pure, and addictively sinful!

Chef's Tip!

For a real sinful treat, cut the chilled cheesecake into slices, and then individually wrap and freeze.

Preparation

1. **Preheat the oven** to 350°F.

2. **To prepare the praline,** place the sugar, water, and lemon juice into a small saucepot, and bring to a rapid boil over medium high heat. Let the syrup cook until it starts to take on a light golden color, then add the nuts and stir with a wooden spoon until the nuts and the sugar turn a medium caramelized color. Immediately pour the hot nut mixture onto a clean nonstick sheet pan, and let it cool undisturbed for at least 15 minutes before touching. When the mixture is cool enough to handle, scrape up the mass with a metal pastry scraper, and place into the work bowl of a food processor fitted with a metal blade. Cover the bowl and pulse the praline until it resembles finely ground breadcrumbs. Pour into a small bowl and set aside.

3. **Prepare a 9-inch** spring form cake pan, by brushing the interior with softened butter, and place a circle of parchment paper onto the bottom of the pan. (Be sure to brush the top of the paper.) Thoroughly combine the crushed graham crackers, sugar, and butter in a small mixing bowl, then pour the mixture into the bottom of the prepared pan. Evenly distribute the graham cracker crust over the parchment paper, and place into the hot oven for 5 minutes to set the crust. Remove the pan from the oven and place onto a round baking sheet. (This will prevent the butter from leaking out of the spring form pan.)

4. **Place the cream cheese** into the work bowl of an electric mixer, and using the paddle attachment, beat on low until smooth. With the machine running, add the sugar, lemon juice, and vanilla in a slow stream. Turn the machine off, and using a plastic spatula, scrape down the sides of the bowl. Turn the machine back on low, and add one egg at a time until fully incorporated. Immediately after the last egg is added, add all of the praline and let the machine run for 1 minute more.

5. **Turn the machine off,** remove the bowl and paddle from the machine, and using a plastic spatula, scrape off any excess filling that is stuck to the paddle. Lightly stir into the mix, then gently pour half the filling into the prepared pan. Level the cheese filling with a spatula, then immediately bake the cheesecake in the hot oven for exactly 40 minutes. After 40 minutes turn the heat off, and open the oven door slightly ajar to remove any excess heat from the oven. Now close the door and let the baked cheesecake sit in the warm oven for another 1¹⁄₂ hours to set. After that time, remove the cake in the pan to a cooling rack for 1 hour, then wrap the entire pan in plastic wrap and refrigerate overnight. (It is imperative that you refrigerate the cake overnight.)

6. **The next day remove** the cake from the refrigerator, and using a sharp boning knife, run the blade around the inside rim of the spring form pan. Unclasp the pan, then carefully remove the bottom with the cake still attached. Carefully holding the cake in one hand, bend the bottom metal circle with the other hand until you can see the parchment paper circle. At that point, slide a thin icing spatula underneath the paper and remove the cheesecake to a serving platter and serve. (The cheesecake will still be on the parchment paper.)

Makes one 9" cake

Chocolate Swirl Cheesecake

Ingredients

6 whole graham crackers, finely crushed
2 teaspoons sugar
4 tablespoons unsalted butter, melted

2 pounds cream cheese
1¼ cups sugar
2 teaspoons vanilla extract
4 large whole eggs
1 tablespoon lemon juice

1 cup semi-sweet chocolate morsels, melted

This chocolate flavored cheesecake is the brother to praline cheesecake. You could easily just add the chocolate morsels directly into the batter, but swirling in the melted chocolate will get enthusiastic raves from your guests.

Chef's Tip!

For a real sinful treat, cut the chilled cheesecake into slices, and then individually wrap and freeze.

Preparation

1. **Preheat the oven** to 350°F.

2. **Prepare a 9-inch** spring form cake pan, by brushing the interior with softened butter, and place a circle of parchment paper onto the bottom of the pan. (Be sure to brush the top of the paper.) Thoroughly combine the crushed graham crackers, sugar, and butter in a small mixing bowl, then pour the mixture into the bottom of the prepared pan. Evenly distribute the graham cracker crust over the parchment paper, and place into the hot oven for 5 minutes to set the crust. Remove the pan from the oven and place onto a round baking sheet. (This will prevent the butter from leaking out of the spring form pan.)

3. **Place the cream cheese** into the work bowl of an electric mixer, and using the paddle attachment, beat on low until smooth. With the machine running, add the sugar, lemon juice, and vanilla in a slow stream. Turn the machine off, and using a plastic spatula, scrape down the sides of the bowl. Turn the machine back on low, and add one egg at a time until fully incorporated.

4. **Turn the machine off,** remove the bowl and paddle from the machine, and using a plastic spatula, scrape off any excess filling that is stuck to the paddle. Pour about half of the cheese mixture into another bowl, and add the warm melted chocolate. Stir with the spatula to thoroughly combine. Pour a little less than half of the light mixture into the center of the pan, and tilt the pan so it spreads out an even layer and covers the crust. Now gently pour a little less than half of the chocolate mixture over the center of the light mixture and let it spread out, without tilting the pan. Keep alternating the batters in the same fashion until they are all used up, then immediately bake the cheesecake in the hot oven for exactly 40 minutes. After 40 minutes, turn the heat off, and open the door slightly ajar to remove any excess heat from the oven. Now close the door and let the baked cheesecake sit in the warm oven for another 1½ hours to set. After that time, remove the cake in the pan to a cooling rack for 1 hour, then wrap the entire pan in plastic wrap and refrigerate overnight. (It is imperative that you refrigerate the cake overnight.)

5. **The next day** remove the cake from the refrigerator, and using a sharp boning knife, run the blade around the inside rim of the spring form pan. Unclasp the pan, then carefully remove the bottom with the cake still attached. Carefully holding the cake in one hand, bend the bottom metal circle with the other hand until you can see the parchment paper circle. At that point, slide a thin icing spatula underneath the paper and remove the cheesecake to a serving platter and serve. (The cheesecake will still be on the parchment paper.)

Makes one 9" cake

High Soufflé Vanilla Cheesecake

The original Polish cheesecake "Paska." You will find this cake at any Polish bakery around the city and, in my opinion, it typifies the refinement of Polish baking at its best. Farmer's cheese, vanilla, and orange are folded into whipped egg whites to produce a light soufflé type cake that rises at least 4 inches. Don't get frustrated if your soufflé falls, because the cake will be just as good.

Ingredients

1¼ cup farmer's or ricotta cheese
6 tablespoons whole milk
3 tablespoons cornstarch
1 egg yolk
1 tablespoon vanilla extract
1 teaspoon grated orange rind

½ cup egg whites

10 tablespoons sugar
2 tablespoons water
Pinch of sea salt

8 whole graham crackers, finely crushed
2 teaspoons sugar
4 tablespoon unsalted butter, melted

Chef's Tip!

The secret to the height of this cake is to make sure that you use cheese that is completely dry, and to fold the egg whites in quickly.

Preparation

1. **The night before** making the cheesecake, place the cheese of your choice into a medium sized fine mesh strainer set over an empty bowl. Cover with plastic wrap and place in the refrigerator overnight to drain excess liquid.

2. **Preheat the oven** to 400°F.

3. **Prepare** an 8 x 8 x 2-inch square cake pan, by brushing the interior with softened butter, and place a piece of square parchment paper, leaving a 3-inch overhang on two sides, on to the bottom of the pan. (Be sure to brush the top of the paper.) Thoroughly combine the crushed graham crackers, sugar, and butter in a small mixing bowl, then pour the mixture into the bottom of the prepared pan. Evenly distribute the graham cracker crust over the parchment paper and set aside.

4. **In a medium-sized** mixing bowl, using a plastic spatula, combine the drained cheese, milk, cornstarch, egg yolk, vanilla, and grated orange rind until thoroughly smooth.

5. **Place the egg whites** in another medium sized mixing bowl and beat with a whisk until soft peaks form.

6. **Place the remaining sugar,** water, and salt into a small saucepan, and bring to a rapid boil until the sugar dissolves.

7. **Remove the dissolved** sugar from the heat, and while whisking the already beaten egg whites with one hand, carefully pour the hot liquid slowly over them. Keep whisking until all the liquid is incorporated. (The egg whites will now take on a shiny appearance.)

8. **Now very carefully,** using a plastic spatula, fold ¼ of the beaten egg whites into the cheese mixture until fully blended. Repeat the process until all the egg white are used, then immediately pour the mixture into the prepared pan.

9. **Place the pan** in the hot oven, and bake on the middle rack for exactly 10 minutes, then lower the heat to 225°F and bake for about 1 hour and 15 minutes more.

10. **When the cake is done,** very gently remove it from the pan by grasping the overhanging parchment paper, and place it onto a cooling rack.

Makes one 8" x 8" cake

Pick Me Up!

Ingredients

1 cup heavy cream
2 large whole eggs
3 tablespoons sugar
1 pound mascarpone cheese
1 cup brewed espresso coffee
3 tablespoons Kahlua
¼ cup cocoa powder

1 recipe Vanilla Sponge Cake *(see page 254)*

A beautiful Italian specialty cake loved by all. Moist and luscious vanilla sponge cake layered with coffee liqueur and Italian cream cheese, then generously dusted with cocoa powder to create an utterly light and delicious dessert. After a few slices, Papa will for sure say to Mama, "Pick me up!"

Chef's Tip!

Feel free to experiment with any coffee-flavored liqueurs you might have laying around in the cupboard.

Preparation

1. **Whip the heavy cream** in a mixing bowl until it forms soft peaks, then place in the refrigerator.

2. **Place a large** mixing bowl over a bain Marie at low heat, and add to the bowl 2 egg yolks, 1 egg white plus the sugar, and beat with a whisk until thick and lemon colored, about 3 to 4 minutes. Remove the bowl from the pot and continue whisking until the sabayon has cooled.

3. **Remove any standing** liquid from the cheese and discard. Now add to the sabayon the mascarpone cheese, whisking the two together just until blended.

4. **Using a plastic** spatula, quickly fold the whipped cream into the mascarpone mixture and set aside.

5. **Combine the espresso** with the Kahlua.

6. **Carefully, using a long** serrated knife, cut the cake into 3 equal and even layers. Now flip the cut cake over so that the bottom is now on top. Place the top layer, cut side up, onto a 9-inch cardboard cake circle, and using a soft pastry brush, paint the cut layer with ¼ cup of the espresso mixture. Using a metal icing spatula, spread a ¼-inch thick layer of mascarpone mixture on top of the brushed cake. Repeat the above process with the other two layers, then ice the sides and top with the remaining mascarpone mixture.

Sift on the cocoa powder and refrigerate for at least 6 hours (24 hours is best).

Makes one 9" layer cake

Biscuit Chopin

I dedicate this cake to Chopin, the famous Polish composer. Chocolate sponge cake is layered with Kahlua, light chocolate mousse, and espresso flavored butter cream. One bite of this cake is like a perfect symphony.

Chef's Tip!

This cake is traditionally made in a rectangular shape because it is so rich, but feel free to bake the sponge cake in a 9-inch round pan.

Ingredients

1 recipe Chocolate Sponge Cake baked in a
  10 x 15-inch jelly roll pan *(see page 254)*

$^1/_2$ cup water
$^1/_4$ cup sugar
2 tablespoons Kahlua
1 teaspoon vanilla extract

1 pound semi-sweet chocolate morsels
$1^1/_3$ cup heavy cream

$^3/_4$ cup sugar
$^1/_3$ cup water
8 egg yolks
1 cup unsalted butter, soft
$1^1/_2$ tablespoons instant coffee
2 teaspoons water

Preparation

1. **To make the brushing** syrup, place the water, sugar, Kahlua, and vanilla extract into a small saucepan, and heat over medium fire until the sugar is dissolved, then remove from the heat.

2. **Place the chocolate** into a medium sized mixing bowl. Bring the heavy cream to a boil in a small saucepan, then pour over the chocolate, and let it sit for 1 minute. Using a plastic spatula, stir the mixture until completely smooth, and then let the mixture cool at room temperature for about 1 hour.

3. **To make the coffee butter** cream, dissolve the instant coffee into the 2 teaspoons of water and set aside. Now place the egg yolks into the work bowl of and electric mixer and attach the balloon whisk to the machine. Do not whip the eggs yet.

4. **In a small saucepan,** boil the sugar with the water until it reaches 250°F on a candy thermometer. Keep a careful eye on the thermometer.

5. **When the temperature** reaches 240°F, turn the electric mixer on medium speed, and whisk the yolks. When the thermometer reaches 250°F, remove the sugar-water from the heat, and pour in a slow steady stream over the whisking eggs. Continue beating the eggs until the mixture is cool, about 3 to 4 minutes. When the bottom of the mixing bowl is cool to the touch, add the softened butter, piece by piece, and continue to whip the mixture at low speed for 5 minutes more. Now add the dissolved coffee and turn

the machine off. Scrape the coffee butter cream out of the work bowl into another bowl, and set aside.

6. **Clean the work bowl,** scrape the chocolate mixture into it, and then place back on the machine with the balloon whisk. Beat the mixture on medium high speed until light in color and fluffy.

7. **Place the baked** cake onto a clean work surface, and using a long serrate knife, cut the cake vertically into 3 equal pieces. Trim any rough edges if necessary. Using a soft pastry brush, paint all 3 of the cut layers with the brushing syrup. Now using a metal icing spatula, spread a thick layer of the whipped chocolate onto one of the painted layers. Flatten the top lightly with the spatula. Now gently stack another cut layer on top of the chocolate covered one. Again, using a metal icing spatula, spread a thick layer of the coffee butter cream onto this layer, and flatten the top slightly with the spatula. Place the last piece of cake on top of the coffee butter cream layer, and again, ice with the remaining coffee butter cream. Smooth out the top and sides as evenly as possible, then place the whole cake into the refrigerator for about 20 minutes. Remove the cake, and spread the remaining chocolate on top of the coffee butter cream as evenly as possible, as this is the last layer of icing. Refrigerate the cake for at least 6 hours before serving. When the cake is cold, trim up the 4 sides with a long serrated knife.

Makes one 4" x 8" layer cake

Chocolate Raspberry Torte

Ingredients

1 Chocolate Sponge Cake (*see page 254*)

¹⁄₂ cup water
¹⁄₄ cup sugar
2 tablespoons raspberry liqueur
1 teaspoon vanilla extract

1 pound semi-sweet chocolate morsels
1¹⁄₃ cup heavy cream
2 tablespoons raspberry liqueur

¹⁄₂ cup seedless raspberry preserves
2 tablespoons water

1 cup bittersweet chocolate morsels
³⁄₄ cup heavy cream

The original "chocolate orgasm." Chocolate sponge cake layered with a light chocolate mousse, raspberry liqueur, and Polish preserves, then a shiny bittersweet coating of, you guessed it, chocolate!

Chef's Tip!

This cake actually tastes better if left overnight to chill. You can also substitute Kahlua for the raspberry liqueur.

Preparation

1. **To make the brushing** syrup, place the water, sugar, raspberry liqueur, and vanilla extract into a small saucepan, and heat over medium fire until the sugar is dissolved, then remove from the heat.

2. **Place the chocolate** into the work bowl of an electric mixer. Bring the heavy cream and raspberry liqueur to a boil in a small saucepan, then pour over the chocolate, and let it sit for 1 minute. Using a plastic spatula, stir the mixture until completely smooth, then let the mixture cool at room temperature for about 1 hour.

3. **Carefully, using a long** serrated knife, cut the cake into 3 equal and even layers. Now flip the cut cake over so that the bottom is now on top. Place the top layer, cut side up, onto a 9-inch cardboard cake circle, and using a soft pastry brush, paint the cut layer with the brushing syrup. Using a metal icing spatula, spread a thin layer of the raspberry preserves on top of the brushed cake.

4. **Now take the work** bowl filled with the chocolate and place onto the machine. Attach the balloon whisk, and beat the mixture on medium high speed until light in color and fluffy. Add the vanilla and turn the machine off.

5. **Using a metal icing** spatula, spread a ¹⁄₄-inch thick layer of chocolate mixture on top of the brushed cake. Repeat the above process with the other 2 layers, then ice the sides and top with the remaining whipped chocolate. Place the tort in the refrigerator for about 1 hour to chill.

6. **Bring the remaining** heavy cream to a boil in a small saucepan, then pour over the remaining chocolate. Let it sit for 1 minute, then smooth with a plastic spatula. Let it cool slightly at room temperature, about 20 minutes. Remove the torte from the refrigerator and place it onto a cooling rack set over and sheet pan. Now gently pour the chocolate glaze over the chilled torte to cover. Refrigerate the torte.

Makes one 9" layer cake

Chocolate Raspberry Torte

Strawberry Layer Cake

Ingredients

1 Vanilla Sponge Cake *(see page 254)*
1 recipe Vanilla Pastry Cream *(see page 256)*

½ cup water
¼ cup sugar
1 tablespoon dark rum

2 cups heavy cream
2 tablespoons sugar
2 teaspoons vanilla extract

½ cup red currant jelly
1 pint fresh strawberries, cleaned and hulled

When I was growing up, the Fourth of July was a huge event, and it always seemed that we celebrated someone's birthday on that day. This was the cake of choice. Cool layers of sponge cake, pastry cream, whipped cream, and strawberries always cooled down those hot summer nights. Hey, fireworks, sparklers, outdoor grilling, and cake; what more can I say?

Chef's Tip!

I highly recommend having everything prepared and well-chilled before assembling this cake. A packet of Whip-it can be added to the whipped cream to keep it firm.

Preparation

1. **Thoroughly dry** the strawberries after they have been cleaned and hulled then pick through the berries and reserve 10 of the best for the cake garnish. Thinly slice the remaining berries and set aside.

2. **In a large** mixing bowl, whip the heavy cream, sugar, and vanilla until they form soft peaks, then place in the refrigerator.

3. **To make** the brushing syrup, place the water, sugar, and rum into a small saucepan, and heat over medium fire until the sugar is dissolved, then remove from the heat.

4. **Carefully,** using a long serrated knife cut the cake into 2 equal and even layers. Now flip the cut cake over so that the bottom is now on top. Place the top layer, cut side up, onto a 9-inch cardboard cake circle, and using a soft pastry brush, paint the cut layer with the brushing syrup. Using a metal icing spatula, spread a ¼-inch thick layer of pastry cream on top of the brushed cake. Now arrange all of the sliced strawberries on top of the pastry cream.

5. **Place the second** layer of cake, cut side down, over the berries, and paint the top with the brushing syrup. Now using a metal icing spatula, spread about half of the whipped cream onto the top and sides of the cake, making sure that the top is flat, and that there is enough icing on the sides so that you can't see through to the cake.

Fit a pastry bag with a #7 star tube (large star tip), fill with the remaining whipped cream, then pipe 10 to 12 stars on top of the cake in a decorative design.

6. **Heat the red** currant jelly in a small saucepan over medium heat until it dissolves, and stir until shiny and smooth then remove from the fire. Now carefully grasp one of the garnish strawberries by the hulled end, and swirl into the melted jelly to coat the berry. Let the excess drip, then place the berry on top of the cake between the piped stars. Repeat with the remaining berries, then refrigerate the cake for a couple of hours before serving.

Makes one 9" layer cake

Bittersweet Chocolate Tart

Slim, dark, and delicious is the way most chefs describe this simple tart. A silky chocolate ganache is slowly baked in a sugar crust to produce an utterly chocoholic experience.

Ingredients

1 recipe Sweet Pastry Dough *(see page 255)*

³/₄ cup heavy cream
¹/₃ cup milk
1 heaping cup bittersweet or semi-sweet
   chocolate morsels
1 whole large egg
2 tablespoons unsweetened cocoa powder

Chef's Tip!

This chocolate tart is decadently rich, so I recommend serving it in small slices with just a dollop of slightly sweetened whipped cream.

Preparation

1. **Place the dough** on a lightly floured work surface, and using a rolling pin, roll out the dough into a 12-inch circle, ¹/₈-inch thick. Now carefully fit the dough into a 9-inch fluted tart pan with a removable bottom, and using your index finger, press the pastry well into the sides of the pan and make sure there are no tears. Now using a kitchen fork, lightly make indents into the base of the dough. Cover with a piece of parchment paper, then weigh down the base with baking beans, and chill in the refrigerator for 1 hour.

2. **Preheat the oven** to 375°F while the dough is resting.

3. **Place the tart** shell onto a baking sheet, and bake for 10 minutes in the hot oven. Now remove the shell from the oven, discard the parchment and baking beans, and trim the edges of the excess pastry using a sharp knife. Return the shell back to the oven, and bake for another 5 minutes to firm up the dough. Remove from the oven and set aside.

4. **Place the chocolate** morsels into a medium sized bowl. In a small saucepan, bring the heavy cream and milk just to the boil, then pour over the chocolate, whisking until the chocolate is completely melted and smooth.

5. **When the chocolate** is cooled to lukewarm, add the lightly beaten whole egg, and whisk until thoroughly blended. Pour the mixture into the baked pastry shell, and bake on the middle rack for 12 to 15 minutes until the filling is almost firm, but still trembling in the center. Remove and cool on a wire rack, then dust the top with the cocoa powder.

Makes one 9" tart

Hot Apple Tart with Vanilla Bean Ice Cream

Ingredients

¹/₂ pound puff pastry dough
1 large whole egg
Pinch of sea salt
4 large Granny Smith apples; peeled, cored,
    and cut in half
2 tablespoons sugar plus ¹/₄ teaspoon cinnamon
¹/₂ cup apricot jam
2 tablespoons water

1 recipe Vanilla Bean Ice Cream (*see page 239*)

"Szarlotka," or Polish apple cake, is easily the Polish equivalent to what we would call apple pie in this country. The original calls for cooked cinnamon apples to be baked between 2 sheets of sugar pastry dough, but some find it too rich and filling. This is my simple, but elegant interpretation of that dish. The flavors are the same, however it's easier on your waistline.

Chef's Tip!

You can prepare the tarts a few hours in advance—just re-heat in the oven for 5 minutes, re-glaze, and then scoop on the ice cream.

Preparation

1. **Lightly flour** a work surface, and place the dough on top of it. Using a rolling pin, gently roll out the dough into a 12 × 12-inch square about, ¹/₈-inch thick. Carefully brush off all excess flour from the dough, and slide the square onto a sheet pan lined with parchment paper. Place the pan in the refrigerator for about 1 hour to rest.

2. **Whip the egg** and salt together.

3. **Thoroughly combine** the sugar with the cinnamon.

4. **Preheat the oven** to 375°F.

5. **Remove the dough** from the refrigerator, and using a round cutter or a small plate as a guide, cut the dough into four 5-inch circles. Now carefully, using a 1-inch round cutter, cut out a hole in the center of each circle to form rings. Transfer the cut circles to another parchment lined sheet pan, equally spaced apart. Slice the apples into thin semi-circles, then lay the slices around the inner edge of each pastry ring, leaving a ¹/₈-inch border.

6. **Using a soft** pastry brush, paint the outer edges of the pastry circle with the egg wash.

7. **Lightly sprinkle** the cinnamon sugar onto the cut apples, then place the pan into the hot oven for about 20 minutes until the tarts have risen and are golden brown.

8. **While the tarts** are cooking, prepare the glaze. Put the apricot jam and water into a small saucepan and bring to a boil, then lower the heat and simmer slowly until the glaze coats the back of a spoon.

9. **When the apple** tarts are golden brown, remove them from the oven, and brush them with the warm apricot glaze. To serve, place a scoop of vanilla bean ice cream in the center of each tart.

Serves 4

Red Fruits in Flaky Pastry

Ingredients

½ pound puff pastry dough
1 whole large egg
Pinch of sea salt

1 recipe Vanilla Pastry Cream *(see page 256)*

1 cup heavy cream
2 tablespoons sugar
1 teaspoon vanilla extract

1 recipe Fresh Strawberry or Raspberry Sauce
  (see page 253)

1½ cups assorted sliced berries
¼ cup powdered sugar

Flaky pastry, or puff pastry, desserts are usually served in most upscale restaurants that charge upscale prices for them. This dessert is a distant cousin of the famous "Napoleon slice," with the addition of freshly whipped cream, berries, and a cool fruit sauce that somehow brings it all together.

Chef's Tip!

Any combination of fresh red fruits can be used—strawberries, raspberries, blackberries, even blueberries go well with the cool pastry cream.

Preparation

1. **Lightly flour** a work surface, and place the dough on top of it. Using a rolling pin, gently roll out the dough into an 8 × 8-inch square about ⅛-inch thick. Carefully brush off all excess flour from the dough, and slide the square onto a sheet pan lined with parchment paper. Place the pan in the refrigerator for about 1 hour to rest.

2. **Whip the egg** and salt together.

3. **Preheat the oven** to 350°F.

4. **Remove the dough** from the refrigerator, and using a round cutter or a small plate as a guide, cut the dough into four 3-inch circles. Now transfer the cut circles to another parchment lined sheet pan, equally spaced apart. Using a soft pastry brush, paint the pastry with the egg wash. Now bake the feuillettes until they are risen and beginning to feel crisp, about 15 minutes, then lower the heat to 300°F and continue baking another 10 minutes until they are dry and very light. Remove from the oven and place on a cooling rack.

5. **In a medium-sized** mixing bowl whip the heavy cream, sugar, and vanilla until they form soft peaks.

6. **Now, gently using** a serrated knife, cut the baked pastry in half horizontally and remove the top. Using a kitchen spoon, place

about ¼ cup of pastry cream onto the bottoms of the pastry, then equally divide the sliced berries on top of the pastry cream, slightly pushing down on the fruit so that it adheres to the cream. Quickly scrape the whipped cream into a pastry bag fitted with a ½-inch tube, and pipe on to the fresh berries. Gently replace the tops.

7. **Using a small ladle,** pour equal amounts of strawberry sauce onto 4 individual dessert plates. Very gently place a feuillette onto the dessert plate, then sprinkle with sifted powdered sugar.

Serves 4

Profiteroles with Chocolate Sauce

Ingredients

½ cup plus 1 tablespoon whole milk
½ cup plus 1 tablespoon water
1⅛ teaspoon sea salt
1½ teaspoons sugar
8 tablespoons unsalted butter
1½ cups all-purpose flour
5 whole large eggs

1½ cups semisweet chocolate morsels
½ cup whole milk
2 tablespoons unsalted butter, chilled
2 tablespoons Tia Maria or Kahlua, optional

1 quart Vanilla Bean Ice Cream (*see page 239*)

One heavy sheet pan lined with parchment paper

This is really an old French standby dessert that has become very fashionable over the last couple of years. Lightly baked cream puff shells are stuffed with a rich homemade vanilla bean ice cream, and then topped with a decadently warm chocolate sauce. It's kind of like a grownup chocolate sundae, but better!

Chef's Tip!

Do not open the oven door while the puffs are cooking or they will fall. Also, freeze the cooked puffs to facilitate easier handling and slicing.

Preparation

1. **Preheat the oven** to 425°F.

2. **In a medium saucepan,** bring the milk, water, salt, sugar, and butter to a rolling boil. Then stirring with a heavy wooden spoon, add all the flour, and stir hard until the mixture forms a ball. Cook for exactly 1 minute more, stirring all the while to avoid sticking. Remove the pot from the fire, then one by one, add an egg to the pot, and stir vigorously with a wooden spoon to fully incorporate the egg. Repeat the procedure with the rest of the eggs until the dough is smooth and glossy. Now scrape the dough into a pastry bag fitted with a ½-inch plain tube, then pipe the dough onto the parchment lined pan making about 16 to 20 puffs of equal size evenly spaced apart.

3. **Bake for 15 minutes** at 425°F, then lower the oven temperature to 350°F, and bake for another 20 to 25 minutes until the puffs are golden brown. (Do not open the oven while the puffs are cooking). Remove the puffs from the oven and cool on a wire rack.

4. **To make the sauce,** bring the milk to the boil in a medium sized saucepan, then remove from the heat and stir in the chocolate and butter. Keep stirring with a wooden spoon until the mixture is smooth, then set aside.

5. **Now cut the puffs** horizontally in half, and line them up on a platter. Working quickly, scoop out a small ball of ice cream and place it onto the puffs, then replace the tops, and cover with the warm chocolate sauce and serve.

Makes about 16 pieces

Vanilla Bean Ice Cream

A great chef that I worked for used to proclaim that you can always tell a real Vanilla ice cream because it will be pale yellow and speckled with tiny black seeds. I agree. I was never partial to ice cream until I began making it fresh from scratch, and of all the flavors I could prepare, the simple vanilla bean has always been everyone's favorite. The pure, rich, and unaltered taste and texture of this classic will make you think twice about buying from the store.

Chef's Tip!

Fresh vanilla bean ice cream is best eaten within a week's time as it contains no preservatives.

Ingredients

2 cups half and half
1 vanilla bean split open lengthwise
⅔ cup sugar
6 egg yolks
1 cup heavy cream

One medium sized bowl full of ice

Preparation

1. **In a saucepan** over medium heat, bring the half and half and vanilla bean to a simmer, stirring occasionally to make sure the mixture doesn't burn.

2. **Meanwhile in a large** mixing bowl, beat the egg yolks and sugar together until pale yellow.

3. **Now very carefully,** pour a little of the hot milk into the bowl with the egg yolk-sugar mixture, whisking constantly as the liquid is added, then pour the egg-milk mixture back into the saucepan containing the rest of the milk.

4. **Cook over medium** low heat, stirring continuously with a wooden spoon, until the mixture thickly coats the back of the spoon. (To test for the right consistency, lift the spoon out of the mixture on a tilt, and run your finger down the back of the spoon to draw a line. If the strip stays clear, it's ready. If it doesn't, cook it a little more.)

5. **When the mixture** is thickened, immediately place the saucepan into a bowl of ice and while still stirring, cool as quickly as possible. When it is cool, strain through a fine mesh conical sieve into a new clean bowl, and whisk in the heavy cream. Refrigerate for at least 4 hours tightly covered with plastic wrap. Then freeze according to the directions of your ice cream maker.

Makes about 1 quart

Chocolate Almond Ice Cream

Ingredients

¹/₂ cup semi-sweet chocolate
1 cup shelled almonds, lightly copped
3¹/₄ cups half and half
6 tablespoons unsweetened cocoa powder
²/₃ cup sugar
6 egg yolks

One medium sized bowl full of ice

Chocolate ice cream is really good, but the addition of chocolate-coated almonds takes this recipe to a higher level. For all of you chocolate and nut lovers out there, this is the ultimate sinful delight!

Chef's Tip!

Don't be tempted to smash the chocolate-coated almonds too finely. If you do, the pieces won't be apparent in the ice cream when it's finished.

Preparation

1. **In a small saucepan,** bring about a cup of water to the boil, then reduce the heat to a slow simmer. Place the semi-sweet chocolate into a medium sized mixing bowl, and place that directly over the simmering water. Now using a plastic spatula, stir the chocolate around until it is completely melted. Now add the lightly crushed almonds to the chocolate and stir around, to thoroughly coat all sides. Pour the chocolate-almond mixture onto a platter, and spread out with the spatula. Place the mixture into the freezer to cool.

2. **Now in a saucepan** over medium heat, bring the half and half and cocoa powder to a simmer, stirring occasionally to make sure the mixture doesn't burn.

3. **Place the egg yolks** and sugar in a medium sized mixing bowl, and beat together until pale yellow.

4. **Now very carefully,** pour a little of the hot milk into the bowl with the egg yolk- sugar mixture, whisking constantly as the liquid is added, then pour the egg-milk mixture back into the saucepan containing the rest of the milk.

5. **Cook over medium** low heat, stirring continuously with a wooden spoon, until the mixture thickly coats the back of the spoon. (To test for the right consistency, lift the spoon out of the mixture on a tilt, and run your finger down the back of the spoon to draw a line. If the strip stays clear, it's ready. If it doesn't, cook it a little more.)

6. **When the mixture is thickened,** immediately place the saucepan into a bowl of ice, and while still stirring cool as quickly as possible. When it is cool, strain through a fine mesh conical sieve into a new clean bowl. Refrigerate for at least 4 hours tightly covered with plastic wrap.

7. **Remove the chocolate almonds** from the freezer, and very carefully place them into a Ziploc bag. Seal the bag and using a small heavy-duty pot, crush the chocolate almonds into small bite size pieces, and return the bag back to the freezer.

8. **Now according to** the directions of your ice cream maker, start to churn the chocolate ice cream mix until it gets to the point where it is almost fully frozen, then add the whole bag of crushed chocolate almonds to the churning ice cream to finish.

Makes about 1 quart

Pistachio Ice Cream

When I was a kid, I remember standing in line for what seemed like hours at an ice cream shop called Peacock's. Everyone thinks of chocolate and vanilla as the most popular flavors and more times than not they are. However, I remember on those hot summer nights that people would be lined up to get a huge scoop of Pistachio nut ice cream for refreshment!

Ingredients

3¼ cups half and half
3 tablespoons sliced almonds, finely ground
¾ cup shelled pistachios, finely ground
⅔ cup sugar
6 egg yolks

One medium sized bowl full of ice

Chef's Tip!

This recipe produces a smooth pistachio ice cream so feel free to add a half-cup of coarsely chopped pistachio nuts to the ice cream maker while it's churning.

Preparation

1. **In a saucepan** over medium heat, bring the half and half, almonds, pistachios, and half of the sugar to a simmer; stirring occasionally to make sure the mixture doesn't burn. Then remove from the heat, and cover, and let the mixture infuse for 30 minutes.

2. **Meanwhile in a** large mixing bowl, beat the egg yolks and remaining sugar together until pale yellow.

3. **Once the milk** and nuts have finished infusing, pour the mixture through a fine mesh conical sieve into a clean saucepan and bring it back to a slow simmer.

4. **Now very carefully,** pour a little of the hot milk into the bowl with the egg yolk-sugar mixture, whisking constantly as the liquid is added, then pour the egg-milk mixture back into the saucepan containing the rest of the milk.

5. **Cook over medium** low heat, stirring continuously with a wooden spoon, until the mixture thickly coats the back of the spoon. (To test for the right consistency, lift the spoon out of the mixture on a tilt, and run your finger down the back of the spoon to draw a line. If the strip stays clear, it's ready. If it doesn't, cook it a little more.)

6. **When the mixture** is thickened, immediately place the saucepan into a bowl of ice, and while still stirring cool as quickly as possible.

When it is cool, strain through a fine mesh conical sieve into a new clean bowl. Refrigerate for at least 4 hours tightly covered with plastic wrap. Then freeze according to the directions of your ice cream maker.

Makes about 1 quart

Caramel Strawberry Ice Cream

Ingredients

2 pint baskets of fresh strawberries
⅓ cup sugar
⅓ cup water
1 tablespoon raspberry liqueur

9 tablespoons sugar
5 drops lemon juice

3 cups half and half

6 egg yolks

One medium sized bowl full of ice

One time I prepared this ice cream for my friend Julia Child, who after one taste proclaimed in French, "C'est magnifique!" She then ordered a serving for everyone in the restaurant. The rich texture of the caramel blended with the sweetness of the strawberries is a winning combination that I think you will enjoy.

Chef's Tip!

Be very careful when you cook the caramel base. If it gets too dark, your ice cream will have a bitter taste to it.

Preparation

1. **Combine the fresh strawberries** with the sugar and water in a saucepan over medium heat. Bring to a boil and simmer until slightly thickened, about 15 minutes. Puree the sauce in a food processor, strain through a fine mesh conical sieve to remove the seeds and cool. Stir in the liqueur and set aside.

2. **To make the caramel base,** place the sugar and lemon juice into a medium sized heavy saucepan and cook stirring over low heat until the sugar starts to melt. Now raise the heat a little, and cook the sugar until it starts to turn a light golden color, stirring occasionally. Cook for another minute until you get a rich golden color, and immediately remove the pan from the heat.

3. **In a saucepan** over medium heat, bring the half and half to a simmer, stirring occasionally to make sure the mixture doesn't burn.

4. **Meanwhile in a large mixing bowl,** beat the egg yolks together until pale yellow.

5. **Now very carefully,** pour the hot milk into the pot with the caramelized sugar stirring as the milk is being added. Return the caramel pot to the fire over low heat and continue stirring the mixture until all of the caramel has dissolved.

6. **Now very carefully,** add a little of the hot milk-caramel mixture into the bowl with the egg yolks, whisking constantly as the liquid is added, then pour the egg-caramel mixture into the saucepan containing the rest of the milk.

7. **Cook over medium** low heat, stirring continuously with a wooden spoon, until the mixture thickly coats the back of the spoon. (To test for the right consistency, lift the spoon out of the mixture on a tilt, and run your finger down the back of the spoon to draw a line. If the strip stays clear, it's ready. If it doesn't, cook it a little more.)

8. **When the mixture is thickened,** immediately place the saucepan into a bowl of ice and while still stirring cool as quickly as possible. When it is cool, strain through a fine mesh conical sieve into a new clean bowl. Refrigerate for at least 4 hours tightly covered with plastic wrap.

9. **Now churn the ice cream** according to the directions of your ice cream maker. When the ice cream is sufficiently frozen, remove it from the work bowl, and using a small plastic spatula, place about ¾ of a cup into the bottom of a five-cup capacity plastic freezer container. Now pour on some of the reserved strawberry puree, and then add another layer of ice cream on top of that. Repeat the layering until all of the ingredients are used. Seal and freeze.

Makes about 1 quart

Coffee Treats

Orange Honey Roof Tiles

Ingredients

3½ tablespoons unsalted butter, melted
Scant ½ cup sugar
⅓ cup fresh orange juice
1 tablespoon Krupnik or orange liqueur
6 tablespoons all-purpose flour
Heaping ¼ cup blanched almonds, sliced

Preparation

1. **Line a few large** heavy-duty baking pans with parchment paper, and then set aside.

2. **In a small mixing bowl,** combine the butter, sugar, juice, and liquor until well blended, then add the rest of the ingredients and stir until smooth. Cover with a piece of plastic wrap, and let rest at room temperature for exactly 20 minutes.

3. **While the batter** is resting, preheat the oven to 400°.

4. **After 20 minutes,** using a tablespoon, scoop 6 portions of the batter equally spaced apart onto the prepared sheet pan. (I recommend making only 1 pan at a time.) Now using the back of the spoon gently spread out the batter until each cookie forms a rough 4-inch circle. Immediately place the pan into the hot oven, and bake on the middle rack for 5 to 6 minutes until the tiles start to color at the edges.

5. **When the cookies** are evenly browned, remove the pan from the oven, and using a thin icing spatula, carefully lift the baked tiles to a cooling rack. (The baked tiles can also be placed onto the back of a rolling pin to give them a curved shape when removed hot from the oven.) Repeat with the rest of the batter.

Makes about 18 pieces

Candied Grapefruit Peel

Ingredients

2 large ruby red grapefruits
1¼ cups sugar
1 cup bittersweet chocolate morsels, melted

Preparation

1. **Cut a small slice** off the top and bottom of each grapefruit, and then cut each grapefruit into quarters. Using a sharp boning knife, remove the fruit from the peel, being sure to leave a little bit of the white membrane on the peel. Now carefully slice each quartered peel diagonally into strips about ½-inch wide.

2. **Place all the strips** into a medium sized saucepan filled with enough water just to cover the peels. Bring the water to a boil, then immediately drain the peels into a fine mesh sieve placed over the sink.

3. **Now repeat step # 2** three more times being sure to use fresh water each time. (Using fresh water removes all the bitterness from the peel.)

4. **After the fourth boil,** return the drained peels to the saucepan, add the sugar, and enough water to again cover the peels by ½-inch.

5. **Simmer the pot** with the peels and the sugar over low heat for about 1 hour, or until they are translucent and the syrup is very thick. Carefully using a kitchen tong, remove the peels, and place them onto a wire rack set over a baking sheet to dry and remove excess syrup. After a few hours, the peels should be firm to the touch and can be dipped into the melted chocolate.

Makes about 60 pieces

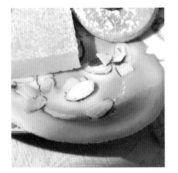

Chocolate-Dipped Strawberries

Ingredients

$^1/_2$ pound semi-sweet or white chocolate morsels
12 large, ripe but firm long-stemmed strawberries

Preparation

1. **Place the semi-sweet** chocolate morsels into a bowl set over a double boiler, and slowly melt until the chocolate is smooth.

2. **Cover a small** baking sheet with a piece of parchment paper.

3. **Remove the melted** chocolate from the heat and place it next to the parchment-lined pan.

4. **Now carefully grab** the strawberry at the base of the stem and dip it into the melted chocolate, covering it halfway. With a quick twist of the hand, remove the berry from the chocolate and let the excess drip for a few seconds, and then place it directly onto the parchment-lined pan. Repeat with the remaining berries, then place the entire pan into the refrigerator for at least 40 minutes to chill before serving.

Makes 12

Easy Almond Brittle

Ingredients

$^1/_2$ cup sugar
1 stick unsalted butter
1 tablespoon water
1 cup blanched almonds, sliced
$^1/_2$ cup semi-sweet chocolate morsels

Preparation

1. **Using a clean paper towel,** wipe off any residual dirt or grease from a heavy-duty non-stick baking pan.

2. **Place the sugar,** butter, and water into a medium sized heavy-duty pot, and bring the mixture to a boil over medium high heat. Using a small wooden spoon, stir the sugar until it completely melts and starts to turn amber in color, and reached 290° on a candy thermometer.

3. **Now quickly add** all of the sliced nuts, and again stir with the wooden spoon, then immediately remove the pan from the fire, and pour the caramelized nuts directly onto the clean sheet pan, being sure to spread the nut mixture around with the wooded spoon.

4. **After 15 to 20 minutes,** melt the chocolate morsels, and then evenly spread the chocolate over the tops of the almond brittle. Place the whole pan into the refrigerator and after 30 minutes, cut the brittle into bite size pieces.

Makes $^1/_2$ pound

Mushroom Meringues

Ingredients

3 large whole egg whites, room temperature
³⁄₄ cup sugar
¹⁄₄ teaspoon cream of tartar

¹⁄₃ cup semi-sweet chocolate morsels, melted

¹⁄₄ cup unsweetened cocoa powder

Preparation

1. **Preheat the oven** to 250°, and then line a large heavy-duty sheet pan with a piece of parchment paper and set aside.

2. **Place the egg whites** and tartar into a clean mixing bowl, and using a hand mixer set on high speed, whip the egg whites until they are white opaque and begin to hold a soft peak, about 3 to 4 minutes.

3. **Now slowly add** all of the sugar in a steady stream, and continue whipping the meringue until it is smooth, glossy, and holds a stiff peak.

4. **Carefully scoop** the meringue into a large pastry bag fitted with a ¹⁄₂-inch tip, and holding the bag perpendicular to the paper-lined tray, use half of the meringue to pipe the mushroom stems. (Your mushroom bases should be about 1¹⁄₂-inches tall, tapering to a small point at the tip.)

5. **To pipe the** mushroom caps, again hold the bag perpendicular to the paper and make 1¹⁄₂-inch wide domed caps. (While piping, lift the bag slightly so that the center of the cap is about ¹⁄₂-inch tall.)

6. **Lightly sift** the powdered cocoa onto the mushroom caps, then place the pan directly into the preheated oven to bake for exactly 15 minutes. Turn the heat off, and leave the pan in the oven for a few hours until the mushroom pieces are hard.

7. **After a few hours** remove the pan from the oven, and wearing thin latex gloves, carefully remove the caps from the baking pan. Using a small paring knife, cut a small hole directly into the bottom of each mushroom cap. Dip the pointed end of the mushroom base into the melted chocolate, then place a mushroom cap on top of that and set aside to cool. Repeat with the rest of the pieces.

Makes about 40 to 50 pieces

Polish Kolaczki Light and Flaky

Ingredients

¹⁄₂ pound unsalted butter, softened
4 ounces cream cheese, softened
1 egg yolk
1 teaspoon vanilla extract
Large pinch of sea salt
1³⁄₄ cup cake flour, sifted
Assorted Polish fruit preserves for filling such as: raspberry, peach, bilberry, apricot, black currant, strawberry, blackberry, sour cherry, plum, or gooseberry
Powdered sugar for dusting

Preparation

1. **The night before** preparing the Kolaczki make the dough. To mix the dough in a heavy-duty mixer, place the butter, cream cheese, egg yolk, vanilla, and salt in the mixer bowl, attach the paddle, and mix on low speed for 1 minute to blend the ingredients. Turn the machine off, and using a plastic spatula, scrape down the sides of the bowl.

2. **Now with the machine** running on low, pour in the flour and mix just until a crumbly, shaggy mass forms. Turn the machine off.

3. **Lightly flour** a clean work surface, and scrape the dough out onto the countertop. Now very carefully using floured hands, gently knead in a little bit more flour just until you feel comfortable in handling the dough. (Do not over mix. At this point, the dough will be soft and sticky but that's the way it should be). Carefully place the dough into a Ziploc bag and refrigerate overnight.

4. **The next morning,** remove the dough from the refrigerator to a clean work surface, and let it come to room temperature. After about 1 hour or so, check the dough and if it gives a little with the push of your finger, it is ready to be kneaded. Lightly flour a clean work surface, and place the dough on top. Gently knead the dough with the flour until you have a smooth elastic but soft dough, then cut it into 2 pieces. Again lightly flour the work surface, and using a rolling pin, roll out the dough to a ¹⁄₈-inch thickness. Brush off any excess flour, then cut the dough using a sharp chef's knife into 2 by 3-inch rectangles. Using an offset spatula, transfer the rectangles to parchment paper lined sheet pans. Preheat the oven to 375°F.

5. **While the oven** is preheating, fill the center of the Kolaczkis with the preserves, carefully using a baby spoon. Gently fold one corner of the cut dough over the filling, then fold the other corner over that.

6. **When the oven** is hot, cook the Kolaczkis for 12 to 15 minutes, until the pastries are light golden brown. When cooked, remove the pans, and let the Kolaczkis cool on baker's racks. Sprinkle on the powdered sugar.

Makes about 40 to 50 pieces

Dainty Lemon Squares

Ingredients

Crust

1 stick unsalted butter, softened
1/4 cup sugar
1 cup all-purpose flour
Pinch of sea salt

Filling

2 large whole eggs
3 1/2 tablespoons fresh lemon juice
Grated rind of one lemon
1 cup sugar
Dash of sea salt
2 tablespoons all-purpose flour
1 tablespoon cornstarch

Preparation

1. **Preheat the oven** to 350°, and then line a 9 by 9-inch square baking pan with parchment paper and set aside.

2. **To make the crust,** cream the butter and sugar, then add the flour and salt and mix until well combined. Using your hands, gently press the dough into the bottom of the prepared baking pan, and bake for exactly 20 minutes.

3. **Remove the pan** from the oven and lower the temperature to 325°. Place the rest of the ingredients into a medium sized mixing bowl, and using a whisk, beat vigorously until thoroughly combined, then immediately pour the filling into the pre-baked shell and return to the oven to bake for another 25 to 30 minutes. When the lemon squares are cooked, remove the pan from the oven, and chill for at least 24 hours before cutting into pieces.

Makes about 20 pieces

Apricot Rugelach

Ingredients

Dough

1/2 pound unsalted butter, softened
8 ounces cream cheese
1/4 cup sugar
Pinch of sea salt
1 teaspoon vanilla extract
2 cups all-purpose flour
1/2 teaspoon baking powder

Filling

1/4 cup light brown sugar
1/4 cup sugar
1/2 teaspoon cinnamon
3/4 cup walnuts, finely chopped
3/4 cup raisins
1 cup apricot preserves

Egg wash

1 large whole egg beaten with 1 tablespoon milk

Preparation

1. **To make the dough,** place the butter, cream cheese, sugar, salt, and vanilla into the bowl of a heavy-duty mixer fitted with the paddle attachment. Slowly mix the ingredients until well combined. While the machine is still running, add the flour and baking powder, and mix again until all the ingredients just come together. Do not over mix.

2. **Remove all** the mixed dough from the work bowl, and place it onto a lightly floured work surface, then knead gently just until it forms a cohesive ball. Cut the ball into 2 equal pieces, wrap each piece in plastic wrap, lightly flatten, and then place into the refrigerator to chill for at least 4 hours.

3. **When the dough** is sufficiently chilled, preheat the oven to 350°, and line 2 heavy-duty baking pans with parchment paper. Place the chilled dough balls onto a lightly floured work surface, and gently roll each one out into an 8 to 10-inch circle. Now using a tablespoon, gently spread the apricot preserves evenly onto the top of the circles.

4. **Now combine** the brown sugar, sugar, cinnamon, walnuts, and raisins in a small mixing bowl, and then sprinkle evenly over the apricot covered circles. (Reserve some of the filling for the topping.)

5. **Carefully using** a pizza cutter, cut each circle into 12 equal wedges. Starting with the wide edge, roll up each wedge, then place the cookies point side down onto the baking sheets. Gently brush on the egg glaze, sprinkle on any remaining filling, and bake in the hot oven for 15 to 20 minutes until lightly browned. Remove to a baking rack to cool.

Makes about 30 pieces

Wedding Cookies

Ingredients

¹/₂ cup sugar
³/₄ cup unsalted butter, softened
2 teaspoons vanilla extract
1³/₄ cups all-purpose flour
Dash of sea salt

Egg wash

1 egg yolk beaten with a little water
¹/₄ cup sugar

Preparation

1. **Place the sugar,** butter, and vanilla into the work bowl of a heavy-duty mixer fitted with the paddle attachment, then slowly mix the ingredients until well combined. While the machine is still running, add the flour and salt, and mix again until all the ingredients just come together. Do not over mix.

2. **Remove all** the mixed dough from the work bowl, and place it onto a lightly floured work surface, then knead gently just until it forms a cohesive ball. Now using lightly floured hands, carefully roll the ball into a fat cigar shape exactly 12-inches long by 1¹/₂-inches thick. (Try your best to keep the roll in a uniformly round shape.) Using a pastry brush, remove as much excess flour from the log as possible, place it onto a piece of plastic wrap, roll up tightly, and refrigerate for at least 3 hours to chill and get firm.

3. **When the dough** is sufficiently chilled, preheat the oven to 400°, and line 2 heavy-duty baking pans with parchment paper. Remove the plastic from the dough, and using a pastry brush, liberally brush the entire surface of the dough with the egg wash, then roll it in or sprinkle on the excess sugar until the log is completely coated. Now carefully using a sharp chef's knife and a ruler as your guide, cut the dough into ¹/₄-inch slices, and then place the slices on the parchment paper. Bake in the hot oven for exactly 12 minutes or until the cookies are lightly browned.

Makes about 40 cookies

Oatmeal Chocolate Chip Cookies

Ingredients

³/₄ cup shortening (butter flavored)
3 tablespoons unsalted butter, softened
1 cup firmly packed light brown sugar
¹/₄ cup sugar
2 tablespoons whole milk
1 tablespoon vanilla extract
1 whole large egg
1³/₄ cups all-purpose flour
¹/₂ cup oatmeal, finely ground
¹/₂ teaspoon sea salt
³/₄ teaspoon baking soda
1¹/₂ cups semi-sweet chocolate chips
¹/₂ cup semi-sweet chocolate, finely chopped

Preparation

1. **Preheat the oven** to 375°, and line 3 heavy-duty baking pans with parchment paper, and set aside.

2. **Place the shortening,** butter, and sugars into the work bowl of a heavy-duty mixer fitted with the paddle attachment, and mix the ingredients until well combined. While the machine is still running, add the milk, vanilla, and egg and mix until smooth. Turn the machine off.

3. **In a medium-sized** mixing bowl, combine the flour, oatmeal, salt, and baking soda then stir together with a fork to mix. Turn the mixer back on and add the dry ingredients, ¹/₄ cup at a time until the dough just comes together. Do not over mix. Now add the chocolate chips and chocolate pieces, and mix a little bit longer. Turn the machine off, remove the paddle, and using a spatula, scrape down the sides of the mixing bowl until all of the dough is in the middle.

4. **Using a small spoon,** scoop balls of the dough onto the parchment lined baking sheets. (I recommend 12 to 15 on each pan depending on how big you want your cookies.) Bake in the hot oven on the middle rack for 12 to 15 minutes until the cookies are nicely browned around the edges. Repeat with the rest of the dough.

Makes about 40 cookies

Pecan Crescents

Ingredients

2 sticks unsalted butter, softened
$\frac{1}{3}$ cup powdered sugar
2 tablespoons sugar
$\frac{1}{2}$ teaspoon sea salt
1 tablespoon vanilla extract
1 egg yolk
2 tablespoons chilled water
$2\frac{1}{2}$ cups cake flour
$\frac{1}{2}$ teaspoon baking powder
1 cup pecans, finely chopped

Powdered sugar for dusting

Preparation

1. **Place the butter,** powdered sugar, sugar, salt, vanilla, egg, and water into the work bowl of a heavy-duty mixer fitted with the paddle attachment, then slowly mix the ingredients until well combined and fluffy. While the machine is still running, add the flour, baking powder and pecan pieces, and mix again until all the ingredients just come together. Do not over mix.

2. **Remove all the mixed** dough from the work bowl, place it onto a lightly floured work surface, and knead gently until it forms a cohesive ball. Divide the dough evenly into 4 equal pieces, and then using lightly floured hands, roll each piece into a cigar shaped log about 12 inches long by 2 inches wide. Wrap each log in plastic wrap, lightly flatten, place on a flat baking sheet, and store in the refrigerator to chill for at least 4 to 5 hours. (These cookies are best if left to refrigerate over night.)

3. **When the dough** is sufficiently chilled, preheat the oven to 350°, and line 2 heavy-duty baking pans with parchment paper. Remove the plastic from the logs, and using a sharp chef's knife, cut pieces of dough that are about $\frac{3}{4}$ to 1-inch thick. (You should get about 14 slices from each log.) Now carefully roll each piece between both palms, and when the cookie forms a small log, bend it to a half moon shape, and place it on the parchment lined sheet pan. Repeat with the rest of the dough.

4. **Bake in the hot oven** on the middle rack for about 20 to 25 minutes or until the crescents are nicely browned. Remove to a baking rack to cool, and when the cookies are completely cool, dust with powdered sugar. Store in an airtight tin.

Makes about 60 cookies

Lemon Sables

Ingredients

2 sticks salted butter, softened
1 scant cup powdered sugar
1 whole large egg
Zest of one whole lemon, minced
Dash of lemon extract
$2\frac{1}{4}$ cups all-purpose flour

Preparation

1. **Place the butter,** powdered sugar, egg, lemon zest, and extract into the work bowl of a heavy-duty mixer fitted with the paddle attachment, then slowly mix the ingredients until well combined. While the machine is still running, add the flour and mix again until all the ingredients just come together. Do not over mix. Let the dough rest for 1 hour.

2. **Preheat the oven** to 375°, then line 2 heavy-duty sheet pans with parchment paper. Carefully scrape the dough into a pastry bag fitted with a small star tube, and then pipe out the dough onto the paper lined pans. Bake the cookies for 10 to 12 minutes until lightly browned. Remove to a baking rack to cool.

Makes about 40 pieces

Chicken Stock

Ingredients

4–5 pounds raw chicken bones or one large stewing
  chicken of equal weight
3 quarts cold water
2 large garlic cloves
1 medium onion, chopped
2 medium carrots, chopped
1 medium celery stalk, chopped
1 leek, white and some of the green part, chopped
1 bay leaf
6 sprigs parsley
6 sprigs thyme
1 teaspoon sea salt
8 black peppercorns

Preparation

1. **Rinse the chicken bones** under cold water for 5 minutes to
remove impurities, and then put them in a large stockpot. Add the
water and set the pot over high heat. Bring to a boil and then skim
off any froth that comes to the top.

2. **Reduce the heat** so that the liquid is barely simmering.

3. **Add the rest** of the ingredients and simmer for 2 hours. Skim
off any froth that has risen to the top with a kitchen spoon.

4. **Strain through** a fine mesh conical sieve into a bowl and cool it
as quickly as possible.

Makes about 2 quarts

Veal or Beef Stock

Ingredients

8 pounds veal or beef bones
One half calf's foot, split lengthwise, chopped,
  and blanched
2 large garlic cloves
1 medium onion, chopped
2 medium carrots, chopped
1 medium celery stalk, chopped
1/2 cup mushrooms, sliced
2 bay leaves
3 sprigs tarragon
6 sprigs parsley
6 sprigs thyme
4 tablespoons tomato paste
1/2 cup dry white wine
1 teaspoon sea salt
8 black peppercorns
6 quarts cold water

Preparation

1. **Preheat the oven** to 425°F.

2. **Rinse the bones** under cold running water for 5 minutes to
remove any impurities.

3. **In a large roasting pan,** place the bones in the pan. Roast about
35–45 minutes until browned. Add the tomato paste and
vegetables and toss to coat and return to the oven and roast until
the vegetables and bones are well browned, about 20 minutes
more. Keep tossing and checking.

4. **Remove from the oven** and transfer the bones and vegetables to
a large stockpot.

5. **Pour off the fat** from the roasting pan and deglaze with the
white wine scraping up all of the sediment. Set the pan over high
heat and reduce the wine by half, then pour the wine into the
stockpot.

6. **Pour the water** over the bones and the vegetables, then add the
bay leaves, tarragon, parsley, thyme, sea salt, and black peppercorns and bring just to a boil over high heat.

7. **As soon as the liquid** boils, reduce the heat so that the liquid is
barely simmering. Skim off any froth that has risen to the top with
a kitchen spoon.

8. **Simmer the stock** for 3 1/2 to 4 hours skimming as necessary.
Strain through a fine mesh conical sieve into a bowl and cool it as
quickly as possible.

Makes about 3 quarts

Polish Spice #1

Ingredients

2 teaspoons sea salt
$\frac{1}{2}$ teaspoon freshly ground black pepper
1 teaspoon garlic powder
1 teaspoon Hungarian sweet paprika
1 teaspoon dried marjoram
1 teaspoon onion powder
$\frac{1}{2}$ teaspoon ground allspice
$\frac{1}{2}$ teaspoon ground juniper
$\frac{1}{2}$ teaspoon mushroom powder
2 pinches ground savory
2 pinches cayenne pepper

Preparation

1. **Place all** of the ingredients in a small mixing bowl and stir with a fork to combine. Store in a small glass jar.

Makes about $\frac{1}{4}$ cup

Polish Spice #2

Ingredients

1 teaspoon caraway seeds, mortar crushed
2 teaspoons sea salt
$\frac{1}{2}$ teaspoon freshly ground black pepper
1 teaspoon garlic powder
1 teaspoon Hungarian sweet paprika
1 teaspoon dried marjoram
1 teaspoon onion powder
$\frac{1}{2}$ teaspoon ground allspice
$\frac{1}{2}$ teaspoon ground juniper
$\frac{1}{2}$ teaspoon mushroom powder
2 pinches ground savory
2 pinches cayenne pepper

Preparation

1. **Place all** of the ingredients in a small mixing bowl and stir with a fork to combine. Store in a small glass jar.

Makes about $\frac{1}{4}$ cup

Polish Spice #3

Ingredients

$1\frac{1}{2}$ teaspoons Hungarian sweet paprika
$\frac{3}{4}$ teaspoon onion powder
$\frac{3}{4}$ teaspoon garlic powder
$\frac{3}{4}$ teaspoon dried oregano
$\frac{3}{4}$ teaspoon dried marjoram
$\frac{1}{4}$ teaspoon dried thyme
$\frac{1}{4}$ teaspoon freshly ground black pepper
$\frac{1}{4}$ teaspoon freshly ground white pepper
$\frac{1}{4}$ teaspoon cayenne pepper

Preparation

1. **Place all** of the ingredients in a small mixing bowl and stir with a fork to combine. Store in a small glass jar.

Makes about $\frac{1}{4}$ cup

Seafood Seasoning Spice

Ingredients

2 tablespoons sea salt
1 tablespoon cayenne pepper
1 tablespoon freshly ground black pepper
1 tablespoon Hungarian sweet paprika
2 teaspoons onion powder
$1\frac{1}{2}$ teaspoons garlic powder
$\frac{1}{2}$ teaspoon dried basil
$\frac{1}{8}$ teaspoon dried thyme
$\frac{1}{8}$ teaspoon dried tarragon
$\frac{1}{8}$ teaspoon gumbo file powder
$\frac{1}{4}$ teaspoon dry mustard
Pinch of dried oregano
Pinch of dried rosemary

Preparation

1. **Place all** of the ingredients in a small mixing bowl and stir with a fork to combine. Store in a small glass jar.

Makes about $\frac{1}{2}$ cup

Kanapki Seasoned Cheese Base

Ingredients

16 ounces cream cheese, softened
2 tablespoons heavy cream
1 teaspoon garlic powder
¼ teaspoon onion powder
½ teaspoon celery salt
¼ teaspoon freshly ground white pepper
Dash of paprika
Dash of Tabasco

Preparation

1. **Place the cream cheese** and heavy cream into a medium sized mixing bowl, and using a heavy wooden spoon, blend until smooth and well combined. Now add the rest of the ingredients and stir vigorously until well incorporated. Store in the refrigerator until needed.

Herbed cheese base—To the seasoned cheese base, add 2 tablespoons of freshly chopped assorted herbs such as, parsley, dill, basil, and chives.

Horseradish cheese base—To the seasoned cheese base, add 2 tablespoons of pink horseradish.

Smoked salmon cheese base—To the seasoned cheese base, add 2 to 3 ounces of finely minced smoked salmon.

Makes about 2 cups

Savory Polish Topping

Ingredients

4 tablespoons unsalted butter, melted
1 slice hickory smoked bacon, minced
2 large garlic cloves, minced
1 small onion, finely diced
1 cup fresh breadcrumbs
2 hardboiled eggs, diced
2 tablespoons parsley, minced
¼ cup dill, minced
Dash of sea salt
Dash of freshly ground black pepper

Preparation

1. **In a large** nonstick skillet over medium high heat, heat the butter, add the bacon, and cook for exactly 1 minute.

2. **Now add** the garlic and onion, and cook for another minute until the onion is slightly soft.

3. **Add the breadcrumbs** and eggs, and gently toss the skillet until the mixture is well blended. Turn the heat off, and stir in the rest of the ingredients until well seasoned.

Makes about 1 cup

Beet Horseradish Dressing

Ingredients

1 cup mayonnaise, full fat
1½ to 2 tablespoons beet horseradish
2 teaspoons Dijon mustard
⅛ teaspoon celery salt
¼ teaspoon garlic powder
⅛ teaspoon freshly ground black pepper
Large dash of Worcestershire sauce
Large dash of Tabasco

Preparation

1. **At least 2 hours** before serving the dressing, place all the ingredients into a medium sized mixing bowl, and combine with a plastic spatula until well blended. Cover and refrigerate.

Makes about 1 cup

Whipped Horseradish Cream

Ingredients

1 cup heavy cream
¼ teaspoon sea salt
2 tablespoons prepared horseradish, well drained
Dash of Tabasco

Preparation

1. **Place the heavy cream**, salt, and Tabasco into a medium sized chilled mixing bowl, and using a balloon whisk, whip the cream vigorously until it forms stiff peaks. Gently fold in the horseradish, then put into a decorative sauceboat and serve.

Makes about 2 cups

Spicy Tomato Sauce

Ingredients

2 tablespoons olive oil
2 large garlic cloves, minced
1 medium onion, sliced
1 medium red or green pepper, sliced
¾ teaspoon dried thyme
1 bay leaf
3 tablespoons tomato paste
1½ cups tomato sauce

1½ cups beef or chicken stock
¼ cup dry white wine
Dash of cayenne pepper
Dash of Tabasco
Dash of Worcestershire sauce
¼ teaspoon sea salt
Freshly ground black pepper

Preparation

1. **Heat the oil** in a medium pot over medium heat, add the garlic, onion, and peppers and cook, stirring until softened, about 3 minutes. Do not let the vegetables brown.

2. **Now add** the bay leaf and thyme and cook for exactly 1 minute to release their oils.

3. **Add the rest** of the ingredients to the pot and bring it to a boil, and then reduce the heat and simmer slowly for about 10 minutes.

Makes about 3 cups

Apple, Honey, and Rosemary Sauce

Ingredients

1 tablespoon unsalted butter, melted
2 large shallots, sliced
2 tablespoons honey
1 large sprig fresh rosemary
2 small Granny Smith apples, peeled, cored, and diced

2 cups veal stock
Sea salt
Freshly ground black pepper
Dash of lemon juice
1 tablespoon unsalted butter, chilled

Preparation

1. **Heat the butter** in a medium sized nonstick saucepan over medium high heat, then add the shallots and cook stir for exactly 1 minute. Add the honey to the pot, and cook until the honey takes on a light brown caramel color, then immediately add the apples and rosemary and cook for about 2 minutes more until well coated. Add the stock and bring it to a boil, then reduce the heat and simmer the sauce slowly for 15 to 20 minutes until it thinly coats the back of a spoon. Season the sauce with the salt, pepper, and lemon juice, then strain through a fine mesh conical sieve into a clean saucepan. Swirl in the butter just before serving.

Makes about 2 cups

Pesto

Ingredients

2 cups fresh basil leaves
¼ cup fresh Italian parsley, stems removed
2 medium garlic cloves, peeled
¼ cup pine nuts or walnuts, lightly toasted
½ cup extra virgin olive oil
¼ teaspoon sea salt
¼ cup grated Parmigiano-Reggiano cheese

Preparation

1. **Place the basil,** parsley, garlic, and nuts into the work bowl of a food processor fitted with a metal blade, attach the lid, and pulse 5 to 6 times. Remove the lid, and scrape down the sides with a plastic spatula, then pulse again. Now with the machine running, add the rest of the ingredients in a slow steady stream until the pesto is smooth. Carefully remove to a clean glass mason jar and store in the refrigerator.

Makes about 1 cup

Freash Strawberry, Raspberry, or Blueberry Sauce

Ingredients

2 to 3 cups berries (fresh or frozen without syrup)
4 to 6 tablespoons sugar
1 tablespoon lemon juice
1 teaspoon cornstarch

Preparation

1. **Combine the fresh** or frozen berries with the sugar, lemon juice, and cornstarch in a saucepan over medium heat. Bring to a boil, reduce the heat, and simmer until slightly thickened, about 7 to 10 minutes. Purée the hot sauce in a blender, strain through a fine mesh sieve, and cool until needed.

Makes about 2 cups

Vanilla Sponge Cake

Ingredients

4 whole large eggs
Pinch of sea salt
$\frac{1}{2}$ cup sugar
1 teaspoon vanilla extract
$\frac{1}{2}$ cup cake flour
$\frac{1}{2}$ cup corn starch
3 tablespoons unsalted butter, melted

Preparation

1. **Preheat the oven** to 350°F.

2. **Prepare a 9-inch** round cake pan, by brushing the interior with softened butter, and place a piece of round parchment paper onto the bottom of the pan. Now add 1 tablespoon of all-purpose flour to the pan and swirl around to coat the brushed on butter, then gently tap out all of the excess flour from the pan and set aside.

3. **Break the eggs** into the work bowl of an electric mixer, add the salt, sugar, and vanilla extract, and place over a warm bain Marie. Beat the eggs with a whisk until light in color and slightly warm to the touch. Now remove the work bowl to the machine, and beat on high speed with the whip until thick and triple in volume, about 3 to 5 minutes.

4. **While the eggs** are beating, sift the flour and corn starch together 3 times through a fine mesh sieve, then set aside.

5. **When the eggs** are thick, remove the work bowl from the machine, and sift in $\frac{1}{3}$ of the flour. Gently fold the flour into the eggs using a plastic spatula, and continue sifting and folding until all the flour is used. Now quickly fold in all the melted butter and immediately pour the cake batter into the prepared pan, and bake on the middle rack for $\frac{1}{2}$ hour. When nicely browned, remove the cake from the oven, run a small spatula around the inside edge of the pan, then invert onto a cooling rack. Leave the paper on. When the cake is completely cool, flip it over onto a 9-inch cardboard cake circle, place into a Ziploc bag, seal, and freeze.

Makes one 9-inch layer cake

Chocolate Sponge Cake

Ingredients

$\frac{1}{3}$ cup unsweetened cocoa powder
$\frac{1}{4}$ cup water

4 whole large eggs
Pinch of sea salt
$\frac{1}{2}$ cup sugar
1 teaspoon vanilla extract
$\frac{3}{4}$ cup cake flour
3 tablespoons unsalted butter, melted

Preparation

1. **Preheat the oven** to 350°F.

2. **Prepare a 9-inch** round cake pan, by brushing the interior with softened butter, and place a piece of round parchment paper onto the bottom of the pan. Now add 1 tablespoon of all-purpose flour to the pan and swirl around to coat the brushed on butter, then gently tap out all of the excess flour from the pan and set aside.

3. **Place the cocoa powder** and water in a small saucepan, and cook stir over low heat until thoroughly dissolved and smooth. Remove from the heat and cool slightly.

4. **Break the eggs** into the work bowl of an electric mixer, add the salt, sugar, and vanilla extract, and place over a warm bain Marie. Beat the eggs with a whisk until light in color and slightly warm to the touch. Now remove the work bowl to the machine, and beat on high speed with the whip until thick and triple in volume, about 3 to 5 minutes.

5. **While the eggs** are beating, sift the flour 3 times through a fine mesh sieve, then set aside.

6. **When the eggs** are thick, remove the work bowl from the machine, and scoop out 1 cup of the beaten eggs to the cooled chocolate mixture, and gently fold together until smooth. Now quickly sift $\frac{1}{3}$ of the flour over the rest of the beaten eggs, and gently fold in using a plastic spatula. Continue sifting and folding until all the flour is used, then fold in the chocolate mixture and melted butter and immediately pour the cake batter into the prepared pan, and bake on the middle rack for $\frac{1}{2}$ hour. When nicely browned, remove the cake from the oven, run a small spatula around the inside edge of the pan, then invert onto a cooling rack. Leave the paper on. When the cake is completely cool, flip it over onto a 9-inch cardboard cake circle, place into a Ziploc bag, seal, and freeze.

Makes one 9-inch layer cake

Sweet Pastry Dough

Ingredients

1 cup plus 2 tablespoons unsalted butter, softened
¾ cup plus 2 tablespoons sugar
1 teaspoon vanilla extract
2 whole large eggs, beaten
3½ cups all-purpose flour
¼ teaspoon sea salt

Preparation

1. **Using an electric mixer,** beat the butter, sugar, and vanilla together in a bowl until smooth and creamy.

2. **With the beaters** running on a slow speed, gradually add the beaten eggs until well incorporated.

3. **Sift the flour** and salt together, and with the mixer set on the slowest speed, gradually add the flour until the mixture just comes together and forms a shaggy mass. Now turn the mixer off, pour the dough out onto a clean work surface, and then gently knead with your hands until the dough is smooth, about 1 to 2 minutes. (Don't over knead the pastry.)

4. **Divide the dough** into 2 to 3 batches, tightly cover them with plastic wrap, and then refrigerate for at least 2 hours before using.

Makes enough for 2 to 3 9-inch shells

Vanilla Pastry Cream

Ingredients

1 cup whole milk
⅓ cup sugar
2 tablespoons cornstarch
3 egg yolks
1 teaspoon vanilla extract

Preparation

1. **Combine** ¾ cup of the milk and all the sugar in a medium saucepan, and bring to the boil.

2. **In a mixing bowl,** whisk together the remaining milk, cornstarch, eggs, and vanilla.

3. **Now carefully pour** about ¼ cup of the hot milk into the mixing bowl, and whisk until smooth. Place the hot milk back onto the fire and reduce the heat to medium. Pour the egg-milk mixture into the hot milk, and whisk constantly until the pastry cream begins to thicken. Keep whisking until the pastry cream comes to a boil, taking care that the whip reaches all corners of the pan, to prevent the cream from scorching. Continue whisking for about 1 minute more, then pour the pastry cream into a glass bowl. Cover with plastic wrap and refrigerate immediately.

Makes about 1½ cups

Polish Danish Dough

Ingredients

3½ cups all-purpose flour
1 cup cake flour
6 tablespoons sugar
1 teaspoons sea salt
¼ teaspoon cardamon
4 teaspoons active dry yeast
6 tablespoons unsalted butter, softened
2 whole large eggs
½ teaspoon vanilla extract
1 cup half and half (about 110 degrees)
½ pound unsalted butter, softened

Every once in awhile on rainy days, I get the urge to knock out some fresh Danish but I can never decide which animal to make. Everyone has their favorite so I've included two that I like the best. Once you've tried homemade, you'll never go back to store bought again.

Chef's Tip!

Danish dough is extremely versatile and can be frozen for up to a month until needed. I recommend cutting the dough in half as this recipe makes a generous portion.

Preparation

1. **Place the all-purpose flour,** cake flour, sugar, salt, cardamon, and yeast in the bowl of a food processor fitted with a metal blade, then pulse several times to combine. Add the shortening and pulse 6 to 8 times until it is absorbed, then add the eggs and pulse 4 times more. Now add the warm half and half, and continue to pulse until the dough forms a ball. If the dough is excessively soft and sticky, add 1 to 2 tablespoons more flour, one at a time, and knead a little longer. Let the dough rest in the bowl for 5 minutes, then scrape the dough out onto a lightly floured work surface. Using floured hands, gently knead the dough until it is smooth, elastic and not at all sticky (if the dough is still sticky, add 1 to 2 more tablespoons of flour). Place the ball into a Ziploc bag, and let it rest in the refrigerator for a few hours.

2. **Remove the dough** to a lightly floured work surface, and roll it out into a 6 by 12-inch rectangle, ⅜-inch thick. Using your hand, smear the softened butter evenly over the lower two thirds of the dough, leaving a ½-inch unbuttered border around the side and edges. Fold the upper third of the dough toward the center of the rectangle, then fold the lowest third over that. With your fingers, crimp the short edges and the seam on top to seal in the butter. Turn the dough so that the long, crimped edge is on your right.

3. **Lightly flour the work surface** and the dough, and using a rolling pin, press a series of horizontal lines in the dough to flatten it gently. Now gently, without rolling over the edges, roll the dough to make a 12 by 24-inch rectangle. Fold the two narrow ends of the dough to within ¼-inch of the middle, leaving a ½-inch space between their ends. Fold over again at the space to make four layers. Give the dough a quarter turn so that the seamed edge is on your right.

4. **Completely repeat** step #3, then place the dough in a Ziploc bag and refrigerate overnight.

5. **Follow** the preceding recipes.

Sweet Whipped Cream

Ingredients

1 cup heavy cream
2 tablespoons sugar
1 teaspoon vanilla

Preparation

1. **Place the heavy cream,** sugar, and vanilla into a medium sized stainless steel mixing bowl that has been well chilled, and whip the cream with an electric mixer until the cream holds a soft peak and is thickened.

Makes about 2 cups

Cheese Filling for Danish

Ingredients

1 cup farmer's or ricotta cheese
4 tablespoons sugar
$\frac{1}{8}$ teaspoon sea salt
1 teaspoon orange zest
1 egg yolk
2 tablespoons unsalted butter, melted

Preparation

1. **The night before** making the Danish, place the cheese of your choice into a medium sized fine mesh strainer set over an empty bowl. Cover with plastic wrap and place in the refrigerator overnight to drain excess liquid.

2. **The next day** in a medium sized mixing bowl, thoroughly combine all the ingredients with a plastic spatula. Do not over mix.

Makes about 1½ cups

Walnut Filling

Ingredients

$\frac{1}{3}$ cup fresh almond paste
1 tablespoon unsalted butter
$\frac{1}{4}$ cup light or dark brown sugar
$\frac{1}{4}$ cup sugar
1 tablespoon all-purpose flour
$\frac{3}{4}$ teaspoon ground cinnamon
1 teaspoon vanilla extract
$\frac{3}{4}$ cup lightly crushed walnut pieces

Preparation

1. **Combine all the ingredients** in a medium sized mixing bowl, and working quickly, cut the butter into the mixture with a pastry blender until the mixture is evenly distributed. Do not over mix.

Makes about 1 cup

Fresh Almond Paste

Ingredients

$\frac{2}{3}$ cup finely ground almonds
Dash of almond extract
$1\frac{3}{4}$ cup powdered sugar
1 small egg white

Preparation

1. **Place all the ingredients** into the bowl of a food processor fitted with a metal blade. Pulse several times until the mixture is smooth and paste like.

Makes about ¾ cup

Cinnamon Filling

Ingredients

1 stick unsalted butter
1 tablespoon ground cinnamon
1¾ cups powdered sugar
1 large egg white

Preparation

1. **Place the all the ingredients** into the bowl of a heavy duty mixer with the paddle attached, and beat for 2 to 3 minutes until the mixture is light and fluffy.

Makes about 1 cup

Streusel

Ingredients

1 tablespoon unsalted butter, chilled
¼ cup light brown sugar
¼ cup sugar
1 tablespoon all-purpose flour
¾ teaspoon cinnamon
¾ cup crushed walnuts or sliced almonds

Preparation

1. **Combine all the ingredients** in a medium sized mixing bowl, and working quickly, cut the butter into the mixture with a pastry blender until the mixture is evenly distributed. Do not over mix.

Makes about 1 cup

Vanilla Sugar

Ingredients

1 cup sugar
1 fresh vanilla bean

Preparation

1. **Place the sugar** and vanilla bean into the bowl of a food processor fitted with a steel blade. Cover and pulse 5 times, then pulse again another 5 times. Remove the cover and sift the sugar through a fine mesh sieve into a clean bowl. Return to the food processor any lumps that won't go through the sieve, then pulse again until fine. Re-sift, then store the vanilla sugar in a clean glass mason jar with a tight fitting lid.

Makes about 1 cup

Cinnamon Sugar

Ingredients

1 cup sugar
1 tablespoon cinnamon

Preparation

1. **Place the sugar** and cinnamon into a clean glass mason jar with a tight fitting lid, and shake vigorously until well blended. Store in a cool place.

Makes about 1 cup

Clear Glaze

Ingredients

1/2 cup sugar
1/4 cup water
1 tablespoon light corn syrup

Preparation

1. **Place the ingredients** in a small saucepan over medium heat and bring to the boil. Remove from the heat and cool.

Makes about 1/2 cup

Chocolate Glaze

Ingredients

1 1/4 cups powdered sugar
3 tablespoons unsweetened cocoa powder
1 1/2 teaspoons light corn syrup
1 tablespoon shortening, melted
2 tablespoons water
1 teaspoon vanilla extract

Preparation

1. **Combine all the ingredients** in a medium sized mixing bowl, then set over a warm bain Marie. Stir with a wooden spoon until completely smooth and warm.

Makes about 1 cup

Butter Cream Icing

Ingredients

5 tablespoons shortening
3 tablespoons sugar
3/4 cup powdered sugar
1 egg white
1/8 teaspoon vanilla extract

Preparation

1. **Combine all the ingredients** in a medium sized mixing bowl, then set over a warm bain Marie. Whisk until completely smooth, and then remove from the heat.

Makes about 1/2 cup

Warm Chocolate Sauce

Ingredients

1 1/2 cups semi sweet chocolate morsels
3/4 cup whole milk
2 tablespoons unsalted butter, chilled
2 tablespoons Tia Maria or Kahlua

Preparation

1. **To make the sauce,** bring the milk to the boil in a medium sized sauce pan, then remove from the heat and stir in the chocolate and butter. Keep stirring with a wooden spoon until the mixture is smooth, add the liquor, stir again, and then set aside.

Makes about 2 cups

glossary of cooking terms

Al Dente

Slightly underdone with a chewy consistency, from the Italian phrase "to the tooth." The term is usually applied to the cooking of pasta, but can also refer to vegetables that are blanched or not fully cooked.

Bain Marie

Also called a hot water bath. The process of placing a mixing bowl over a simmering pot of warm water to keep sauces warm on top of the stove without curdling.

Bake

To bake is to cook foods by surrounding them with hot, dry air.

Baste

To keep foods moist during cooking by spooning, brushing, or drizzling with a sauce, pan juice, or wine.

Beat

To mix ingredients rapidly so that air is incorporated, resulting in a smooth creamy mixture.

Blanch

To briefly plunge vegetables, fruit, or meat products into boiling water to bring out the color, loosen skins for peeling, mellow flavors, or remove excess salt or fat.

Blend

To combine ingredients until well mixed and smooth.

Braise

To brown meat in fat over high heat, then cover and cook slowly in the oven in a small amount of liquid.

Breading

To dredge or coat food with fresh breadcrumbs.

Brown

To cook food quickly in a preheated hot skillet with a little bit of oil or butter to seal in the juices.

Caramelize

To dissolve sugar syrup slowly, then heat until it turns a caramel brown color.

Chop

To cut food into coarsely cut pieces, which can range from small finely chopped to large coarsely chopped in size.

Clarify

To clear a soup by straining it through cooked egg whites, or to make butter clear by heating, separating, and discarding milk solids.

Cream

To mix 2 softened ingredients together with a whisk until completely blended and smooth.

Crimp

To decorate the edge of a piecrust by pinching dough together with the fingers, or to seal a pastry dough seam together.

Dash

A very small quantity usually associated with 2 quick shakes of liquid or a small pinch of spice.

Deep Fried

To cook foods by completely submerging them in a large quantity of lard or vegetable oil until completely browned.

Deglaze

To add water, wine, or broth to a pan in which food has been cooked, stirring and scraping up and dissolving the brown bits from the bottom of the pan.

Degrease

To carefully skim the layer of fat from the top of a soup, sauce, or stock.

Dice

To cut food into equal size small cubes from $\frac{1}{4}$-inch to $\frac{1}{2}$-inch.

Drain

To remove excess liquid from food through a fine mesh strainer.

Dredge

To lightly coat food, usually with flour or fresh breadcrumbs.

Drippings

The juices, fat, and browned bits that are left in a pan after meat or poultry has been roasted or sautéed.

Drizzle

To slowly pour a very thin stream of liquid lightly over food.

Dry Mashed Potatoes

That is to cook peeled potatoes in lightly salted water until tender, then strain off all the water and mash with no added liquid to the pot.

Dust

To sprinkle very lightly with powdered sugar or flour.

Fold

To incorporate one ingredient into another without stirring or beating but instead by gently lifting from underneath with a rubber spatula.

Grate

To reduce a large chunk of hard cheese into smaller bits by rubbing it against a hand grater.

Gratinée

The term that is given to food that is cooked in a shallow gratin dish, and browned in the oven until bubbly.

Grill

To cook foods on a rack over very hot coals or wood.

Grind

To use a small food processor to transform a solid piece of food into finer pieces.

Julienne

To cut fresh vegetables into thin matchstick size strips of uniform length.

Knead

To work dough in a heavy-duty mixer until it is smooth and elastic.

Line

To cover the surface of a baking sheet with parchment paper to prevent sticking.

Marinate

To place food in a seasoned liquid overnight to tenderize and flavor.

Mince

To cut or chop into very fine pieces.

Pinch

The amount of a dry ingredient you can hold between your thumb and finger.

Pipe

To decorate cakes or food by forcing frosting or filling through a pastry bag.

Poach

To cook food gently in simmering liquid that does not boil.

Pound

To flatten or tenderize meat between two sheets of waxed paper with a heavy mallet.

Preheat

To set an oven at the desired temperature 20 minutes before use so that the oven is hot.

Purée

To mash solid food through a fine mesh strainer until it is smooth.

Reduce

To thicken or concentrate a liquid by boiling it down, which lessens the volume and intensifies the flavor.

Roast

To cook in a hot oven without any liquid added to the pan.

Sauté

To cook food in butter or fat in a skillet until lightly browned.

Score

To make very thin slashes along the surface of meat to help tenderize it.

Sear

To brown the surface of meat very quickly in a hot pan to seal in the juices.

Sift

To pass dry ingredients through a fine mesh strainer to remove any lumps.

Simmer

To cook liquid over low heat so that it never boils.

Skim

To spoon off fat or scum that rises to the surface of a cooked liquid.

Stew

To slowly cook meats and vegetables in liquid in a covered pan.

Stir-cook

To quickly sauté meat or vegetables while stirring constantly in a hot pot or skillet.

Stock

A long simmered, well-flavored broth made from meat, poultry, or fish.

Strain

To remove solids from liquids by pouring through a colander or sieve.

Toss

To quickly and gently mix assorted ingredients in a mixing bowl until well combined.

Truss

To tie the legs and wings of poultry close to the body with string.

Whip

To beat rapidly with an electric mixer to add air and increase volume.

Zest

To remove in fine strips the outer most colored peel of citrus fruits, not including the bitter white pith underneath.

conversion charts

If you need to convert measurements into their equivalents in another system, this is how to do it:

ounces to grams   multiply ounce figure by 28.3 to get number of grams

grams to ounces   multiply grams figure by .0353 to get number of ounces

pounds to grams   multiply pound figure by 453.59 to get number of grams

pounds to kilograms   multiply pound figure by 0.45 to get number of kilograms

ounces to milliliters   multiply ounce figure by 30 to get number of milliliters

cups to liters   multiply cup figure by 0.24 to get number of liters

fahrenheit to celsius   subtract 32 from the Fahrenheit figure, multiply by 5, then divide by 9 to get Celsius figure

celsius to fahrenheit   multiply Celsius figure by 9, divide by 5, then add 32 to get Fahrenheit figure

inches to centimeters   multiply inch figure by 2.54 to get number of centimeters

centimeters to inches   multiply centimeter figure by .39 to get number of inches

U.S. weights and measures

liquid measures

1 cup	=	8 fl. oz.	=	½ pint
2 cups	=	16 fl. oz.	=	1 pint
4 cups	=	32 fl. oz.	=	1 quart
2 pints	=	32 fl. oz.	=	1 quart
4 quarts	=	128 fl. oz.	=	1 gallon

8 quarts = 1 peck

4 pecks = 1 bushel

1 dash = 3 drops or less than ¼ teaspoon

dry measures

3 teaspoons	=	1 tablespoon	=	½ oz.
2 tablespoons	=	⅛ cup	=	1 oz.
4 tablespoons	=	¼ cup	=	2 oz.
5⅓ tablespoons	=	⅓ cup	=	2.6 oz.
8 tablespoons	=	½ cup	=	4 oz.
12 tablespoons	=	¾ cup	=	6 oz.
32 tablespoons	=	2 cups	=	16 oz.
64 tablespoons	=	4 cups	=	32 oz.

temperatures

°Fahrenheit (F) to °Celsius (C)

-10°F	=	-23.3°C (freezer storage)
0°F	=	-17.7°C
32°F	=	0°C (water freezes)
50°F	=	10°C
68°F	=	20°C (room temperature)
100°F	=	37.7°C
150°F	=	65.5°C
205°F	=	96.1°C (water simmers)
212°F	=	100°C (water boils)
300°F	=	148.8°C
325°F	=	162.8°C
350°F	=	177°C (baking)
375°F	=	190.5°C
400°F	=	204.4°C (hot oven)
425°F	=	218.3°C
450°F	=	232°C (very hot oven)
475°F	=	246.1°C
500°F	=	260°C (broiling)

conversion charts

solid weight conversions

imperial to metric

½ oz.	=		15 g.	
1 oz.	=		30 g.	
2 oz.	=		60 g.	
3 oz.	=		90 g.	
4 oz.	=	¼ lb.	=	125 g.
5 oz.	=		155 g.	
6 oz.	=		185 g.	
7 oz.	=		220 g.	
8 oz.	=	½ lb.	=	250 g.
9 oz.	=		280 g.	
10 oz.	=		315 g.	
11 oz.	=		345 g.	
12 oz.	=	¾ lb.	=	375 g.
13 oz.	=		410 g.	
14 oz.	=		440 g.	
15 oz.	=		470 g.	
16 oz. = 1 lb. = 500 g. = 0.5 kg.				
24 oz. = 1½ lb. = 750 g.				
32 oz. = 2 lbs. = 1,000 g. = 1 kg.				

liquid conversions

½ fl. oz.	=	15 ml.	=	1 tbsp.
1 fl. oz.	=	30 ml.	=	⅛ cup
2 fl. oz.	=	60 ml.	=	¼ cup
4 fl. oz.	=	125 ml.	=	½ cup
5 fl. oz.	=	150 ml.	=	⅔ cup
6 fl. oz.	=	175 ml.	=	¾ cup
8 fl. oz.	=	250 ml.	=	1 cup
10 fl. oz.	=	300 ml.	=	1¼ cups
12 fl. oz.	=	375 ml.	=	1½ cups
16 fl. oz.	=	500 ml.	=	2 cups
20 fl. oz.	=	600 ml.	=	2½ cups
1¾ pints = 1 liter = 1 quart = 4 cups				
2 pints = 1.25 liters = 1 quart				

yeast to flour conversions

cups of flour		packets of dry yeast		teaspoons of dry yeast
0–4 cups	=	1 pk.	=	2¼ teaspoons
4–7 cups	=	2 pks.	=	4½ teaspoons
7–10 cups	=	3 pks.	=	6¾ teaspoons

fresh compressed yeast to active dry yeast

1 oz. cake	=	1½ tablespoons active dry yeast
2 oz. cake	=	3 tablespoons active dry yeast
4 oz. cake	=	6 tablespoons active dry yeast

index

La Baruch

The *New* Polish Cuisine

TheNewPolishCuisine.com

Mike the chef would like to hear your thoughts about this book
so please contact him at:

LBCM Publishing, Inc.
P.O. Box 55, Del Mar, Ca 92014-0055

or join us on our interactive Web site at:

TheNewPolishCuisine.com

I would love to exchange stories and recipes about Polish cooking.